Information Obesity

CHANDOS
INFORMATION PROFESSIONAL SERIES

Series Editor: Ruth Rikowski
(email: Rikowskigr@aol.com)

Chandos' new series of books are aimed at the busy information professional. They have been specially commissioned to provide the reader with an authoritative view of current thinking. They are designed to provide easy-to-read and (most importantly) practical coverage of topics that are of interest to librarians and other information professionals. If you would like a full listing of current and forthcoming titles, please visit our website www.chandospublishing.com or email info@chandospublishing.com or telephone +44 (0) 1223 891358.

New authors: we are always pleased to receive ideas for new titles; if you would like to write a book for Chandos, please contact Dr Glyn Jones on email gjones@chandospublishing.com or telephone number +44 (0) 1993 848726.

Bulk orders: some organisations buy a number of copies of our books. If you are interested in doing this, we would be pleased to discuss a discount. Please email info@chandospublishing.com or telephone +44(0) 1223 891358.

Information Obesity

ANDREW WHITWORTH

Chandos Publishing
Oxford • Cambridge • New Delhi

Chandos Publishing
TBAC Business Centre
Avenue 4
Station Lane
Witney
Oxford OX28 4BN
UK
Tel: +44 (0) 1993 848726
Email: info@chandospublishing.com
www.chandospublishing.com

Chandos Publishing is an imprint of Woodhead Publishing Limited

Woodhead Publishing Limited
Abington Hall
Granta Park
Great Abington
Cambridge CB21 6AH
UK
www.woodheadpublishing.com

First published in 2009

ISBN:
978 1 84334 449 0

© A. Whitworth, 2009

British Library Cataloguing-in-Publication Data.
A catalogue record for this book is available from the British Library.

Typeset by Domex e-Data Pvt. Ltd.
Printed in the UK and USA.

For Clare and Joe, whose future this is all about.

Contents

The website

This book is a teaching resource as well as a work of social theory. Throughout, mention is made of a website that resides at *http://www.informationobesity.com* (this URL is repeated in the "running head" at the top of each page, as you can see).

The website is there mainly to:

- provide additional illustrative material which is important, but not really suited to the print format;
- hyperlink to many online resources, whether academic papers, websites or official documents;
- provide a space in which debate about the issues raised in this book can be continued, whether by myself or by readers.

To aid navigation, the site is divided into sections that correspond to the book's chapters. There is also a general section.

Do have a look at it, and do feel free to contribute. No single person these days (if they were ever able to) can serve as the definitive authority on any given field: inevitably, others will have access to criticisms, experience, knowledge or other material that is relevant and important. Communicating and sharing this is how knowledge is developed in a consensual way.

Introduction

This book argues that we are suffering from a condition called "information obesity".

Physical obesity currently worries health analysts and educators. It may become the prime cause of premature death in the developed world, overtaking smoking. It is said to threaten our physical and mental health and the economic wellbeing of society. However, obesity is not simply the result of an overload of food. It is also caused by a decrease in quality. It is behavioural, linked to how we treat both food and our bodies (e.g. exercise, lifestyle).

This is a useful analogy for our relationship with information. Mass production has given us easy access to very large stocks of information. Finding information is no longer the problem, but being discriminating, filtering it out, and managing it is difficult. Quantity rises, but quality and balance drop. The long-term impact of these changes on the health of people and societies has yet to be seen, but many believe it will be negative unless we find a way to manage the flow of information into our minds and around our organisations.

Physical obesity and information come together in an interesting research project reported by Peter Levine (in Hess and Ostrom, 2007[1]). Levine engaged high school children in Maryland, USA, as researchers, investigating how obesity has causes at different levels of society. First, there are contributions from global, structural factors. The multinational food industries, particularly fast food, target children and other vulnerable groups with cheap, tasty but unhealthy food. These strategies have been explored elsewhere, notably by Spurlock's film *Supersize Me* (and book, *Don't Eat This Book*), Vidal's *McLibel* and Schlosser's *Fast Food Nation*.

---

[1] All books cited in the text are listed, in traditional form, in the bibliography. There is also an annotated reading list at the end of the book, which focuses on those books that are most relevant to students and teachers of these subjects. This reading list is repeated on the website, which contains many additional online references.

However, individuals cannot ignore their responsibilities. We do not have to eat the hamburger. We could go to the gym more often. We could educate ourselves about how to live healthily, develop a critical attitude to advertising, filter out unhelpful information, and make choices that might keep obesity at bay.

However, between these, there was another interesting possibility. Levine's students collected obesity data from different parts of town, finding that rates varied from one neighbourhood to another. Though obesity continued to be related to what people ate and how often they exercised, *those* variables were correlated with others such as crime rates; the presence, or otherwise, of local food stores; the number of playgrounds; and even the proportion of streets that had sidewalks (pavements, in the UK). If people felt safe – from street crime and from traffic – they would walk to the local food store to buy produce, which led both to healthier eating, and more exercise; if parents felt safe in the same way they would let their children do these things. If they did not, everyone stayed in and phoned for a pizza.

Obesity is usually cast as the consequence of either personal or corporate neglect. A "personal responsibility" approach considers the obese person as someone who has failed to control their own appetites; who is ignorant generally and, more specifically, ignores health and fitness advice. Conversely, a "corporate responsibility" approach casts obesity as the result of the industrialisation of food production, which both stimulates consumption (as this makes money) and decreases quality (unhealthy ingredients are added to enhance taste or because they are cheaper).

Both views have some truth in them. But what Levine and his teenage researchers suggested is that the causes of obesity – and hence, ways of addressing it – can potentially be found *between* these two levels. Things like sidewalks, the location of food stores, and street crime rates, are *community responsibilities*. They are the result of decisions taken at a level that is not individual, but nor is it that of the state or market, though it is influenced by both. Community solutions are found in the interconnections between people and their local environment, and are achievable in ways that do not cost a lot of money, do not require global changes to a system uninterested in changing from the top, and may well not be very controversial.

What exactly I mean by the "community" is open to debate. It is a nebulous idea because many different things contribute to it. There are individual psychological elements, a sense of belonging, and a sense of things shared. There are formal aspects, such as local government institutions, bodies that decide where sidewalks will be built (or taken away) and allocate local taxes to pay for these public works. There are other institutions such as schools (particularly), sports clubs, places of worship, voluntary organisations, gathering places such as pubs and cafes, and families: elements of *social capital* (see Putnam, 2000), which seem old-fashioned in this information age but which still occupy a great deal of people's time.

Wenger's work on "communities of practice" (1998) shows also that workplaces are communities. At work, people interact not just for social reasons but to *learn* about how they do their jobs, and how their work environment helps and hinders them in this. Additionally, workplaces supply resources to, and shape the environment of, local communities. When the workplace is recognised as an essential part of, and basis for, community life, then one can persuasively argue that everyone lives within several communities.

Communities can be strengthened by recognising the links between them. A teacher in a school, or a university, is a "teacher", but that role is defined largely by the state, market and media. But the teacher is also a *person* and a member of a school or university community (of employees, and of parents/learners/teachers as a whole). She is a member of a family (as a parent or a child), and other informal groups and learning networks. Similarly, we do not lose our connection with formal education simply because we are no longer registered on a course. Informal learning, communities of practice and individual creativity allow us to apply formal training and qualifications in actual life situations. *Actively learning about how we apply knowledge developed elsewhere* is a crucial aspect of our everyday activity, and in it lies a key difference between the active citizen and the passive consumer. It is in this distinction that I will seek answers to the problem of information obesity, and exploring it requires these solutions to be sought not only in formal education (schools, universities and work-based training) but in the other communities and environments within which we learn.

This book is divided into four parts. Part 1 discusses the nature of information and technology generally: Part 2 considers information and communication technology (ICT) more specifically, then develops the idea of *literacy* as something which has always been considered a foundation of information management, and takes its development forward into the information age. Computer literacy and information literacy are, historically, the favoured educational solutions to the problems ICT poses. I will review them, and conclude that any "literacy" risks becoming a passively applied set of skills: a "checklist" that graduates or workers can present as a qualification, without it representing a creative and active relationship with information. Part 3 explains why this tendency is so strong in our education systems, connecting this to the way organisations and technologies affect the way we think. Part 4 then suggests some educational means to combat information obesity that reside in communities as well as structures and individuals. Like physical obesity, the causes of information obesity reside in all three levels of society: therefore, so must the solutions. Long-term *creative regeneration* of the community and its informational resources is not unforeseeable. If we are to flourish in the information society then we have to think about how to make our relationship with information healthier and sustainable, and this is intimately connected to the need to create a more sustainable, healthy world.

I will say some things about what this book is not, as well as what it is.

This is not a "how to" book about teaching or learning information literacy or ICT skills. Many such books have already been written, with several reviewed in Part 2. Although the book is certainly intended to be read by teachers (amongst others), my aim is more to develop a theoretical model for teaching information-related skills in a way different from how they are usually taught. I therefore discuss the history of how we have organised ourselves, our technologies and ultimately our minds around information. I then use this history to suggest why current educational approaches to ICT, and information more generally, fail to meet expectations, *both* from the point of view of government and the economy, *and* from local, personal perspectives. A historical perspective also shows that these criticisms have often been made before. This is somewhat depressing, but this repetition, and the constant failure of policy makers to acknowledge the criticisms, can be better explained by the theory I develop.

This book is not about new or future technologies. It does not discuss "Web 3.0", the semantic Web, permission-based information agents, organisational taxonomies nor any other examples of emerging ICTs. Rather, it is about where we are and how we got here[2]. Perhaps this may lead to its quickly going out of date, but I hope the opposite is true. By mostly avoiding making predictions about the future, instead describing what we know about the past, it should remain a record of a specific period in history.

---

[2] For reference, it was written mainly between March–August 2008.

Besides, have we learnt to use *today's* ICTs effectively? Telling teachers that all their current technical knowledge will rapidly be outdated by the super-semantic-intelligent-personal-web-agent-software just round the corner is exactly what has beset the use of ICT in schools and colleges since the 1960s. The constant focus on the new, on the next generation of ICT (and of learners), risks blinding us. It is harder to look at, and really *think* about, what is old and familiar than what is new and strange. But the world of the present is based only on the past. Familiarity may not breed contempt, but it can breed an unconscious, passive acceptance of things, and thus a failure to challenge basic assumptions when necessary.

I do not declare a (party) political position. Some bits of the book may appear left wing, some right wing – I cannot tell, as these positions are usually assigned rather than declared. Also, as a book intended for a worldwide audience, it is not country-specific. But I need to qualify that. I am British – specifically, English – and have spent all my life in the UK's education system (apart from 2 months at a US college). My examples are unavoidably influenced by UK politics and perspectives. I try to extend my view outwards, but the reader should be aware of this innate bias. It would have been more artificial to remove it, to affect an international "accent" not my own.

This book is not an "agenda for change". History shows that such agendas are frequently worse than what they seek to change, particularly when co-opted by those whose position was based on the "old" way of thinking. Education is already plagued by endless reforms that disrupt the working practices of both teachers and learners but leave the basic system intact (for reasons which will be elaborated on throughout the book). I do not propose a glorious revolution that has no chance of occurring.

However, it *is* addressed to the individual – the individual teacher, student, parent, and any other interested party – concerned about why the education system fails to live up to promises made regarding quality and working conditions, and about society's wider ability to control the ICTs which now permeate most aspects of work and leisure. It may depress at times but it is not meant to be a depressing book, a mere critique. Instead I hope that, at least in some ways, it will interest, inspire and perhaps empower: empower the individual teacher trying to bring back creativity and fun into their pupils' and their own lives, empower the parent trying to help their child come to terms with information and ICT, empower the librarian trying to embed information literacy in his or her work but frustrated by institutional obstacles, and empower the student, trying to understand how these technologies change us.

Enough positioning, and making excuses in advance. Let's get on with it.

About the author

Andrew Whitworth was born 10 days after Woodstock and 6 days before the Internet (the first working demonstration of packet-switching, more precisely). As is probably obvious from some passages in this book, he grew up in Sussex, England. After a time working as a computer programmer for an insurance company, which was about as exciting as it sounds, he moved to Yorkshire in 1991. He eventually arrived at Leeds University to study Politics. While there he became increasingly interested in the Internet, his contemporary, which at this time was coming into public view, and began developing ideas about the connections between organisation, technology, education and the environment, which are the basis of this book.

After a time working at Leeds he moved to the University of Manchester in 2005 to become Course Director for what is now called the MA: Digital Technologies, Communication and Education (*http://www .MAdigitaltechnologies.com*). This course tries to develop in students a critical, questioning attitude to the use of ICT, the Internet and other technologies, regarding their use (and abuse) in teaching and learning environments. He has published many papers and chapters in this field, but this is his first single-authored book. He lives in Hebden Bridge, Yorkshire, England, with his wife Clare, son Joe, and a library of old movies, the latter two of whom are currently growing at a healthy rate.

Thanks

This book has been 10 years in the making. Many people have contributed, in ways large and small, to its creation. It has my name on it but it is a joint effort.

Thanks go to:

Shima Al-Otaibi	Annalisa Manca
Susie Andretta	Helen Manchester
Marilena Aspioti	Maggie McPherson
Angela Benson	Peter Millican
Ricardo Blaug	Sobia Nawaz
Roger Boyle	Doug Paulley
Gráinne Conole	Jim Petch
Hannah Dee	Katerina Polivanova
Jill Duggleby	Pete Reffell
Hugh Dyer	Gail Taylor
Elvira Evgenyeva	Julian Williams
Fred Garnett	The patrons of the Railway Inn,
Caroline Haythornthwaite	Hebden Bridge
Alan Jervis	Mum and Dad
Cormac Lawler	Carol and Dave
Rose Luckin	Clare and Joe:

...all of whom know how, and why.

Part 1:
Information and technology in the world

Information as a resource

> ...the banal fact of the Earth's roundness... [means that] idea will encounter idea, and the result will be an organised web of thought... a piece of evolutionary machinery... (Julian Huxley)

This chapter addresses the fundamental, but not straightforward, question: *what is information?* We need to understand the role information plays in our world in order to appreciate why it has certain effects on us, and therefore, grasp the nature of information and communication technology (ICT), information literacy, and information obesity.

Information is part of our environment, as this chapter is mainly concerned with explaining. But it is more than something lying around waiting to be used. Jonassen *et al.* (2003: p. iii) say: "Since evolving from primordial ooze, humans have interacted with the world and struggled to make sense out of what they experienced; this is as natural to humans as breathing". Information, defined very broadly, is the product of this interaction. It includes data, technical specifications, laws and procedures, works of art, emotional responses, statements of morality and ethics, and more, produced then communicated by human beings interacting with the world and each other. As we will see, one of the learning issues regarding "information" is whether something like a factual statement can and should be distinguished from things like expressions of emotion, stories or paintings. The thinking tasks on the website for this chapter help address this question.

Therefore, information may be consciously produced and communicated for specific reasons, or it may arise accidentally, or as a spontaneous response to an event. It may be communicated without either party being aware of it. It may be unambiguous and easy to understand, or difficult, requiring a high level of prior knowledge in recipients. It may have multiple layers of meaning and possible interpretations.

Information can also be *stored*. Indeed it could be argued that humanity's facility for information storage is what largely distinguishes us from other species and has allowed us to develop civilisation. We store information in many places: in our minds, in language, in technology. Through their interactions, the environment itself becomes a storage medium. Information is a *resource drawn from the environment*. This "environmental model" of information is the basis of this book.

This idea is not necessarily intuitive, but is the key to understanding why information affects our lives the way it does. Let us explore it in more depth, starting with some basic facts about human existence. At this stage in our history there is one thing – and, beyond basic genetic material, it is the only thing – that, unarguably, every human being shares. That is, we all live on the planet Earth. From a personal point of view it is quite large. For example, from my house to Beijing is about 8400 km, a journey that, on foot, would take me many months. However, with air travel I could reach Beijing in a day, and ICT can put me in contact with someone there almost immediately. In those terms the Earth is fairly small. It is also finite, and mostly a closed system. Things made or born here tend to stay here, interacting with many other things occupying the same space. This has profound implications.

One is *evolution*. Darwin's *Origin of the Species* has an elegant central idea; that *through countless small changes iterated over and over again at the microscopic scale, profound and wide-ranging change can occur in a system*. Although Darwin did not invent this principle (philosophers such as Zeno were there 2 millennia earlier), he did successfully apply it to biological systems. On a finite, closed space such as the Earth, as many systems interact over eons, the result is the great diversity of Earth's lifeforms and environmental niches.

The Earth is more than just a container for organisms, however. The environment itself can be considered a living system. Life exists at many scales, from the genetic level to organisms, species, and ecosystems. At the top lies the *biosphere*. Earth itself is a single living planet, and life a single phenomenon. This is not as fanciful as it sounds; if an alien astronomer had the right equipment, they could detect in our atmosphere the existence of organic compounds, substances which would almost certainly prove that life existed here. The biosphere absorbs energy from the Sun and processes it to maintain itself; it is self regulating, hugely diverse, and it evolves.

The biosphere idea was best described by a Russian scientist, Vladimir Vernadsky (and, later, James Lovelock with his notion of "Gaia": see Samson and Pitt, 1999 for an excellent general resource). Later, in 1945, Vernadsky went further, writing a paper called "The Biosphere and the Noösphere". As well as a living planet, Vernadsky observed that Earth was also a *thinking* planet. Again, the simple truth of this is demonstrated by realising that, with the right equipment, one could receive information from Earth, even light years away, that could only have come from a planet of intelligent beings. Radio and TV waves move out into the cosmos and could be detected: as imagined in the novel and movie *Contact* (Sagan, 1986; see also Chapter 5).

Just as genetic information moves through the biosphere, so human communication moves through the noösphere[1]. The noösphere is wholly integrated with Earth's other spheres. It depends on their natural resources for sustenance, and simultaneously influences change in these other spheres. It is, in short, fully part of the environment, as essential a resource for human activity as the atmosphere, hydrosphere (water), lithosphere (rocks, minerals) and biosphere (life). On the website are further illustrations of the way these spheres interact.

Before I explain the relevance of this, let us conduct a thought experiment to illustrate the noösphere's reality. Consider the Mona Lisa. Almost everyone surely has a vague idea of what this painting looks like and many will bring it to mind quite accurately. This already suggests that the *concept* of the Mona Lisa surpasses the physical object, the canvas in Paris. However, if someone were to breach the Louvre's security and destroy it, we would probably agree that the Mona Lisa would have been "lost". It exists in countless other versions – digital files, printed reproductions and painted copies – but as far as we know there is only one original.

Now, could you similarly destroy *Romeo and Juliet*? What if, through an heroic effort of will, you tracked down every book, DVD and online text, and destroyed them? Would the play disappear? This is less certain than with the painting. Where is the "original"? What of the Shakespearean scholars and actors with the text in their heads? Even if one person could not remember it all, collaboration could salvage the play fairly quickly. (Ray Bradbury uses this point in *Fahrenheit 451*.)

The best conclusion is that *Romeo and Juliet* exists, but in some place other than simple physical reality. This place, intangible but real, is the noösphere. And though the Mona Lisa is more rooted in physical reality than *Romeo and Juliet*, its primary sphere of existence is also the noösphere.

Much of what we see in the world around us is the result of interactions of the noösphere with other parts of the environment. This

---

[1] The word comes from the Greek *nous*, meaning "mind". Pronounce it something like "Noah-sphere", with the two "o"s separate.

is clearly true of constructed, urban landscapes, in which different types of information interact with natural environments to produce cities and towns (see Chapter 3 for a specific example). But even a rural landscape will have been shaped by the knowledge required to farm and manage it, and a wilderness may only be such because it is protected by human legal constructions which "fence" it off from development. Information is as much embedded into, say, a railway viaduct as into a page of the London *Financial Times*. Indeed, considering why railways were built, it is, at least in part, the same kind of information.

It is hopefully clear that all environments have an informational element. It is in these environments and the structures, procedures and technologies that comprise them that information is stored. Storage media include books, newspapers, the World-Wide Web and television, and less obvious media such as computer programs, laws, and a transport infrastructure. These media, and the information within them, are amongst the resources we draw from our environment in order to act in the world, live everyday lives, work in jobs, relate to friends and study. In turn, information influences the world and changes its many environments. And this process is rapidly accelerating.

Information is not like other resources such as oil, land or machinery. Mason *et al.* spend a few pages (1995: pp. 41–5) describing the differences. Note, incidentally, their reference to information as a source of *power*; we will return to this in later chapters.

> Unlike weapons, money, and many other sources of power... information is not a thing. It is not materialistic. Information obeys different laws...
>
> Because it originates in the mind and is intangible, information has some surprisingly different characteristics that clearly distinguish it from other kinds of resources and from other sources of wealth. Cleveland (1982) has identified seven special characteristics of information: Information, he asserts, is human, expandable, compressible, substitutable, transportable, diffusive and shareable. Collectively, these make information a unique resource, the use of which creates some rather unique ethical issues.

As they do, let's expand on these characteristics, which help explain why information has the importance that it does, and why we find it difficult to resist getting fat on it. (All page references in this section refer to Mason *et al.*)

Information is human. This is not strictly true, as animals can communicate to spread information (e.g. "the nectar is this way"). But it is certainly true that information is *mental.* Although information can be stored in tangible objects, it gains meaning "only in the… mind – what it observes, remembers and can retrieve – and what it then analyses, intuits, and integrates" (p. 42). Because information is mental, that also means it is ambiguous, personal, and subject to multiple interpretations.

Information is expandable. Because it is difficult to destroy, it tends to expand through use. As a result, "abundance and overload are greater problems than scarcity" (p. 42), and it is essential for us to *filter* information if we are to make our way through the world (an important point which will be frequently returned to).

Information is compressible. Its usefulness and power also arise because information can be summarised and concentrated. It can change its form: for example, spoken words, written text and a picture can express roughly the same message.

Information is substitutable. This is discussed in Chapter 2, but for now let us note that information "can replace labour, capital or physical materials in most economic processes… To cite one example, information is replacing aluminium in beverage can production. From 1972 to 1990 the number of cans produced per pound of aluminium increased almost 40% due to scientific developments…" (p. 43).

Information is transportable. Most resources can be moved to some extent, the exceptions being things such as land and other location-specific resources (like a good view). However, recent improvements in our ability to transport information have been "explosive" (p. 44), and through communications technologies we can move information around the globe at virtually the speed of light, far faster than we will ever be able to move physical resources.

Information is diffusive. "It is hard to contain. It tends to leak. Because it is intangible, it naturally oozes through the pores of things and radiates, spreads out, and disperses…. This is one of the reasons that many traditional methods of containing the flow of information, such as provisions for confidentiality, secrecy and intellectual property rights, are, in practice, so difficult to apply effectively today…" (p. 44).

Information is shareable. "Perhaps the most significant economic feature of information is that it is *not* depleted with use…. Cleveland adds: '*Things* are exchanged: if I give you a flower or sell you my automobile (or a book or video tape), you have it and I don't. But if I sell you an idea, we both have it. And if I give you a fact or tell you a story, it's like a good kiss: in sharing the thrill, you enhance it…'" (pp. 44–5).

Let us end this discussion of information as an environmental resource by further exploring parallels between the noösphere and other spheres of the world.

None of these spheres are static. Instead, the Earth is in a constant state of dynamic change. In the environmental model, in principle, any part of the world has a chance to eventually interact with any other part of the world. In the solid sphere (lithosphere) this may take many millions of years. The exchange rate of the sphere's basic substance – rock – is very slow. In other spheres it happens more quickly. The biosphere is in fact less dynamic than the atmosphere and hydrosphere. The basic substance of the biosphere, genetic material, is exchanged through a process limited by geography and which takes, ultimately, quite a long time for most species. Hence evolution's extremely slow rate of change compared to the weather, but its reasonably fast rate compared to continental drift.

In the noösphere, information can be exchanged in a second, and on a worldwide scale. Enormous amounts interact every day, producing new circumstances to which we must immediately adapt. These conditions have been brought upon us by technology, though not all at once; exchange rates have accelerated throughout the evolution of communications technologies, from language itself through writing, printing, telecommunications, broadcasting and now ICT. Each step in this process gave a profound boost to the speed at which information can be exchanged, and made the world's environments more dynamic as a result. The good news may be that because we are exchanging information as physically fast as we ever can do – the speed of light – we may have reached a time of maximum dynamism. However more we enhance ICT in other ways, this is a basic fact of the universe. To exchange information any faster would be to prove Einstein wrong[2].

We might still increase the *volume* of information exchanged at lightspeed. But we will still need to absorb and understand that information: to *learn*, in other words. Just because we might be able to

---

[2] The Theory of Relativity is probably science's most rigorously-proven theory. But there is evidence from quantum physics, which still stands separate from relativity, that under certain conditions information can be exchanged between objects faster than the speed of light at the sub-nuclear level. Tapping into this medium of information exchange is the aim of *quantum computing*. If a genuine quantum computer could be built, it may access a sixth sphere of the Earth, which interconnects at a subatomic level – the *microsphere*, maybe. Whether it would make information exchange any faster, however, is unlikely, for at the local astronomical scale of the Earth information exchange is already effectively instantaneous.

download the whole of, say, *2001: A Space Odyssey* or *Zen and the Art of Motorcycle Maintenance* in half a second, and perhaps, ultimately, be able to "watch" or "read" them in half a second (as the characters in *The Matrix* download knowledge straight into their brains), this is not going to make it easier to understand either of these difficult works, it is not going to make either of them more aesthetically and intellectually pleasing, and it is not going to end debate on whether they are important, or pretentious irrelevances. *Any information we absorb only becomes knowledge if we assign it some kind of value and actively construct this knowledge through an educational process.* To bypass the place where we ask, "Do I need this? Do I like this?" is one way our ability to filter information is taken from us: and a lack of effective filtering is one cause of information obesity. (I will summarise the elements of information obesity at the end of Chapter 3.)

We may indeed develop further technologies to help us manage, analyse and produce information; enhancing our ability to *tune* this sphere, to filter out waste and to make effective use of its resources. Indeed these are probably essential to our continued ability to learn. However, these technologies will not remove the need to address other environmental questions. Will they help us retain the noösphere's diversity? Will parts of it degrade through our exploiting it, what parts, how, and what can we do to regenerate them? Will everyone have a right to access, manage and produce the resources they need? Will they be able to exercise these rights in real-life situations? The noösphere may not become any more dynamic, but it may become polluted, degraded and enclosed. Discovering how to use this priceless resource sustainably, to benefit the maximum number of people, is an educational issue. We need to learn how to manage information; not just reactively as we go along, but by attending to the nature of the environment itself: for *what we embed into our environment influences later evolution.* Resources are often considered as things to be used, or at least transformed, but they should instead be viewed as things that we *build for the future.*

In *The Selfish Gene* (1976), Richard Dawkins described the notion of the *meme.* Memes are the informational equivalent of genes; "bits" of information propagated through the noösphere. Dawkins wrote (p. 191):

> ...for an understanding of the evolution of modern humanity, we must begin by throwing out the gene as the sole basis of our ideas on evolution.... Darwinism is too big a theory to be confined to the narrow context of the gene.

Remember Darwinism's premise: the iteration of small changes leading to wider systemic change. It's the same, says Dawkins, with cultural evolution. Diverse ideas – memes – encounter each other, interact, and spread. Good ones are sustained, bad ones die out, the noösphere evolves, and possible futures are shaped.

The question is, of course, what criteria are used to judge "good" and "bad". The environment is not a neutral space in which things may or may not flourish mostly through lucky chance. Instead, conditions are created in which *certain* memes – values, beliefs, ideas, ways of working and thinking – thrive and spread. Information becomes embedded into technologies and therefore contributes to environmental conditions that are more favourable to some memes than others. In this point lies our whole modern relationship with information, and how it affects our lives and the world.

The next chapter elaborates on these issues, showing how the environmental model of information helps explain the different ways in which information is *valuable*. Through appreciating these, and how they often conflict, we can develop a framework for analysing the development of information technology, and education's response to it.

2

Valuing information

"Where am I?"
"In the Village."
"What do you want?"
"Information...."
"You won't get it!"
"By hook or by crook, we will."

(Opening dialogue from each episode of *The Prisoner*)

I said earlier that to call works of art or moral principles "information" may seem to demean them. If it does, then this because of ideas about *value*. We value information in many ways, usually not dependent on quantity, but *qualities*. This chapter explores that idea in more detail, then develops the environmental model into a general scheme of value for information.

Below are various sequences of 30 bytes. A byte is a unit of information storage that (with text) equates to one letter, number, symbol or space. In terms of quantity, the phrases are equal. But what of their value?

fqw2**;K>:py&% Wnjwi96#,8$HC0+
East gerbils leave Scotland no
Portsmouth won the 2008 FA Cup
Nissan shares went up 8¢ today
We will be on holiday tomorrow
Love thy neighbour as thy self

The first is completely meaningless. The second is readable, but nonsense. The third has meaning and is actually about something: it is a *fact* and therefore information in a human sense. On one level it is fairly trivial, valuable perhaps if one needed an answer in a quiz. However, the statement summarises many things, such as the hundreds of games that comprised the competition (the FA Cup is the English Football Association's yearly knockout contest open to all teams in the Football League) and the money exchanged as a result, directly (gate receipts, TV income) and indirectly (transport costs, gambling). It will also provoke an emotional response in some people, whereas others will find it irrelevant.

The fourth statement is also factual, and might be extremely valuable to investors in this company, not to mention its employees. It is this kind of information which flows through the world's financial systems, forming a basis for the exchange of huge amounts of money, as investors and brokers seek to maximise returns. The significance of these flows for the development of ICT is returned to below and in Chapter 4.

The fifth statement may also be a fact, but is different from the previous two in terms of its significance. Nevertheless it summarises a reasonably complex process involving the movement of several kinds of resources. It wraps inside it a set of values relevant to the whole idea of "going on holiday" (vacation) and what this means for life in the modern era. It may also be information which makes someone happy, and that alone gives it value.

With the final statement, we move beyond simple facts. Regardless of one's religious beliefs this is a deeply profound observation about how we might learn to live together peacefully. Consequently, it touches on the controversial question of what makes for "truth" and how different interpretations of these "truths" can be valued.

What should be clear from this exercise is that the *quality* of any piece of information is variable and its value largely depends on context and interpretation. To get a grip on this diversity let us explore four different ways in which information is valued.

- personal, or *subjective* value;
- scientific, or *objective* value;
- economic value; and
- community value, both of which are *intersubjective* values.

It is impossible to generalise about the ways information might be valued at the subjective level. Personally, I am indifferent to Portsmouth Football Club (FC) and rather more interested in the next club east along England's coast, Brighton & Hove Albion FC (see also below). I don't own a car, so information about the cost and punctuality of the local rail service is more important to me than it might be to my neighbours. I care about how my son gets on at school and whether he and my wife are currently happy. I could go on, of course. In short I have a *configuration* of interests in the world that make up my personal environment. It will change over time, but at any point there will always be some information that in practical terms is valuable to me but not necessarily to others.

It is not just a matter of current circumstance, however. Like everyone else I have a personality, a set of moral values and beliefs, and likes and dislikes, which are a consequence of many things including my family background, education and other prior experiences. Any new piece of information does not simply fall into my mind as it would into a hole in the ground but interacts with what is already there, with what I know, remember and understand. (Here lies a key distinction between "behaviourist" and "constructivist" education, but that is for later. See also the website, where thinking tasks help you explore your personal perspectives.)

Subjective value is very significant. How could it not be? For anyone, it is going to be their primary filter for information. To filter, one must inevitably ask: "Do I *care* about this? Do I *value* this?". As a result, the subjective form of value forms the basis of much of the teaching of information literacy, currently the favoured strategy for combating information obesity (see Chapter 5).

Nevertheless there are problems with relying solely on subjective value, and these have long been recognised. One problem is how to aggregate these subjective values into collective decision making; a problem on which the art of *politics* is based. At some point the values, needs, or circumstances on which I base my life may come into conflict with others'. Interpretations of the same information may differ. We may be competing for resources. These conflicts arise all the time and we have, as a society, developed various means for dealing with them: from simply talking differences through (amicably or not), through arbitration, voting, decree, litigation and – though sensible people should hope it never reaches this – exercising force to get one's way. Learning about the strategies that exist for resolving conflict is a substantial part of what it means to grow out of childhood, past the stage where we believe ourselves the centre of the world. It is one link from the individual into their communities.

It is also difficult to treat all personal, subjective values equally. To refuse to pass judgement on particular points of view, through a belief that individual opinions must be respected, is a philosophical stance known as *relativism*. Most people would probably accept that at times, a relativistic stance is hard to maintain, such as when faced by outright racial or religious prejudice, the hatred of women, or the glorification of violence and murder. Yet even here it is difficult sometimes to draw clear lines between "right" and "wrong". Is abortion justified, or murderous? Is it wrong to kill someone if they demand the right to die? Questions such as these may be resolved by individuals who develop an opinion one way or the other, but are more difficult to resolve at the level of a group or society. They are ongoing questions of morality or ethics, and good examples of the kind of knowledge that has *intersubjective* value. We will return to this below.

There is another reason to treat relativism with suspicion. Information held in an individual mind – or a community's, organisation's or society's stock of knowledge – may be "wrong" in an objective sense. In *Counterknowledge* (2008), Damian Thompson forcefully makes this point by discussing a range of what he considers dangerous and unscientific points of view, and how these damage the intellectual resources of society. He attacks, amongst others: creationism; alternative histories (such as the idea that lost civilisations existed before the Ice Age); alternative therapies such as homoeopathy; conspiracy theories; and more. Thompson's book will be discussed in more detail in Chapter 5, but for now, let us look at why he feels this kind of knowledge is without value. His judgment is based on how the procedures of scientific method *validate* certain beliefs, theories or practices. Scientific method is a rigorous means of valuing information objectively: that is, not subject to the biases, whims or misconceptions of individuals. The following quotes make Thompson's basic point:

> We are lucky to live in an age in which the techniques available for evaluating the truth or falsehood of claims about science and history are more reliable than ever before…. One of the greatest legacies of the European Enlightenment is a scientific methodology that allows us to make increasingly accurate observations about the world around us. (pp. 1–2)

> The tests applied to empirical statements are, for the most part, impressively rigorous, and they are applied by a scientific community that… is made up of individuals from diverse ethnic, religious and cultural backgrounds… from time to time scientists arrive at the wrong explanation of natural phenomena; but these mistakes are usually rectified by later hypotheses that better fit the data. So, when scrupulous researchers overwhelmingly agree that a particular claim is a statement of fact, the probability that they are right is extremely high. (p. 28)

However, there are limits on how useful scientifically validated knowledge can ever be in our everyday lives. Because these forms of knowledge are objective, they cannot and never will be able to explain or support subjective forms of value such as aesthetics or the sublime (the sort of experience one has when watching a perfect sunset, or listening to great music). Second, they are often inadequate for understanding complex social phenomena, and are not usually to hand when one needs to apply oneself to a new or unexpected situation where an immediate response is required. None of this affects the objective value of scientific knowledge, but it clearly affects other forms of value. (See Chapter 5.)

The structure of scientific method, and the organisations that have grown up around it, are also *social systems*, and objectivity can therefore be distorted within them. This point was famously made by Kuhn in *The Structure of Scientific Revolutions* (1970). Kuhn observed that science could entrench itself in *paradigms*, systems of belief which had become institutionalised into an "establishment". However well justified and validated through scientific method, knowledge which challenged this paradigm – thus, the stature of scientists with positions and careers based on the values embedded in the paradigm – could be rejected or ignored; its publication and validation refused. Paradigms rarely changed unless evidence became overwhelming: or, more likely, those entrenched in the paradigm retired or passed on. A significant example was Wegener's theory of continental drift, deduced from strictly-conducted observations in geology and palaeontology. Geologists prior to Wegener had been taught that the Earth's crust was rigid, and observations and theories were grounded in this fundamental principle. Now we know that the lithosphere, like the Earth's other spheres, is dynamic, but due to the establishment's adherence to the previous paradigm, it was decades after Wegener's death in 1930 before his theories were fully accepted. (See Chapter 1 of Redfern's excellent layperson's guide (2000).)

The point is not that scientists are engaged in some giant conspiracy to keep new ideas down. As Thompson says, this sort of conspiracy theory is itself a form of counterknowledge. It is merely to say that certain ways of thinking can become embedded into institutions and organisations and resist changes in the manner of an immune system fighting off a virus (see also Chapter 9). It is a classic example of how information can become embedded in the environment and form conditions that are not conducive to the spread of certain (rival) memes.

Objective values can be distorted in another significant way, one Thompson castigates throughout his book, particularly when discussing pseudohistory and quack medicine. That is, there is a *market* for it. Publishers have a greater interest in producing counterknowledge for consumption than they do in refusing to distribute it due to its unscientific nature. This criticism refers to another significant form of value; indeed, the most significant in the modern era: economic or market value.

Information is something with potentially unlimited economic value. We live in a capitalist economic system, based on the use of resources in the pursuit of profit. In a production process, value is (ideally) *added* at various points by producing something that can be sold for more than the sum cost of its parts. Information is just one resource that enters this process (others include raw materials, energy, labour and technology), but it is becoming the most significant one. Mason *et al.*'s observation that information can substitute for aluminium in cans is only one example. Information about how to market a product, gathered from surveys of consumers and their spending or other habits; information about what one's competitors will release for Christmas; advance knowledge of legislation which may affect business; even information about the weather forecast, so a supermarket can move disposable barbecues to a prominent shelf should sunny weather be due. All these and more are vital for conducting business in a competitive market. Fuelling it all is information about stock, currency and commodity prices, endlessly circulating and constantly influencing the world's financial exchanges. On top of this is the value of information about our personal lives, our credit history, even our movements, constantly gathered and stored by companies and governments. Finally there is the vast amount of information produced purely for consumption. Rolling 24-hour news channels need news, so news is written; magazines need pictures, so pictures are taken; and so on. In "information industries" such as the arts, media and indeed education, almost all added value comes from the exploitation, packaging and production of information. Information in such a setting becomes valued not because of its "truth" (scientific or otherwise), nor even its aesthetic values, but because it will sell (Lyotard, 1984: p. 84).

Like the scientific establishment, markets are human constructions, media for the transmission of information. Markets are not objective like mathematical operations, which help calculate exchange values, are objective. Economics is a social science, not an objective one, and the measures of value it develops are the result of interactions between people: neither objective, nor subjective, but *intersubjective*.

Information and communication are the basis of our social nature. We learn *with others* to adapt to the world and other people within it. Jonassen *et al.* say (2003: p. 5) that as well as being individual (changes in the brain, behaviour etc.), learning is distributed amongst *communities*, with knowledge built and held by groups and organisations as well as individuals:

> As we interact with others in knowledge-building communities, our knowledge and beliefs about the world are influenced by that community and their beliefs and values.... Communities of learners, like communities of practitioners, can be seen as a kind of widely distributed memory with each of its members storing a part of the group's total memory...

Note the link between the two words "community" and "communication". Both come from the Latin word *communis*, meaning to hold in common, to share; also the root of "communal" and "commune". All are based on the principle of *sharing*, and amongst the things that are shared (see below) are values. It is in this process that information becomes valued at the intersubjective level.

Communities are not simply gatherings of otherwise unconnected people. Clarke (1996: p. 24) says communities share things such as symbols, myths, stories, significant moments, and some form of place or location; often, but not necessarily, where community members live. Communities support and give meaning to individual lives, in many different ways. A good illustration is the community of the sports club fan. I have already mentioned that I support Brighton & Hove Albion football club, a relatively minor English team. It, and thousands of similar clubs across the world, fit Clarke's definition of "community" perfectly. Even if you have no interest in football, try to see that fans of a club will share:

- *significant moments*: all Brighton fans identify with the FA Cup Final of 1983 and a certain game at Hereford in 1997 where the team avoided relegation (demotion from the Football League to non-league status), at least;

- *shared symbols*: the club badge; the seagull motif and nickname; the blue and white striped kit; the song *Sussex by the Sea* sung by supporters (shared with Sussex County Cricket Club, tying both into the wider identity of Sussex and its people);

- *significant people*: star players – or hate figures, whether rival football clubs (Crystal Palace... boo!), players, or despised owners...;

- ■ ... one of whom was defined as a *shared threat* in 1997, as fans campaigned against unpopular chairman Bill Archer (see North and Hodson, 1997);

- ■ *shared ongoing events*: each game, obviously;

- ■ *shared sense of place*: the community of fans is distributed throughout the UK and the world. But there's an obvious connection back to Brighton and/or wherever the team plays each away game.

These resources are active ingredients of the community's identity, culture and history. It is through their being shared that the community exists. These values are not wholly subjective, as they do not depend only on individual feelings. But one cannot be *told* one is a member of a community in any real way. Membership of a community also has to be *felt*. Nor, then, are community values objective. Instead they are intersubjective, existing in the connections between people: existing, in short, in the noösphere.

I used a relatively trivial and local example here, though sports fandom gives rise to strong feelings and (as Brighton fans have proved: North and Hodson, 1997) can change environments. This kind of communal dynamism has been called *social capital*, most notably (but not only) by Putnam (2000), who bemoans the decline of institutions such as sports clubs in which such values were historically embedded. Actually, football fan culture is a prime example; the brand of each team is now used to market products, increasingly owned by the global marketplace rather than the community that spawned it. For a few clubs (communities) the result is rapid growth but a perceived loss of "soul"; for most, slow decline as a community asset. On a smaller scale, the network of community organisations such as churches, local sports clubs and family connections is likewise in decline.

Some may see this as just part of the evolution of the world. We might replace local (and parochial) forms of social capital with global ones, building identities with people anywhere should we feel an affinity with them. But Putnam's book is a warning, and the environmental model of information helps justify the concern. It is at the intersubjective level, communities and communication, that we validate the values and ethics that help govern our lives. This role is increasingly undertaken not by public debate and agreement, but by controlled, technical methods such as the vote, economics, marketing, and control over media for information exchange. This *colonisation* process is a fundamental challenge to the sustainability of the noösphere: it is the basis of the argument of Part 3.

How to recognise valid or *rational* ways of thinking and acting has occupied philosophers for thousands of years, from Plato to Hume, Kant, Habermas and more. I introduce some of their work at this point, with the caveat that this can only be an introduction: I strongly recommend the interested reader consult other books which cover these matters in more detail and sophistication than I can manage (see the annotated reading list).

One way of validating an action or decision is to ask whether it is the most effective tool, technique, strategy or plan. This has been called *instrumental rationality*. Here, what counts as "effective" will be judged against criteria such as: What works best? What is cheapest, quickest or most efficient? To make these judgements, a constant stream of information is required, information that ideally has objective value. As Bonnett says (in McFarlane, 1997: p. 148):

> We constantly seek to evaluate, predict, control, our environment the better to exploit it…. We manipulate our social and natural environment… to serve our purposes more efficiently…. [Instrumental rationality] is the sort of thinking that enables us to "get things done" and its success in this regard is highly seductive. Few of us would lightly forgo many of the products of this kind of thinking, which even at a basic level range from on-the-shelf food to potable water and anaesthetics.

But as the previous discussion has hopefully made clear, though we could not do without instrumental rationality, other kinds of thinking help us make our way through the world. For instance, we need some motivation for beginning a technical inquiry: a *reason* to do so. Although this may develop through other technical enquiries it is always going to be at least partly subjective and/or intersubjective. Egan's *Romantic Understanding* (1990) is a useful guide to the educational value of these other ways of thinking. I will refer to it frequently when discussing teaching methods that may help combat information obesity (particularly in Chapter 10). For now, let us consider his basic point. The romantic point of view does not seek to manipulate the environment around us, but to appreciate it: it does not seek "one best" way of thinking and acting, or "universal, uniform standards supposedly inherent in nature", but celebrates diversity (Egan, 1990: Chapter 2). It recognises the value of emotion as motivation for action and learning, and how both action and learning help individuals determine what knowledge and information is to them *authentic*, meaning relevant to one's own outlook, experience and activity (also Bonnett, in McFarlane, 1997: p. 149). Relevance can be identified in advance but is also established through *using* information and then evaluating the results in an ongoing cycle of learning.

Egan is fully aware that appeals to romantic understanding in the current educational environment, where emphasis is placed on the relevance of teaching to the needs of the economy and business, risks seeming an anachronism, a kind of idealistic appeal to the emotions. Worse, it may be "sentimental whimsy" (Egan, 1990: p. 34) which can all too readily degenerate into the counterknowledge that Thompson is so concerned about. Yet as Egan points out on the same page:

> [T]he constituents of Romanticism... are not historical curiosities; they are a part of the ways we now see, hear and make sense of the world.

It is not romanticism that is problematic, but rather, an overemphasis on *either* romantic or instrumental rationality: in other words, neglecting subjective value in favour of objective or vice versa. What is best, and this is Egan's point throughout, is "a combination of imagination and systematic method working together" (Egan, 1990: p. 22).

Nevertheless, the idea of intersubjective value can help establish a way of thinking about information that recognises the way it is embedded in the world. To develop a rationality based on intersubjective value it is necessary to return to the idea of information as a resource. Let us think about the ways in which different resources exist and are used in the world, and how information follows these patterns just as do other resources such as water, oil and gold. (There is more detail on each of these principles, as well as illustrative thinking tasks, on the website.)

No resource evenly diffuses itself throughout available space; not even air, the *quality* of which varies markedly from place to place. Water, minerals and information flow along specific routes. They may gather in one place – an oil field, gold jewellery, a Swiss bank account – and we consider this *wealth*. Access to wealth, and the right to exploit it, may be controlled and policed. These have always been key political issues and continue to provoke wars and conflict.

In general terms, resources can be renewable or non-renewable. Renewable resources are not depleted by use, and information would seem to fall into this category. But the division is unclear. Soil, for example, is technically renewable, but through bad *management* can lose so much quality that it can no longer support crops, and the land turns to desert. Management of renewable resources is therefore a key principle in the *sustainable* exploitation of environments, and it can take many forms, from preservation, through legal restrictions, to the active nurturing and regeneration of damaged environments.

Environments also have different levels of healthiness. An environment polluted by chemicals or litter will be less likely to thrive than a cleaner one. Diversity is also important. This is not a judgement based on currently fashionable appeals to "biodiversity". It is a basic principle of environmental health. A monoculture – an environment containing only one species – is more vulnerable to collapse through pest, disease or changing environmental conditions than a more diverse ecosystem. Much the same applies to a company dependent on one product; a town dependent on one employer; and a political system dependent on one idea. If that product, employer or idea gets into trouble, the wider system is threatened. *Diversity is what enables adaptation* and that is why it is so fundamentally worrying that our political and educational systems are now embedding one single set of principles into the technological infrastructures which underlie them. But I get ahead of myself.

These terms then:

- access;
- sustainability;
- management;
- diversity;
- healthiness

...are more than just metaphors. They are key criteria for judging the quality of an environment and the resources within it. They can and should be applied to the noösphere as well; for that sphere, despite all its complexity, is only a subset of the wider environments in which we live and on which our future depends. More precisely, it depends on the sustainability and future usefulness of the resources we are building within them.

A model of how information acts as a resource in the world has previously been developed by Elinor Ostrom (see Hess and Ostrom, 2007: pp. 3–14). Information can be considered a "public good"; a resource that, in principle, is shared between all, but which as a result is "subject to social dilemmas" (Hess and Ostrom, 2007: p. 3). Some studies (most notably Hardin, 1968) of traditional commons-based resources such as fisheries, grazing land and the like concluded that such commons are threatened through people's inability to manage their use. Threats to commons include behaviour such as freeriding (people reaping the benefit of the commons without working to maintain or nurture the resource), congestion, pollution and exhaustion. Hess and Ostrom point out, however, that commons-based resources are not historically characterised by "free for alls" but instead "require strong collective-action and self-govering mechanisms, *as well as a high degree of social capital*" (p. 5: I have added the emphasis to make a specific link between the management of common resources and the importance of community-based and intersubjective forms of value and activity).

Information is not quite like other commons-based resources, in that it is "non-rivalrous". Technically, because of its infinitely reproducible nature, an information commons can be accessed constantly and by all without threatening the ability of anyone to access that resource in the future (see Suber's chapter in Hess and Ostrom, 2007). But this is a theoretical principle only. Information might lose quality and effectiveness simply through exposure. Suber also refers to the idea of a "tragic stalemate" in which no user of the commons has any incentive to take the initiative in protecting or nurturing it. A non-rivalrous resource can therefore still become depleted in quality. As this is one basic cause of information obesity, combating it requires, at one level, attending to how an information commons may be regenerated. This is one role of education.

Another significant threat to commons is *enclosure*: or, from another perspective, privatisation. Hess and Ostrom say in their introduction (2007: p. 10): "New technologies can enable the capture of what were once free and open public goods". While not all information has ever been "free and open", no discussion of the impact of information on our lives and minds can neglect developments such as copyright, patenting, "freedom of information" acts and other means by which access to the information commons is often institutionally restricted.

In summary, and though this statement must be supported in more detail – the task of Part 3 of this book – the history of our attempts to manage the world's resources are largely characterised by instrumental rationality. As a result, they have disrupted community life in various ways. Some communities have not survived the experience at all. The embedding of this way of thinking into our technologies and strategies is similarly influencing our management of the noösphere. It is the aim of this book to explain why such methods are now dangerous. Because the noösphere is at its peak level of dynamism, we cannot increase the "efficiency" of information transfer any further without one of two things happening: we either produce technologies to do the job for us, or we become smarter ourselves. Either way, a learning process is required.

I will conclude this chapter by reiterating points made by Egan, which also support claims that a diverse environment is needed to retain adaptability to change. We should not privilege any *one* of these forms of value over others. What is needed is to recognise the value of diverse strategies in particular circumstances and contexts; to understand when one way of thinking is *appropriate* whereas another may not be.

However, not every system of value or belief has equal facility to affect the world. Information becomes embedded into the technological systems within which we act and live and sets conditions for future understanding. How and why that happens is the subject of the next chapter.

3

The shaping of information and technology

...ways of generating, storing and processing ideas and information are never neutral... are the central values that are embodied in certain kinds of IT application really compatible with those of the classroom context into which they are being imported? (Bonnett, in McFarlane, 1997: p. 145)

This chapter is concerned with how information becomes embedded into technology. Remember that "information" is defined in the broadest sense, to include values, beliefs and moralities. I will also use "technology" in the broadest sense, to mean more than just machines and computers. Technology is found throughout the whole infrastructure, like buildings and transport. The idea should also encompass the organisations in which we work, study and teach.

The chapter, and Part 1 of the book, end with a statement about the importance of creativity and innovation for both our lives as individuals and as members of organisations. It is in the tension between these that further causes of information obesity lie, as well as difficulties we have with addressing it. This basic idea will then be explored in detail throughout part 2.

I want to start with three case studies which illustrate the principle of the *social shaping of technology*. This idea has already been presented by Mackenzie and Wajcman (1985), Williams and Edge (1996) and Winner (1986). I merely summarise and illustrate the idea here. For more detail read any of these other excellent works. See also the links on the website.

Case 1: Hebden Bridge, Yorkshire, UK

I know this place well, because it's where I live. It's about 25 miles (40 km) north of the city of Manchester, in the Pennine Hills. It's a good example of how diverse factors can influence design, producing a unique *configuration* of technology – in this case, architecture. Just as individuals can develop unique configurations of values, possessions, friendships and so on, so technology can grow to fit a specific environment, partly through conscious design and partly through adaptation by its users.

There are some photos of Hebden Bridge on the website and I hope these show that the town is built in a steep-sided valley. Until about 1830 there was little there except an inn and the eponymous bridge. Almost the entire town was constructed between then and 1900. Why?

In short, the Industrial Revolution. The Calder valley is one of the easiest Pennine passes, hence a valuable route for goods to cross the north of England. First the canal then the railway penetrated early in the 19th century, and the steep walls of the valley then encouraged the development of mills, an industrial technology which at the time was still largely water-driven. The town was built to house workers for the mills; the railway and canal were built mainly for the movement of goods, not people. Already we see geography, economics and infrastructure shaping a design decision: namely to site a new town here at all.

Things were not straightforward, however. There was insufficient flat land on the valley floor for housing. But building on the valley walls risked being uneconomic, as houses needed a great deal of shoring up to prevent their sliding down the slope. Simply put, they would cost too much to build, prices and rents being what they were. The *technological* response to these (social, technical and economic) problems was to build houses into the shoring walls. Many houses in the town (including mine, and most of those you can see in the photos) are therefore two dwellings, one above the other; top houses face onto one street, bottom houses another. Builders and landlords could get two rents for the same plot, making it economical to build in this way.

There are hundreds of these houses in the town, yet the configuration is found almost nowhere else in Britain. A unique combination of circumstances – geographical, economic, historical (the fact the town was constructed almost in one go), and technical (engineering-based) – has created a technological "system" for living in which is more or less unique.

Case 2: The Long Island Expressway

The Long Island Expressway (LIE) has become the "classic" case of the social shaping of technology, due to its being discussed in Winner's influential article, "Do Artefacts Have Politics?". He answers that question with a definite *yes*, and the LIE clearly illustrates why, as the social rationale embedded into its form is highly divisive.

The LIE was built with very low bridges, as low as 9 feet (under 3 metres) of clearance. This means that only passenger cars can use the road. Buses and trucks are excluded. Why was it built in this way?

The LIE connects New York City with the Long Island beach resorts, frequented by affluent folk of Manhattan. Even now, and certainly when it was built, few of New York's poorer inhabitants had access to cars. They had to travel by bus or suburban train. The LIE's bridges were specifically designed to exclude bus passengers – thus, poorer people – from visiting Long Island's beach resorts.

Therefore, this is not just a case of a political decision influencing technology at the time, but its becoming *embedded* into the technological infrastructure. Winner includes a quote about Robert Moses, the instigator of this development: he "made sure that buses would *never* be able to use his goddamned parkways". When values are embedded into infrastructure such as this, they penetrate the social fabric on a more or less permanent basis. The social and economic conditions that spawned them are therefore still present too. This is why Susan Leigh Star (1999) writes that technological infrastructure can be "read" as a record of historical events and social and political decisions, just as geology can be used to read a landscape, as an accumulated record of factors such as sedimentation, erosion, tectonics and – nowadays – human influence.

Infrastructure is a medium of information storage, shaped by decisions made in accordance with certain ways of thinking. Values embedded into it will influence subsequent decisions. For example, a manufacturing company wanting to invest in a region is less likely to if it has no high-speed access to major cities and/or ports to get goods to market. The region therefore lacks investment, therefore good jobs, therefore an affluent population: therefore, there is less incentive for the private sector to invest in building the infrastructure it requires, and so the cycle goes on. This is precisely why this sort of region is often targeted by public sector investments, but these are not always successful at relieving the problem, particularly when an area is also physically isolated. In the UK, Cornwall is one case of such a region.

An understanding of the social shaping of technology therefore goes some way towards appreciating these processes. It also helps suggest how technologies influence communities in a general way.

Case 3: The assembly line

This case shows how a particular form of rationality – instrumental rationality – has permeated our organisations. It also clearly shows that "technology" is not just limited to "machinery", but rather, that engineering and design principles seep through organisations at every level, affecting our relationships with information and with other people as well as with built technologies.

A significant exploiter of the assembly line idea was Henry Ford. It enabled him to mass-produce the automobile, driving down its cost by reducing the human resources required to manufacture it. Skilled workers – more expensive, less dispensable – were replaced by machines. But this was not a simple matter of substitution. Rather, the whole organisation was engineered. Ford was influenced by F. W. Taylor, an organisation theorist whose book, *Principles of Scientific Management* (1911), was the first real application of instrumental rationality to the design of organisations. In Taylor's view, the technological and human parts of an organisation were interchangeable. What needed analysis was the *process* of production, breaking it down into smaller and smaller steps that could be performed in sequence. This is how a machine works. Taylor viewed the whole organisation as a machine, each of its processes connected to others but studyable in isolation, scientifically. In homage to both key personalities here, this form of work organisation has become known both as Taylorism and Fordism.

However, the redesign of work did not automatically lead to improved efficiency. In the 1940s, a group of researchers at the Tavistock Institute in London were asked to investigate why the introduction of technology into some coal mines had actually led to falls in productivity. What the Tavistock researchers found was that over the years, coal miners developed complex social systems to help each other work safely in incredibly difficult conditions. The new technology had been designed using Taylorist techniques, which broke down mining analytically, but none of the designers had ever *worked* down the mines into which the machinery was introduced. Nor were these community safety practices part of official procedure, so they were not accounted for by the designers. As a result, the technology interfered with these social networks and, in order to compensate, the miners simply slowed down.

From this study the Tavistock Institute developed the idea of *sociotechnical systems* (see Mumford, 1987). Work-based systems are a combination of human and technological elements. Sociotechnical systems include things like procedures, organisational structures, and ways of thinking, as well as machines and computers: anything that allows an organisation to function. An accounting system, for instance, will use ICTs such as spreadsheets, but will also link people together, by defining a procedure that has to be followed to, say, raise invoices, or pay contractors. Any of these processes can "fail", or at least, work less than optimally. Consequently, redesigns may be called for, just as a machine component may need replacing, or upgrading.

Professional roles, such as business process analysts and training consultants, are tasked with the design of sociotechnical systems using instrumental principles. The design problems in this area are the subject of a great deal of research, which seeks "best practice" in human resources management, or instructional design, to name but two relevant fields of study. However, whatever the work process under study, there will be a community integrated with it which has developed an understanding about how to get the job done using the technologies available, and which gives value to the work in ways other than those intended by the system's designers[1]. These are Wenger's "communities of practice", such as the insurance claims processors he studied (1998).

The processors were supposedly working within the constraints of rules and procedures set for them by the company. They were cogs in a sociotechnical machine, the "human face" of the system. But these procedures, though they *shaped* their work, did not fully *determine* it. They could also draw on other resources; knowledge created in the community of workers, which helped them get round procedure when that procedure proved an obstacle, rather than a facilitator, of their actual work:

> In training, everything looks so strict and black-and-white. But on the floor, everybody learns the shortcuts in order to meet production. For instance, in training, you are taught to start a claim by filling out the forms that will serve as cover sheets for microfilmed records. Yet much of the information on the cover sheet is never used and is redundant with the attached claim record. So experienced processors do not fill out the form completely; they wait until they have completed the entire claim. When they hit the key that indicates they are done, the computer system gives them a batch number. If the number ends with a D, no problem, it will just get paid and archived. If the number ends with a Q, the claim must

---

[1] For a partial compromise here, see the later references to participatory design, particularly in Chapter 11.

be sent to quality review, and so you quickly complete the cover sheet. Everyone learns to do that within the first few weeks after moving to the floor.

You are good at claims processing when you can quickly find legitimate ways to get the charges reimbursed to a reasonable extent... But the shortcuts are not always good for the company or the customer (Wenger, 1998: pp. 30–1).

Communities of practice develop creative solutions to problems caused by the designs of others. But these solutions may challenge those with interests in the current practice. Such challenges are political issues, and one way of dealing with them is to restrict creativity. In Taylor's scheme, innovation was the province only of management and analysts working on their behalf. Standard operatives were allowed no leeway in performing their tasks. Communities of practice, such as those of the coalminers' and the claims processors', would arise anyway, but in most organisations were given no official status in decision making. Nor were the *skills* needed for creative work considered essential characteristics for employees in "low-level" positions. Although creative and flexible workers are still needed at the higher (design, strategic) levels of the organisation, on the assembly line and, increasingly, in "white-collar", office-based jobs as well, creativity is harder to apply. As Robins and Webster bemoan in *The Technical Fix* (1987: pp. 181–3):

...the process of technological innovation this century has been one which has brought about a reduction in the performance skills of the bulk of workers.... The epitome of this process whereby advanced technology has led to reduced skills is the assembly line, that characteristic feature of modern industry, in which machinery and the division of labour have resulted in operatives having next to no skill....

In addition, very large proportions of white-collar work which are assumed to be more professional and skilled than manual labour, are composed of clerical employment that is as routine and mundane as most shop-floor work.

At the same time, mainstream management theory looks to communities of practice as a means by which resources creatively produced at the individual level can be tapped and put to use by the whole organisation (see Part 4). Repressing all creativity within an organisation means that these communities cannot *learn*, and are therefore vulnerable to changing conditions that may leave current practices ineffective. In the dynamic information society, in fact, the value of creativity to the economy is asserted to the extent that creativity is *demanded* of us, both in our personal (as we adapt to new situations, new jobs) and our professional lives (von Osten, quoted in Stalder, 2008). Therefore, there exist deep tensions in how we value and promote creativity in learners. How and where are such individual creative resources produced? In what ways do organisations tap into them and is this always a benign process?

Let us think more about this idea of sociotechnical systems, with the help of *activity theory*. This is not the only way of revealing what goes on inside a sociotechnical system, and how it uses technologies to make knowledge. But it is among the best worked-out of the available theoretical tools[2].

Activity theory (AT), as the name suggests, is a way of thinking about *how things actually get done*. A multitude of processes underpin any activity, at any scale, and AT is a way of describing relationships between these processes; of showing how parts of a system can work harmoniously or be in tension; of how people within the system learn to resolve tensions and problems; and how the whole system evolves as a result. AT is useful for showing how non-technical and technical parts of a system work together, and become indistinguishable from one another as they co-evolve.

There are two schools of AT, useful in different ways. The Socio-Structural Theory of Activity (SSTA) considers AT a tool for analysing systems in a relatively instrumental way: of breaking down their activity-as-a-whole into smaller and smaller blocks, so they can be more easily understood (Bedny and Harris, 2005): in a sense, learning about the system "from outside". Cultural-Historical Activity Theory (CHAT), by contrast, focuses more on understanding relationships and revealing tensions within a system, and exploring how these lead to learning by those "inside", and part of, the system (Engeström *et al.*, 1999). In keeping with the environmental model I will concentrate here on CHAT, though SSTA is by no means ignored: I return to it when discussing how organisations affect the way we think, in Chapter 9.

---

[2] Other relevant theories include *situated action* and *distributed cognition*. All have similarities, and are discussed as a single family by Nardi (1996). This means, however, that they all have similar flaws, to be considered in Chapter 9.

CHAT's history stretches back nearly a century to the work of the Russian educator, Vygotsky, whose elegant primary insight was that learning does not take place through a teacher "pouring" knowledge into the empty mind of a willing recipient. Rather, understanding is *made* by the learner, and this activity is always mediated through some kind of artefact or tool. Through activity, the learner constructs knowledge from resources available in the environment. Tools include technology, but also the knowledge of the teacher (subject knowledge and knowledge of teaching technique), books and other storage media, the existing knowledge base of the learner, communications from friends, families and other community members, and the physical environment in which teaching occurs. (See Part 4 where I return to the idea of an *ecology of resources* (Luckin, 2008).)

This basic model was enhanced by the best-known CHAT school writer, Yrjö Engeström. This diagram first appeared in 1987, and has graced many papers since:

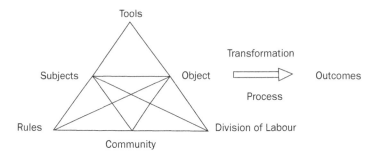

The "triangle" effectively illustrates the different components of an activity system, though not quite the relationship between them. *Subjects* and *communities* are the internal and external persons who initiate activity. This activity has an *object*(ive). *Rules, tools* and *divisions of labour* are the mediating factors.

Tools are, more or less, as described by Vygotsky. Rules are procedural guides built into the structure of a system and to which activity must conform. For example, when I design a course (a task which is part of the wider activity of the department in which I work), I am the subject, and delivering certain learning objectives is the object. I can draw on tools to hand such as ICT, my own subject knowledge, and what I know about pedagogy. But I must also design the course to fit with expectations built into Manchester University as a system: for instance, the need to deliver a grade, to conform to quality assurance criteria, etc. These are *rules*.

It is also likely that the skills or power needed to complete tasks are not all found in individuals, who therefore need to draw on the activity and tools of others to complete tasks. *Divisions of labour*, or roles, restrict or influence activity. One characteristic of many large organisations, including educational ones, is that they draw clear divisions between roles within a system. The Fordist division between workers and analysts is an obvious example. In the university system divisions of labour have historically been based more around the idea of professional autonomy than breaking down work tasks: however, as ICT penetrates our education systems, this is changing. I now depend on software designers and perhaps development assistants to create my course. (There are more illustrations of the usefulness of CHAT on the website, as well as other resources which may help you.)

There may be tensions within the activity system. Values may conflict; my career needs may differ from my development assistants'; what I consider good teaching may not be easily reproduced through the software I am supposed to use. The end product – a new course – may not be well received by the users (students). For Engeström, subjects' and/or the wider community's ability to recognise these tensions are what provoke an ongoing cycle of learning, through which the system evolves. He called this "expansive learning". Through this, it is not just individuals who learn but the system itself, as the results of this learning process are continuously embedded into the system, playing its role as an information storage medium. Tools, rules and roles (divisions of labour) dynamically evolve. In Engeström's own words (in Avis, 2007: 167):

> When an activity system adopts a new element from the outside... it often leads to an aggravated secondary contradiction where some old element... collides with the new one. Such contradictions generate disturbances and conflicts, but also innovative attempts to change the activity.... As the contradictions of an activity system are aggravated, some individual participants begin to question and deviate from its established norms. In some cases this escalates into collaborative envisioning [of alternative ways of working] and as deliberate collective change effort.

In other words, we learn about what happens when systems interact, both as individuals, and communities. Such learning may be absorbed by the wider organisation, or it may be rejected, and restricted to a kind of "subversion" of the system designed (see Benson and Whitworth, 2007).

A criticism of CHAT was raised by Avis (2007: 170), who pointed out that:

> ...such transformations, being tied to localised contexts, may bear only slight relation to wider structural relations, and indeed may support these, becoming conservative practice.

What he means is that learning processes within activity systems may only seek to adapt to changes originating outside the system which cause tension. The system adapts but the *underlying* cause of tension – the "primary tension" as Avis puts it – is not attended to. This criticism is linked to Argyris's (1999) idea of "double loop learning". An organisation engaged in "single-loop learning" is one that questions the *results* of its practices, but does not attend to the premises *beneath* these practices. For example, do declining student numbers on a course indicate that more needs to be spent on marketing (single-loop) – or that the course is less relevant in a changing age (double-loop)? Are increases in energy prices the result of curtailed production by The Organization of the Petroleum Exporting Countries (OPEC) (single-loop), or a sign our oil-based economy is becoming insupportable (double-loop)? (There are more examples on the website which you can apply to your own situation.) Rhetorical as these questions are, they suggest that the problems facing any system may not be resolvable without attention to the basic values underpinning the system. As these become more strongly embedded into technology, however, they may in turn become harder to question, or even to see.

What are the consequences of the social shaping of technology, and activity theory, for the study of ICT and its impact on our lives? First, a technology is not a "black box", sealed up and released into the world where it sits happily working away, exactly as its designers intended and not interacting with its environment. Instead, technologies are changed through use. Evolution may occur that was largely unanticipated. A well-known example is Short Message Service (SMS) text messaging which was originally intended merely as part of the technical side of mobile telephony, but which became so prevalent that it spawned whole new genres of communication, not to mention spelling.

But although Boyle (in Hess and Ostrom, 2007: p. 134) declares that our inability to predict the use of technology in advance means that all systems should, whenever possible, be designed in open, flexible ways that allows users to shape them (see also von Hippel, 2005, and Part 4 of this book), many systems are designed with quite different principles in mind. And as Bonnett says, along similar lines to the quote with which I began this chapter (Bonnett, in McFarlane, 1997: pp. 146–7):

> To what extent might teacher unease and the resulting lack of penetration of IT be the product not simply of resource problems or feelings of lack of expertise, but of some – often tacit, but maybe very real – conflict of values?...

> ... values lie at the heart of issues of thinking quality and... these need to be identified and properly acknowledged if (a) true integration of IT with other areas of the curriculum is to be achieved, (b) the possible effects on children's thinking of the values embedded in IT itself – i.e. of becoming "computer literate" – are to be sufficiently understood.

Whose values shape the technologies with which we must manage information? Therefore, by whom is its design controlled? It is by asking these questions that we start to become critically aware of technology's role in our lives, and the way it influences our response to and use of information.

In academic study, this could first be reflected by looking at the histories, cultures and so on of those who have shaped knowledge and technology. As Egan says (1990: p. 134):

> ...people, like us, made it, invented it, discovered and formulated it, for human purposes, with human motives. For it to be reconstituted in our minds some sense of the role and place it has had in other lives is important, as is some sense of the human motives that stimulated its invention or discovery.

But we can also, as learners, teachers or other stakeholders in education, recognise that telling stories is one thing: *applying learning* is another. It is actual, practical and active *work* with technology, in the broadest sense, which leads to creativity and innovation. Yet innovations emerge into systems in which there is a deeper, primary tension, one which I still need to explore in later chapters.

The theories presented in this chapter show how we embed values into the rules, ways of thinking and divisions of labour that comprise our environment, just as much as we do into machines such as computers. In order to become active, critical users of ICT and information, rather than passive consumers, we need to understand the values that underlie how we organise, educate, and design technologies to do both. The first part of this book has attempted to develop a framework for such a task. The second part will now use it to analyse the development of ICT and of education's response to it.

To conclude Part 1, let me present a summary of the causes of information obesity, and how these fit into the theories and models discussed so far.

Information obesity is a failure to use informational resources in ways that build, within individuals and communities, sustainable foundations for future activity. In other words, the information is not becoming *knowledge* and is not, therefore, becoming embedded by individuals and communities into *their own* environments. This happens, broadly, because of a failure of filtering strategies, caused by:

- a lack of understanding of technological change and its consequences, within individuals, communities and the education system;

- the noösphere having increased its dynamism to a point at which we often do not have, or are not granted, the time to reflect on information before absorbing it: we could be said to live in an era of "fast information";

- economic pressures on us to consume information, due to the profits it makes for the information industries; these pressures encourage us to buy, or at least absorb, information *before* judging its worth, rather than the other way around;

- a lack of management of the informational environment, with many parts of it being exploited in an unsustainable way, rather than being nurtured; this is linked to the deterioration of social capital and our communities, and results in the enclosure of the information commons, a lack of diversity, and a general decline in quality;

- the lack of individual creativity within many organisational roles.

In summary, the modern world promotes economic and financial value as the chief measure of effectiveness and worth, and this applies to the production and consumption of information – thus, the ongoing evolution of the noösphere – as much as to any other activity. We are also encouraged to use subjective value as our main filtering strategy (as Part 2 will explain), but as with food and physical obesity, this is often ineffective in resisting the psychological, economic and organisational influences that push information at us, of highly variable quality. Subjectively valuable information also runs the risk of collapsing into counterknowledge. What is needed is to reassert the position of the two other types of value: objective value, and intersubjective (community) value. Through doing so, I believe we can develop an *educational* strategy for coping with the increased dynamism of the noösphere brought about through ICT, and as a result, build resources which individuals and communities can draw on, for their own empowerment, in sustainable ways.

All the above needs more explanation and justification, but that is the task of the rest of the book.

Part 2:
The impact of information technology

4

A brief history of ICT

To err is human and to blame it on the computer is even more so. (Robert Orben)

The story of how ICT entered our lives, is, perhaps, familiar. Certainly it has been told in detail in several good books (see the reading list, and below). What I concentrate on is not what was developed, but the *motivations* for developing ICT and the *processes* by which this was done. I make no claims that this is a comprehensive review, but I do pick out major milestones in the history of ICT as well as some consequences, where these are significant. These are then assessed with reference to the environmental model of information.

This chapter will look at:

- the long history of computational technology and how it has changed the way we work and organise;
- the development of the Internet, as both an information management tool and a communications tool;
- how these technologies have impacted on the way we make knowledge, particularly with reference to the notion of "information overload".

The first machine to aid computation was probably the abacus, though Stonehenge and similar astrological sites have a claim. However, number systems are also a form of computing technology. Mathematics in a pure sense is an intellectual art, but the commonplace number system is one of many tools through which it can be applied. Numbers had to be *invented*, and the existence of Roman numerals and binary notation, which both remain part of our everyday world, show that there are number tools other than the familiar Hindu–Arabic one. These become part of the infrastructure on which other technologies develop; *rules* and *tools* in the activity theory sense. Of course, they seem perfectly "natural" parts of the environment, impossible now to change, but they remain social constructions. (I make no claims to be a mathematician; the best source for this idea of number systems as evolving technologies is Menninger, 1969. See also Egan, 1990: pp. 267–70.)

Another early computer which is still frequently seen is the *clock*. A clock is a computer because it helps with calculation. A mechanical action – usually, the oscillation of a pendulum – is translated into numerical information (hours, minutes, seconds). Computers which work using mechanical processes like these are called "analogue" computers.

The clock played a significant role in changing the world from an agricultural mode to an industrial one. In agricultural societies the main measure of time was the sun, both its daily rhythms (one rose at sunrise, worked during daylight, and returned home and to bed after dark), and annual ones, with life based around the cycle of the seasons. In factories, however, time was reckoned by the clock: fixed hours of work, pay by the hour, etc. New transport networks like the railways required time to be reckoned the same in London as in Edinburgh and Bristol, or the railways would descend into chaos. Note also the clock's role in solving the last great problem of maritime navigation, the fixing of longitude. Both contributed to the creation of standardised "time zones". It is therefore no exaggeration to say that the clock changed the world and ushered in the Industrial age. Whether it was *intended* to do so is not the point.

Interestingly, Norman, in his classic *The Design of Everyday Things* (2002: p. 196), comes out against the clock's basic design. If one were introduced now, he says, people would probably dislike the arbitrary divisions on the (inter)face, which are often not even numbered, and do two jobs at once (indicating primary divisions, hours, and secondary ones, minutes). The two indicators are confusingly similar in shape and size. And there are 24 hours in a day, so why only 12 on the clock? Having noon at the top makes sense, as it evokes the sun's being overhead at noon, but why midnight as well? Norman admits that, of course, the clock is now too familiar to be radically redesigned, and at least the conventions which display the internal calculations are widespread, so once learnt can be applied anywhere. And of course we now see as many digital timepieces as traditional ones. Digital clocks and watches make telling the exact time easier, though are less good at indicating the *passage* of time, and are often less attractive. At present, the two formats seem to have reached an amicable equilibrium.

None of this argues that modern problems are the fault of the inventor of the zero, or the clock, and in response we might ditch the whole technological basis of computation. Of course not. Rather, these are instances of how technology, culture, ideas and eventually, the whole environment co-evolve over long periods, based on activity, creativity, and the aggregation of these human-scale processes into wider environmental change. They suggest:

- the usefulness of a holistic, environmental view of information;
- that "technologies" are more than just "machines";
- that technologies are not always produced for reasons, and in ways, that future users, or those in different circumstances, will find optimal.

There is another analogue computer which has a realistic claim to have influenced the course of history. This is Colossus, built by British engineers to help crack the German Enigma code in World War II. The machine did not work alone: in fact this is a good example of a sociotechnical system, which included the human codebreakers who established patterns in intercepted communications, not to mention the soldiers who captured an Enigma machine in the first place. Colossus then worked to "compute" the machine's internal workings and so increase the system's *efficiency*, making it possible to crack codes before the information's usefulness expired and its value was lost. Ultimately, this system turned garbage (like the first "30 bytes" example in Chapter 2) into meaningful, and indeed absolutely vital, information.

Computing technology has long been essential to military strategy: calculating missile trajectories, gathering intelligence and launching spy satellites. I mention it here due to the frequent references made to the military's role in developing the Internet. The US military sought a communications system that could survive a nuclear attack. Traditional telephone systems depend on exchanges to connect calls, but if an exchange is taken out of the network – whether by technical problems, or by being blown up – there is simply no other route for the message to take. With *packet-switching*, the technology behind the Internet, the message simply finds another route. The communications system is therefore more dispersed, and less vulnerable to losing key nodes. Although the significance of the military's role in developing the Internet is not universally accepted (Randall, 1997: p. 15, mentions the difference of opinion), it does suggest how technology can enhance information's *strategic* value.

Digressing momentarily, Robins and Webster devote an entire chapter to the military influence over ICT (1987: pp. 233–55), reading which might depress anyone with a liberal bent, especially if they are committed to the idea of ICT in their classrooms and in education generally. Others may shrug, think "realistically" and acknowledge the fact that innovations that emerge from war might subsequently be applied in peacetime. In this difference of opinion lies the moral argument. However, there are other, less divisive grounds on which to criticise the military's role in shaping technology. It is difficult to deny that the military system absorbs a vast amount of resources – financial, human, technological and informational – which might have been invested either on socially-democratic public projects or in the private sector (the military is a major consumer of science and engineering graduates). Military expenditure is often made with minimal public scrutiny and little post-grant accountability. This contributes to a huge level of waste and project failure in the sector[1]. Robins and Webster criticise these issues, and the military's influence over technology and (therefore) education, on moral and ethical grounds, and it is up to the reader to consider whether they agree with these values. But the facts suggest that the military is the classic example of an obese system, consuming huge amounts of technology, information and other resources. Whatever one thinks about the need for a military presence in society, the critically aware user of information must be aware of these issues.

Back to the story. Actually, the military influence over the Internet was less significant than it might have been. In the two decades following the first demonstration of packet-switching, on 1 September 1969, the Internet's development was mainly driven by different people and processes.

Until at least the 1980s, there was no home computing sector to speak of: no affordable hardware, no Internet Service Providers and no easy way to avoid high telephone bills for a home user. Computers remained large and expensive pieces of kit that required good technical knowledge to get working at all, let alone to connect to a network (which lacked easy to use search facilities, à la Google). The expertise and equipment needed to use the Internet did exist in places such as government

---

[1] What constitues "waste" and "effectiveness" is often a matter of opinion, of course, but for critical voices from within the UK military establishment see, for example, Rayment's piece in the *Daily Telegraph*, 12 Nov 2007: "MoD in £1bn battle to stay within budget" (*http://www.telegraph.co.uk/news/uknews/1568980/MoD-in-andpound1bn-battle-to-stay-within-budget.html*, last accessed 19 Aug 2008).

facilities, large businesses, and universities, but these did not give access to users of the sort which would give the developing network commercial value: and while individual computer systems might be kept secure (in principle anyway), the Internet as a whole was open to all and remained largely "ungoverned", at least in any centralised way. How this worked can be shown with the adoption in 1983 of the Transmission Control Protocol/Internet Protocol (TCP/IP) as the single protocol, or standard for communication, on the network. This was an example of how the Internet was not "designed", but rather *grew* through creative activity at the community level. Many classic applications which lubricate the exchange of online information, like e-mail and the World-Wide Web, were written by individuals acting autonomously, and then having their work validated by the Internet community through the *Request for Comments (RFC)* system (Randall, 1997: p. 59). This was a collaborative decision-making process which involved anyone who expressed an interest, rather than being imposed from above. The decision to implement TCP/IP rather than a rival standard, OSI, was actually a direct clash between these two methods of development. I wrote the following elsewhere (Whitworth, 2004: 2):

> RFC was a semi-formal manifestation of the collaborative decision-making model. Individuals proposed protocols, software, systems and other solutions to particular problems. Via e-mail or Usenet newsgroups, any interested party was then free to criticise, augment or otherwise comment upon the proposal. In contrast, [Open Systems Interconnection] OSI was considered an untried, abstract design dreamt up by what the Net community considered an exclusionary group of bureaucrats who lacked genuine experience with the Net. TCP/IP had the advantage of incumbency, with users having both experience of it and a sense of ownership of it. As one (unnamed) scientist said, "Standards should be discovered, not decreed" (cited in Hafner and Lyon, 1996: p. 255).

The evolution of the early Internet, particularly (though not solely) in US universities, was an *educational* process driven by little other than intellectual curiosity at first; later came the recognition that this could help with the *communication* of work to others and thus an *expansion of possibilities* for activity in one's own system. These were bolstered by an intellectual and regulatory environment that encouraged such ways of working and disseminating innovation. Actually, the fact that the early Internet was "owned" (an awkward term, but it will do) by the US

Government probably permitted it to turn into the network we know today with its democratic potentials, as opposed to one commercially controlled from the beginning and on which innovation would thereby have been less free to spread.

When praising "openness" in networks, we should also recognise the possible negative consequences. In the early 1980s the spectre of the "hacker" entered popular consciousness. Before anyone had heard the term "Internet", in 1983 a youthful Matthew Broderick, in *War Games*, played a character whose attempted hack into a games company's system instead provoked the Pentagon's war computer into nearly starting World War III. As bandwagon-jumping movies go, this remains a rather good one, and was not so far off reality. First, it showed the increasing dependence of military decision-making on computers. Here, *War Games* drew themes from *Doctor Strangelove* made 20 years earlier. Though the human intervention is accidental in *War Games* and deliberate (though deranged) in *Strangelove*, both movies show the sociotechnical system that is the thermonuclear war machine proving unable to cope with minute failures in its security systems. All the possible counterstrategies the system can take are locked into procedure or machinery, programmed to accept the security flaw as a real intrusion (*War Games*) or instruction (*Strangelove*) and flinging the world towards Armageddon as a result.

Second, "cyberspace" had become another arena for espionage and covert operations. The reality of this was described by Stoll in *The Cuckoo's Egg* (1990), which recounts his experiences in the 1980s when he worked as an astronomer. Spotting anomalies in the logs of computer access time, Stoll, in the face of bureaucratic indifference from both his employers and government agencies, eventually tracked down the culprit, a German hacker working on behalf of the Communist regime that at the time ruled Bulgaria. Stoll makes an interesting point (1990: p. 188) when observing that a system is only as secure as the *people* that are part of it as well as the technologies. A system can be made more secure, but at the price of being harder to use and less accessible. These show the tradeoffs that must be made with system design. It also illustrates certain political questions, such as how access rights to information are defined, controlled and subverted, and the complex morals and laws which control behaviour here.

These developmental processes had largely defined the technological form of the network by the time the Internet had its huge *cultural* impact. It is worth remembering how recently this happened. In a search

I conducted of the online archive of the London *Times* newspaper, the first mention of the word "Internet" in a news story was on 11 January 1990[2], regarding the release of a computer virus. Even then it was unlikely the word would have meant much to the average person. In the piece the Internet is described as a "computer network, used by thousands of scientists".

Various things happened after this date, almost simultaneously, which provoked the Internet's explosion into popular consciousness. The US Government withdrew from the project and restrictions on the commercial use of the network were lifted. The price and availability of computer technology reduced to the point where it was affordable by households and, with more user-friendly operating systems (such as Microsoft's Windows or Apple's Mac OS), increasingly easy to use. Most significantly, in the World-Wide Web – mainly invented by Tim Berners-Lee (see his 1999 book) – the Internet found its "killer app", an application so popular that people bought or gained access to the technology purely to use it. With this explosion of interest came all the moral panics, new cultural forms, commerce and attempts at control that now characterise our relationship with Internet technology.

However, before this, writers were already noticing the changes that ICT had wrought on global society and its economy. In 1976, Bell published *The Coming of Post-Industrial Society*, suggesting we were undergoing a third major shift in society's economic base. Having moved from a nomadic, to an agricultural, to an industrial economy, Bell declared we were now entering a "post-industrial" world based on the supply of services. Finance, education, information provision, entertainment: these were now the main economic drivers of developed economies, rather than manufacturing. (See the discussion of Bell in Robins and Webster (1987: Chapter 1) and Webster (2002: Chapter 3).)

Additionally, economic processes are now global in scope. A century ago, a manufactured good would have likely been built all in one place, such as Manchester, a cradle of the Industrial Revolution (and now the city where I work). Only then would it have been taken to a port or freight yard and exported. Granted, Manchester was largely built on cotton, an imported good, suggesting these "local" industries were already embedded into a global economic system; in fact, with the trading of spices, precious metals and slaves, we see that resources have long been moved around the Earth. But these processes are now far more dispersed, and occur *within* companies, rather than representing a

---

[2] Some earlier references occur in job advertisements, the earliest I found being 1987.

business-to-business or import/export transaction. The computer on which I type these words may originate from a research and development lab in Seattle or Silicon Valley, but the internal components have been manufactured in Singapore or Taiwan, and then, for the European market, shipped and assembled in Ireland or Hungary. Financial backing will likely have been raised in London; and after that closes for the night, Wall Street then Tokyo, as the world turns. (Chapter 4 of Webster (2002) is an excellent reference.)

Another sociologist, Bauman, has described this age as *Liquid Modernity* (2000). He suggests that in the modern information society, wealth and success (personal and corporate) are best achieved by staying mobile, not tied down to a territory, or fixed capital investments (like office buildings). Modern-day "nomads" stay on the edges of the state system (and its associated costs like taxes and laws) as they did in the past. However, unlike earlier nomads, this is not a disadvantaged life but quite the reverse. ICT lubricates, and enhances the value of, very transportable resources such as money and information, and wealth in this liquid age is based not so much on the ability to control information – there is far too much of it now – but to be skilled at gathering, prioritising, analysing and even anticipating it. Policymakers have long attempted to embed such skills in school and training curricula as a result, with varying success (discussed in more detail in Chapter 6).

There are, however, criticisms of these ideas. Webster (2002) places the term "information society" in quotes throughout to suggest its elusive nature. He says that uncritical use of the concept deflects our attention from an analysis of what is shaping this transition. Although the flow of resources around the information society has become more rapid and location independent, society possesses the same structures and problems that it always has, though manifested differently (civil libertarians now look to surveillance via ICT as a concern, for example; or social exclusion is cast in terms of access to ICT). Information can never act upon the world without being mediated through minds, organisations and socio-economic structures which may be influenced by the information, but which predate it. Is an information society something we all move into, leaving the "old world" behind? Or is it laid over what already exists? I agree with Webster and subscribe to the latter view. The information society has been developing for decades – perhaps even centuries – and though new technologies have accelerated its evolution, the process is far from complete, particularly globally (many people alive today have never made a telephone call, let alone gone online). The information society's future will be shaped by technological and economic influences, but also by social, political and cultural factors which are less easy to predict or direct.

Some have written, for instance, of the way ICTs such as computers, and earlier, the television, affect how we construct identity. Egan (1990: p. 160; see also Levinson, 1999) says:

> The most dramatic claims on this are… Marshall McLuhan's (1962 and *passim*). He sees this sense of identity as an historical phenomenon whose period of tenure is now coming to an end under the force of electronic media – the electronic extension of our senses through the global village.

Identity in this global village is ephemeral. We pick it up and set it down as we please. Though there is still not universal social mobility – people born poor tend to stay poor – it is less easy than it was to predict someone's musical taste, place of work, reading matter, or leisure activity from their income or class. Ideas like sexuality and disability are defined more flexibly than half a century ago. Writers like Turkle (1997) and contributors to collections edited by Smith and Kollock (1999) and Jones (1997) built on these ideas and applied them more directly to the new ICT-based communications networks, developing the academic genre of "cyberculture studies". In cyberculture, media such as blogs, YouTube and Facebook help us have an "online self" parallel with one's "work self" or "family self". In technologies such as *Second Life* (*http://www.secondlife.com*), and even text-based media such as MSN and Usenet, people can play with identity, move in and out of "virtual communities" on a whim, and even pretend to be someone they are not.

The cultural shifts created by wider access to ICT are undeniable, though cyberculture studies tend to exaggerate the impact of these new modes of expression on underlying social structures. One may pretend to be a leggy blonde in *Second Life*, but this is hardly evidence for a radical new form of consciousness or organisation, and it is certainly not an information filtering strategy. Turkle, particularly, is fond of phrases such as "…life on the screen is without origins and foundation" (1997: p. 47) which is plainly false: life "on the screen" depends on a vast array of foundations, from the industrial processes which produced the screen and server hardware, the social, educational and psychological processes which produced the middle-aged male academic (or whoever…) pretending to be the leggy blonde, to the commercial motivations for creating *Second Life* in the first place. Some of the essays in Smith and Kollock are also guilty of this inflation. There is also the assumption that any "identity play" is positive. This will be of little consolation to those who've found agreeable communications spaces destroyed by "trolling", nor younger people who have been the subject of unwanted attention online from those who may have hidden their identity. These are important questions, but we must leave them to one side.

The aim of this chapter so far has been to provide examples of how ICT has been shaped in many ways, technologically, culturally and economically. What I want to do now is discuss more specifically how it impacts on our construction of knowledge, whether individually, in communities, or in society as a whole.

ICT has led to vast increases in information's availability. There has always been a substantial quantity of information stored in the noösphere but as recently as 20 years ago most of it required time and effort to access, through public libraries, newspapers, and so on. Mostly, the searcher needed to have an idea of what they were looking for. But these restrictions have been blown away by the Internet and its search facilities, notably Google. These make enormous quantities of information available for minimal effort. So low is the level of effort required, in fact, that much information now comes to us unbidden, being "ambient noise" in our environments, absorbed, for instance, when we happen to look up at a plasma screen while awaiting a train.

The phrase "information overload" is first credited to Toffler in *Future Shock* (1970). "Overload" suggests a system being fed with too much power or loaded with too much weight: as a result it may break or blow like a fuse. Shenk refers to the phenomenon as "data smog" (Shenk, 1997). This suggests a more insidious intrusion, a polluting by-product of the information revolution, just as air-based smog was and remains an unsightly and possibly dangerous product of the industrial revolution. Smog might not overload and fry our brains, but it could slowly debilitate or even poison us.

Metaphors matter because they provide alternative ways of seeing the same situation (Morgan, 1999). Consider, then, a third metaphor: "information abundance". Here, what is implied is a time of plenty. Resources are available to all with no fear of scarcity. The situation is the same but the view of it is now more positive. Information is a resource, and *could* be managed in ways that not only keep it abundant, but retain its quality, accessibility and the possibility that from it, *knowledge* may emerge in users, and be communicated and shared. That said, neglect could lead to the pollution or deterioriation of this resource. Do we have the capacity to train our minds and adjust our systems to cope with this latest, ICT-generated boost to the noösphere's dynamism and abundance? Or will we and our systems overload and shut down? In this question lies the move from information obesity to a healthier, more sustainable diet of information.

A famous article written in 1945 by Vannevar Bush, called "As We May Think", is one of the earliest discussions of the undesirable effects of information abundance, and the potential technological solutions. You may have already read, or at least heard of, this article which became famous long after being written, as readers saw in it a prophecy of the Internet to come. (See the thinking tasks on the website, which also has hyperlinks to the full article and suggests other relevant resources.)

There are several themes in the piece but the proposal that secured subsequent attention was the machine that Bush envisaged, the *memex*:

> A memex is a device in which an individual stores all his [*sic*] books, records and communications, and which is mechanised so that it may be consulted with exceeding speed and flexibility. It is an enlarged intimate supplement to his memory.
>
> It consists of a desk... On the top are slanting translucent screens, on which material can be projected for convenient reading. There is a keyboard, and sets of buttons and levers. Otherwise it looks like an ordinary desk.
>
> In one end is the stored material. The matter of bulk is well taken care of by improved microfilm... if the user inserted 5000 pages of material a day it would take him hundreds of years to fill the repository, so he can be profligate and enter material freely...
>
> Books of all sorts, pictures, current periodicals, newspapers, are thus obtained and dropped into place. Business correspondence takes the same path....

Lucky guess or no, these words are prophetic. Bush foresaw a personalised, mechanised library, accessible from nothing larger than a normal desktop. The general theme and certain features of the memex sound remarkably like the Web as it exists today. (The exception is that the memex would have only accessed material physically inside it, rather than being a network like the Internet: though in later discussions Bush did suggest that memexes could be so linked.)

Bush had an interest in such a device because as a scientist, he recognised that:

...there is a growing mountain of research. But there is increased evidence that we are being bogged down today as specialization extends. The investigator is staggered by the findings and conclusions of thousands of other workers – conclusions which he cannot find time to grasp, much less to remember, as they appear...

...publication has been extended far beyond our present ability to make real use of the record. The summation of human experience is being expanded at a prodigious rate, and the means we use for threading through the consequent maze to the momentarily important item is the same as was used in the days of square-rigged ships.

The memex was more than just a storage device; it was a technological solution to the problem of information overload. It would help the user locate needed material, by building and storing what Bush called "associative trails". He recognised that this was how the mind actually operated (Nyce and Kahn, 1991: p. 56). Human memory doesn't work in the hierarchical manner of traditional library cataloguing techniques. Rather, we leap from idea to idea as connections form in our minds, developing trains of thought. Unfortunately, we often forget them. Occasionally they might recur, triggered by a word, sound or smell, but are difficult to recall in a disciplined fashion. This was one job of the memex. It would contain a rapid retrieval system to enable the user, struck by a flash of inspiration while reading one text, to quickly retrieve a second, relevant text (from microfilm stored in the memex body). The memex would then store the connection, permitting it to be retrieved later, if either text was accessed. As well as the memex's physical attributes, it is this connective capacity which some see as prefiguring the way the World-Wide Web works, and the idea of *hypertext* as a way to make and store connections between pieces of information[3]. Ultimately, Bush proposed that user and memex would combine in a sociotechnical system for managing information abundance.

Let us look more closely at Bush's arguments, however. Selected passages from the article are given below, with key words highlighted. Think about what these indicate, with reference to what has already

---

[3] This deserves more detailed discussion. The World-Wide Web manifests a limited form of what hypertext could, in principle, become. Meyrowitz (in Nyce and Kahn, 1991) discusses ideas like the *warm link* –in which all links would have to be two-way – and *hot links*, where updating information in one location automatically forces an update in all connected locations: similar to how Excel formulae work. Neither has been implemented on the World-Wide Web as we know it, even in the "Web 2.0" era. See also Landow (1992).

been said about how instrumental rationality encourages a certain way of perceiving the environment:

> For years inventions have extended man's physical **powers** rather than the powers of his mind. Trip hammers that **multiply** the fists, microscopes that sharpen the eye, and engines of destruction and detection are new results, but not the end results, of modern science. Now, says Dr Bush, instruments are at hand which, if properly developed, will give man access to and **command over** the inherited knowledge of the ages. (*This from the Editorial which precedes the article*)
>
> A memex is a device in which an individual stores all his books, records, and communications, and which is **mechanized** so that it may be consulted **with exceeding speed and flexibility**.
>
> There is a new **profession** of trail blazers, those who find delight in the task of **establishing useful trails** through the enormous mass of the common record. The inheritance from **the master** becomes, not only his additions to the world's record, but for his **disciples** the entire scaffolding by which they were erected. **Thus science may implement** the ways in which **man produces, stores, and consults the record of the race.**

The instrumental motives are fairly clear. The memex is a tool designed to give its wielder *mastery* over the noösphere. The implication is that "information abundance" is *not* a positive thing for the scientist who needs to keep abreast of developments in their field, to enhance the (objective) quality of their own work. As the publication rate accelerates, however, the ability to draw these connections is damaged. Hence, the memex. "As We May Think" is written in a utopian spirit, firmly implying that it was the role of science and scientists to guide the world safely from the depths of World War II, which, at the time Bush's piece was published, was a month from its conclusion in Japan. Information was the "new frontier", a place for exploration and expansion (Shenk, 1997: p. 63). But what we have here is not a call for the quality of the information *commons* to be enhanced through the memex. It was not to be available to all, sat in homes alongside (or even instead of) the television. Rather, it was a tool for the "professional", the skilled scientist, used to lay trails through this frontier, classifying and categorising it differently from a library, but imposing a will on it nonetheless. These trails would be followed by "disciples" who would thereby come to new understandings about the world. "As We May Think" therefore reflects well an instrumental, technology-based approach to the solving of problems that originate, essentially, from the intersubjective level.

There is no intent to be unfair here. Bush was a man of his time, an engineer trained in the early 20th century when Taylorism began to transform the world. It is also unfair to criticise a technology that was never built. Had it been, the memex would most likely have had unpredictable social effects, and been turned into something Bush never foresaw: as is the case, potentially, with all technologies. Nevertheless, the values that have historically driven the development of ICT are clearly in view.

Instead of talking about hypothetical technologies, let us return to actual history. What are the impacts of the accelerated production and availability of information? Shenk's *Data Smog* is an interesting and readable guide to this question and its several answers. As already noted, the "smog" metaphor suggests information is a pollutant, obscuring clear vision and making the noösphere a less healthy place. In other words, it is deteriorating in quality.

The magnitude of the increase in information is worth noting. Shenk observes (1997: pp. 26–7) that the amount of information in one *day's* copy of the New York Times is more than the average 17th century person would have come across in an entire lifetime. These changes have resulted not only from the spread of ICT (including earlier forms, like the telegraph), but also the spread of literacy and increased travel, interconnected processes which all broke down parochial, closed communities. Shenk describes how these changes affect us and our society at many levels.

There are individual, psychological effects. For example, many people become addicted to the information flow, and the technologies driving it (Shenk, 1997: p. 43):

> ...computers, the latest and most powerful engines driving the information glut, have provoked a certain compulsive behavior in a large number of people.... The feeling of being driven by the computer to stay *attached*, the manic compulsion to process data as fast and as long as the machine will allow – which is to say, *forever*.

Many computer users also develop feelings of deep dependency on their machines, feeling that they quite literally could not function without them.[4]

Like all addictions, this skews our sense of value, compelling the addicted to do things they know may be damaging bodies, minds and their ability to act in the world. Such addictions can easily lead to obesity, among other unhealthy effects, and are one reason why subjective value cannot always be trusted to produce desirable outcomes.

Whether we become addicted or not, Shenk observes that any technology designed to increase information flows may be incongruous in an educational setting, which is an environment designed to *filter and manage* information (Shenk, 1997: p. 75):

> Education is about enlightenment, not just access.... Schools are stringent filters, not expansive windows on the world. Teachers and textbooks block out the vast majority of the world's information, allowing into the classroom only very small bits of information at any given time. When organised well and cogently presented, these parcels of data are metamorphosed into building blocks of knowledge in the brains of students. The computer, by and large, is designed for a very different purpose... It is not a filter, but a pump.

The key phrase here, of course, is "organised well and cogently presented", equated here with good teaching. (The "organisation" of a learning experience and even its "presentation" are not entirely under the teacher's control, of course: the learning environment is open to influence from a wide range of values. These issues have driven much of this book so far, but only come into the foreground in Part 3.) The filtering role of teaching is psychologically important. It provides vital time and space for *reflection* on found information, as Shenk explains (1997: pp. 152–3):

> Descartes suggested that first we comprehend a notion, and then we either accept or reject it.... In contrast, Spinoza suggested that first we *simultaneously* comprehend *and accept* a notion, and only

---

[4] Shenk does not mention it but another ICT – the mobile phone – produces similar reactions in its users.

afterward, if we have time, are we able to *unaccept* it – that is, reject it.... Though Spinoza's argument is not as intuitive as Descartes', intensive psychological testing has proven Spinoza to be correct. This finding is of critical importance in the context of the information glut, because under conditions of cognitive overload we rarely have the time or the focus to go back and question our initial acceptance of things.... If claims are more likely to be believed in an environment of information glut, consumers are almost certain to be increasingly vulnerable to commercial and political solicitations.

This glut produces vicious circles. Filtering may become based largely on what secures *attention* (Goldhaber, 1997). While attention can be attracted, from beneath data smog, by information of quality, it could also be secured through vulgar appeal: loud shouting in an increasingly noisy informational space. The result is the coarsening of messages, and discouragement to take the time we need to reflect on pronouncements, establish opinions and, thus, choose between alternative points of view.

Advertisers and others seeking to publicise a point of view may seek more subtle means of targeting the message. One route is through exploiting intersubjective, community relationships. Both because of more widespread communication links, and the increasingly dynamic noösphere, these are now less strongly connected to geographical or work-based communities (e.g., professional associations, trades unions), and often defined in more ephemeral ways. Fans of TV programmes, or rock groups, coalesce around certain online spaces. ICT can also collect and analyse information about very specific neighborhoods or communities (Shenk, 1997: pp. 114–8). What results are *microcultures* (Shenk, 1997: p. 127), considered by Shenk as more limited than true communities, and open to being exploited by "niche marketing" which:

> ...coerces people into staying in their social cocoons.... society is imbued with messages conditioning it to stay neatly subdivided into distinct consumer categories... when the world becomes so profoundly splintered into distinct consumer tribles, humankind begins to lose the most valuable thing it has ever had: common information and shared understanding. (pp. 120–1).

A functioning democracy requires "a certain amount of tolerance and consensus, rooted in the ability to understand a wide variety of perspectives..." (p. 127) but microcultures are discouraged from communicating with each other, or having any need to resolve mutually-recognised problems. Indeed, microcultures defined around trivia such as celebrity fandom are based around the eradication of real "problems". About the most significant shared threat they might address would be a network's decision to drop their favourite TV program. Or, their problems become that of the celebrity, his or her social life, chances of getting the next big role, and so on.

The enclosure of the information commons – the noösphere – proceeds apace, but paradoxically, this does not lead to more efficient decision making. Instead we become subject to what Shenk calls "paralysis by analysis" (pp. 89–95) and "stat wars" (pp. 97–100). The cost of producing and researching data has fallen dramatically through ICT: this is one point of an information technology. It is now almost as low-cost to produce one's own data as it is to access the results of others. With self-publication facilities easy to access, those who want to can conduct research and publish it without necessarily needing to draw on the scientific infrastructure in order to do so. There are now so many research projects and lobbying organisations funded by different interests that microcultures spread into politics and academia as well. There is always the "opportunity to crunch some more numbers, spin them a bit and prove the opposite" (p. 91). None of these could be said to be *intended* effects of ICT, but they exist nonetheless, and can be studied with reference to known ways in which the human mind processes information. As people are less likely to filter out information if it reinforces existing beliefs (see Chapter 9), and with there always being some data *somewhere* that can be drawn on to justify an argument, public debate can become paralysed. Political "microcultures" can emerge which simply do not communicate; right-wing people read right-wing newspapers and political commentaries: left wingers, the opposite. People remain in niches, defined now by belief rather than spending profile, but able to be marketed to (by political consultants) all the same. Along with this comes the relative weakening of traditional ways of checking the authority of a position – the institutional affiliation of a researcher; the prestige of a publisher; the objective, scientific rigour of peer review. Who is to be believed? In a dynamic environment, where speedy decision-making may be crucial, do we have the *time* any more to check the credentials of a writer, or an opinion? We must also remember that many interests in society will benefit from promoting the passive consumption of information, at a level beneath conscious awareness, rather than active attention to it. Part 3 returns to this issue in detail.

Regardless of the fine detail, and acknowledging that for many people alive today the "information revolution" is going on without their participation, some clear changes have occurred with our use of, and cultural relationship with, ICT. What might the future hold? What follows, and concludes this chapter, is just one example of a train of intellectual thought one can ride at the present time. It can be considered a case study, showing how our relationship with ICT can be analysed, based on what I have discussed so far.

Computers are no longer found only on desks or our laps, but are now almost literally everywhere, from cars to Christmas cards. Think of the mobile phone found in most people's pockets: is it a phone? A personal organiser? A camera? An mp3 player? This is an excellent example of *convergence*, as are other developments such as radio and TV broadcasts delivered via the Internet, and the release of Hollywood movies being accompanied by promotional campaigns delivered through virtually every communications medium simultaneously (TV, radio, newspapers, magazines, the World-Wide Web, billboards and promotional tie-ins with fast food restaurants).

Convergence moves us towards *ubiquitous computing*, also called pervasive computing, a term popularised first by Weiser. He described ubiquitous computing (1993) as "a method of enhancing computer use by making many computers available throughout the physical environment, but making them effectively invisible to the user". As Parsons writes (2005):

> The manner of this invisibility or disappearance is not primarily that of concealment, although many of the workings of ubiquitous computing may indeed be hidden from view, but familiarity. Such technologies are so familiar, so much a part of everyday life, that they are no longer a focus of conscious attention.

Ubiquitous computing could be represented by, for example, a refrigerator connected to the Internet which detected when it was emptying and logged onto a supermarket website to refill itself. (If the surveillance society keeps developing at its current pace it might also inform a health insurance company of the rate its owners drank cold beer.) But Parsons is also talking about the way these technologies become culturally and psychologically familiar, and thus embedded into the fabric of our sociotechnical systems. Returning to the previous point about convergence, even if the mobile phone could still be considered as "just a phone", this does not account for the enormous cultural changes which mobile telephony has wrought, summarised well by Rheingold in the first chapter of *Smart Mobs* (2003). In fact the mobile may have overtaken the computer as the most culturally pervasive technology in the world. Countries in which easy access to the Internet is still awkward have enthusiastically embraced the mobile phone (for example, the Phillippines). Phones are cheaper, more accessible, more versatile and more reliable than computers.

It is this kind of cultural, rather than technological, familiarity which indicates the real *assimilation* of a technology into the environment. No one needs to be taught how to use the television, or a mobile phone, at the everyday level. Very few people know how they "work" mechanically, who might therefore be able to fix a broken TV or phone. A larger number produce content for these media, though remain in the minority. Still others work to regulate access: for instance, working in systems which perform the task of billing users. But we can all *use* the technology. There are not, nor ever were, training courses in "mobile phone literacy" or "television skills". These technologies are, in short, ubiquitous.

Prensky (2001) made a much-quoted observation; that today's children are "digital natives", growing up in a world where these technologies are ubiquitous, rather than having to adapt to them through education like older "digital immigrants". Yet education is still essential if the "natives" are to make *effective* use of the technologies around them, precisely because of their familiarity. In any situation, it is harder to pay attention to what is familiar, rather than what is new. There is a persuasive argument that it is precisely this kind of cultural comfort with a technology that dulls our ability to think critically about it. Our relationships with these technologies are passive and based mostly on consumption. They are not value-less: the mobile phone, particularly, has boosted the communications networks of many middle-income countries as already noted, made breaking down in countryside at night rather less threatening, and few people now would give theirs up without a fight. But there is a difference between the passive consumption of benefits and the *active exploitation of the possibilities* of any technology. To undertake the latter requires critical awareness.

Without it, cultural comfort and passive consumption of technologies can lead to them doing a lot of our thinking for us. In-car satellite navigation systems are a good example. You can reach a destination more efficiently with personal satellite navigation equipment (sat nav): and at the same time have no idea how you got there. Stories abound (doubtless every community has anecdotes here) of vehicles becoming stuck on impossible bends or godforsaken tracks because "the sat nav said go that way". Drivers have delegated skills to the technology in return for extra efficiency. Of course, map reading and navigation always have been based on systems of information gathering, publication and technological aids: but *the direction taken remained the choice of the navigator*, using his/her own critical judgment. A good map and map reader work together, the map reader absorbing and filtering information in a dynamic way, trusting the map as a resource but also checking information constantly against the terrain and landmarks – or if driving, traffic conditions. The passive user of a sat nav is just taking orders.

The more that these technologies become ubiquitous, the more the values they manifest become embedded into the technological and cultural infrastructure within which we live. Just as the Long Island Expressway more or less permanently excludes certain groups from certain places, will these other technologies be used for similar ends? This is not dystopian speculation, but a fact of crucial importance for our future lives and those of our children. Will our technologies continue to be "cognitively penetrable" – in other words, will we still be able to understand how they work? If they work in ways that do not accord with how we want to live our lives, will we be able to resist or reject their effects? What disadvantages will we face if for some reason we are uncomfortable with a new technology? What if the new technology promotes information obesity, rather than a healthier relationship with our environment?

Rheingold (2003: pp. 106–12) discusses the case of Steve Mann, a researcher, user, and as we can now say, active constituent of a *wearable computing system*. He begins:

> Like most of the wired world, I learned about Steve Mann... when he started webcasting everything he saw. Mann, who had been tinkering with wearable computers since he was a child, had ended up at MIT, where he had equipped himself with a helmet that enclosed his head and showed him the world through video cameras. The video feed was filtered through computers that enabled Mann to add and subtract features from the world he saw around him. Starting in 1994, wireless communications gear enabled him to beam everything he saw to a web page. Mann's wearable computer had many features, including access to his e-mail and the Web, but what was remarkable was his commitment to wearing his wearable computer all the time.

Rheingold, alongside Turkle and others, was one of the prime instigators of the cyberculture genre with his 1993 book *The Virtual Community: Homesteading on the Electronic Frontier*, a title which nicely sums up an early perspective on the Internet, viewing it as a place for discovery and exploration, lauding the value of individual effort. Here, Rheingold clearly sees a kindred spirit, promoting human qualities through technology. Rheingold says that these words from Mann's 2001 manifesto "struck a chord":

> Rather than smart rooms, smart cars, smart toilets, etc., I would like to put forward the notion of smart people.... the goal is to enhance the intelligence of the race, not just its tools.

The intention is to transform our ability to "control the environment that surrounds us":

> Mann can turn the visual background of the world surrounding him into black and white and make his study materials pop up in colour when he wants to study in a public place. Mann's reaction to the technologically enhanced Society of the Spectacle which surrounds him is to use WearComp to filter commercial advertisements out of his visual field. The words and pictures on billboards become invisible at his command...

Advertising on billboards is pervasive. We are culturally comfortable with it. But Mann uses technology to filter it out, to show that it does not have to be *perceived*.

But Mann is not working in the mainstream. He says himself:

> Which road will we go down? The road on which wearable computers create and foster independence and community interaction? Or the road on which wearable computers become part of the apparatus of electronic control which we are ever more subject to, and unaware of?

Rheingold sums up Mann's example as follows:

> The technical question with politically important implications is, Who controls the information that comes into the WearComp and radiates out from the WearComp to sentient devices in the world?....

...and observes that it is important for democracy that wearable computing continue to be developed by individuals as well as the research establishment. While it is hard to believe that his commitment is unexceptional, meaning many will flinch at the lengths to which he has gone in pursuit of his principles, Mann is actively exploiting the possibilities of this technology, and its ability to help him navigate the various environments in which he lives and works, including – most significantly – the informational environment[5].

In summary, this chapter has shown how ICT is not a distinct technological development to which we must respond in a reactive way, but an integral part of our environment, shaped over long periods of time by activity at all levels of society, from the individual, through the community, to our organisations and global economic structures. ICT is not innately dominating and undesirable; but neither is it innately democratic and empowering. It is neither of these things because, like information, its impact depends on how it is used within the organisations and communities through which we interact and communicate with each other and with our wider environment. *Learning* about how ICT can be used, and how it may either increase, or combat, information obesity, is essential, and clearly, this learning process will be driven by the formal and informal educational systems of society.

---

[5] Wearable computing remains an information technology at the current time, but we will eventually see wearable machines that enhance our strength, stamina or other physical characteristics. Arguably, the Speedo LZR swimsuit, which led to a spate of swimming world records falling after its introduction in February 2008, is an example. That it is not a "computing" technology is beside the point: a great deal of information gathering, analysis and modelling has gone into its production and in making it very effective.

5

Literacy and counterknowledge

...it is difficult to overstate the significance of literacy to a modern society... [but] politicians, educators and newsmen have succeeded [in doing so]. (David Olson, quoted in Egan, 1990: p. 85)

Before I discuss the educational responses to ICT, I want to cover the more general field in which they fit, that of *literacy*. Literacy is usually considered the most fundamental of all skills, the first step towards becoming an educated person. It connotes an ability to draw information from the written noösphere: to read, in other words. It is the most basic information management skill, and immensely valuable to individuals, to the extent that if it is not possessed by a person, it almost guarantees they will be restricted to the margins of society and the economy.

Yet agreement on what it, and its antonym "illiteracy", actually mean are not necessarily easy to reach. As Warschauer says (1999: p. 1), "being literate has always depended on mastering processes that are deemed valuable in particular societies, cultures, and contexts". And the assignation of value is, as we have already seen, open to distortion in various ways. Literacy can become defined in very *functional* ways, rather than something that is creative, productive and empowering. Explaining what I mean here is the task of the first part of this chapter. The second part returns to Thompson's *Counterknowledge* and explores his ideas about information management, which highlight the dangers of relativism, but which also prove limited when it comes to combating information obesity.

The printing press, despite effectively bringing an end to the Middle Ages and helping usher in the modern world, did not immediately turn everyone into readers. Mass literacy arrived only after the Industrial Revolution (Warschauer, 1993: p. 3, via Tuman, 1992), and of course, in many countries (particularly among women and the poor), has still not done so.

Literacy does not therefore emerge simply because of new technology. Early manuscripts such as the Book of Kells, and even Gutenberg's printed Bible, were not easy to read even if one could understand the alphabet. Though they were works of art, the lack of familiar conventions like spaces between the words, page numbers, chapters, and indices meant that access to the information within them was limited (see the pictures on the website). Over time, however, these technological features evolved. Different genres of books developed, the information in them better organised and thus more accessible. Compare the characteristics of different books like novels, research monographs, encyclopaedias, the telephone directory, atlases and so on (again, see the website).

Print remains a technology in which a huge amount of information is encoded, and is more durable, more accessible, more flexible, more personalisable and often cheaper than electronic formats. Despite its disadvantages – it is bulkier, less shareable, and harder to produce – these help explain why the age of print is far from over. It is harder to read from a screen than a book, both for technical reasons like resolution and screen flicker, and ergonomic ones, in that it is usually easier to change position while reading a book than sitting at the screen. And no electronic medium will ever exist that is safe to read in the bath. As a result, electronic texts tend to be shorter – overall, and paragraph-by-paragraph – than printed ones (Dorner, 2002: pp. 19–24). Digitisation therefore discourages the use of longer novels and monographs in distance education, for instance.

In the information society, the idea of "literacy" has expanded beyond simply being able to read. At a recent conference, Frances Norton (2008) showed a slide listing at least 15 "literacies", from financial literacy to visual literacy. Doubtless more are being proposed. Partly this happens because there is a career benefit to academics and researchers in claiming a term as one's own and then declaring it to be vital to the success of individuals and economies. Funding and other resources may well then flow one's way. (You may think "information obesity" is another example: I neither confirm nor deny the suggestion.) That said, it is also the result of a measurable growth in the range of skills and competencies that help us navigate the various environments we, and our communities, must now engage with. We need to develop literacies in a *variety* of media (Warschauer, 1999: p. 155), all of which help reverse the tendency towards adopting a passive, and thus obesity-forming, relationship towards information.

For example, numeracy is a form of literacy. At a functional level, it means being able to do mental arithmetic. But beyond this, a numerate person has an ability to analyse claims made using numbers (and related media, such as graphs); for example, knowing how statistics can be abused (see McFarlane, 1997: Chapter 7 and Dewdney, 1996). A related belief is that teenagers should now be taught "financial literacy": how to manage money, recognising the impact of debt on their personal lives. As with the physical obesity question, there are here notions of personal responsibility, but also structural causes, with young people in the developed world being fertile markets for financial institutions, and whole economies driven by credit. (Note also the existence of community-level solutions, like credit unions, as well as education.)

Likewise, the amount of information encoded in visual forms – advertising images, movies, digital photography and so on – leads to calls to teach "visual literacy" (McFarlane, 1997: Chapter 9). Once again, critical elements include the ability to recognise manipulations of meaning through imagery, and showing how techniques such as cropping, colouring and composition can change a message. The era of digital imagery has made it easier both to produce and manipulate the public record, though these concerns are not new (Orwell cited them in his classic, *Nineteen Eighty-Four*). Hence, there is a productive element in visual literacy, and learners can be encouraged to produce as well as analyse their own images. At this point visual literacy can become a career subject, helping nurture the next generation of artists, photographers and graphic designers; who will produce more images in need of critical attention. This shows how the idea of "literacy" is fundamental to both understanding and producing the noösphere – indeed, that these processes are sides of the same coin. With the Web 2.0 concept now extended to visual imagery, through sites such as Flickr and YouTube, the idea that there can be audience collaboration in producing images (and other texts) changes our ideas of what "literacy" might involve.

To draw one final example from Norton (2008), there is "scientific literacy". Faced by developments such as the Human Genome Project and bioengineering, society must develop not only new analytical skills but new ethics. Norton suggested that scientific literacy involves understanding *risk*, *logic*, *probability*, and *numeracy*. This shows that these different literacies can be tied together. (On the website are thinking tasks which illuminate these and other literacies.)

What is common to these many literacies? In combination, they contribute to an *educated* stance towards the noösphere and the resources within it. They mean more than just the ability to absorb information, but to *understand* it, to *filter* it, and *use* it effectively. When one is truly literate, one does more than just "read" – one understands the background of a text (or image, claim, calculation or technological innovation) and the values that went into creating it. There is also a critical element, an ability to reject a text as value-less (to oneself, or generally). Finally there is a productive element, the idea that one both reads *and* writes; and that when one does write (or calculate, or produce an image, or technology), one is doing so with the full knowledge of how this production fits into, and *enhances*, the noösphere.

However, it is not always easy for teachers to move beyond delivering purely functional skills. Early in the 20th century there were moves to make literacy more "progressive", providing the "skills, knowledge and social attitudes required for urbanised commercial and industrial society" (de Castell and Luke, 1986). Progressive literacy would promote self expression and creativity. However, the approach was ultimately subordinated to a "technocratic" model which merely promoted the ability to read set texts and to write legibly, in a grammatically correct way. It was how one wrote, not what one wrote, that mattered (Warschauer, 1999: pp. 3–4).

Of course, there are reasons why it is important to write properly. Grammar and correct spelling are how a writer says what they intended to say. Without these and other functional skills such as the ability to structure a narrative or argument, to divide an essay into paragraphs appropriately and to cite and reference properly, even the most creative work will not be understood. But the reasons behind the domination of the technocratic approach are not really to do with these. Instead, as Warschauer (p. 4) says:

> The technocratic paradigm... both mimicked and served the needs of the dominant Fordist industrial structure of the era. Just as employees were required to carry out carefully programmed, narrowly defined tasks in the workplace, students were taught to do so in the schools.

Literacy, in any of its forms, is not value-neutral. De Castell and Luke write (1986: p. 374 – quoted by Warschauer, 1999: p. 4) that being literate means "having mastery over the processes by means of which culturally significant information is coded". But what *counts* as significant is more likely to be determined by dominant interests in society than it is by individuals or their own local communities. These calculations of "significance" become embedded into our technologies and other social structures, and subsequently influence our ideas of what literacy should involve.

Literacy, however, is as much a matter of *participation*. Literacy may unlock doors, giving access to certain communicative spaces, but does not necessarily *open* these doors, nor give one the ability or right to pass through them and participate in these spaces (Cressy, 1980: p. 189, quoted in Egan, 1990: p. 55). Yet it is in these spaces that the different "languages" of society are evolving (see the discussion of Bakhtin below), and only by participating in the discourse of a community can one learn the rules of, and perhaps contribute to, this evolution. Literacy then becomes not just learning how to read and write, or even how to judge the quality of what others read and write, but to develop skills at "talking, interacting, thinking, valuing and believing" (Gee, 1996: p. 41, quoted in Warschauer, 1999: p. 45). Literacy, viewed as broadly as this, corresponds to what Egan (1990: pp. 44–5) calls *comprehensive* literacy, viewed as:

> ...a social/cultural/political tradition, rather than as a set of skills... the Comprehensive view is sensitive to the relationships of power and politics that are tied up with literacy.

For example, the activist educator Paulo Freire, active since the 1960s in literacy programmes in the developing world, recognised how the languages of native groups were typically repressed by colonisers. Children were denied the right to learn their own languages at school – thus, the culture and history of their community, as encoded into that language – and when they did learn to read and write, this was not undertaken with the aim of developing in them any understanding of their historical situation (see Freire, 1972). The technologies of literacy, whether these be books, broadcast media or ICT, are once again bound up with these power relationships, creating conditions that allow some forms of knowledge (and literacy) to flourish but not others.

These various restrictions on literacy largely explain why Olson said what he did in the quote used above (via Egan, 1990: p. 85): that "it is difficult to overstate the significance of literacy to a modern society... [but] politicians, educators and newsmen have succeeded [in doing so]". Egan explains that limited views of literacy – often argued for by "politicians, educators and newsmen" – in fact *deskill* students (1990: p. 59):

> Conventional "literacy" without historical understanding, for example, is largely meaningless; it destroys the positive features of orality while putting no equivalent sense-making techniques in their place. It provides "skills" of marginal utility that tie one

tightly into the technology that requires them, but provides no empowerment to make sense of that technology nor to control it.

I will soon move on to discuss how these ideas help analyse the more ICT-specific literacies developed in the current time: "computer literacy" and "information literacy". Will they simply "tie us tightly into the technology" on which the information society rests, or will they allow us to "make sense of that technology", and creatively exploit it in our individual and community lives, to construct informational resources for the future?

Before making those arguments, however, let me first return to another analyst of "information overload". ICT is amongst the suggested triggers for what Thompson (2008) sees as the dangerous spread of counterknowledge. Cyberculture studies (see Chapter 4) has, largely, an optimistic view of ICT's allowing the average person to publish online. Recent hype about "Web 2.0" reinforces this, particularly since *Time* magazine made "You" – the individual Web user – its 2006 "Person of the Year". Web 2.0 technologies are so named to contrast them with earlier, more static World-Wide Web publication methods, named "web 1.0" after the fact. Static web pages or other multimedia may have been easy to access but the direction of the message, between author and audience, was still one way. It was the author(ity) who determined what would be said, how it would be said and to what it would be connected, through hypertext links. Although there were some nods made to "interactivity", these were, with hindsight, little different from the sort of interactivity one might get from, say, reading the entries in an encyclopaedia in a self-determined order or following a footnoted reference to another book (a kind of hyperlink). (See Laurillard, 2002.)

Web 2.0 technologies, by contrast, turn the user into the *producer* of web-based content. The most famous (or notorious) Web 2.0 site is probably Wikipedia. Some criticise this site because they believe there is no way that the validity of its information can be confirmed: others laud it precisely because they believe that the information's validity is *more* likely. Wikipedia is constantly checked both by casual readers and, in a more systematic way, by volunteers who check change logs, repair vandalism and post warnings on the site when references are needed. (Here see Lawler, 2008, which has many other references.) Wikipedia is only one example of "wiki" technology, which creates websites that, in principle, anyone can edit (though in practice many require the entry of a password). Many other Web 2.0 tools exist, such as blogging tools, tagging tools like del.icio.us or FURL, user-generated multimedia tools like Flickr and YouTube and social networking sites like Facebook. Doubtless many are already familiar to you. Whether they help create a sense of online community, or whether they instead lead to invasions of privacy and the creation of microcultures, is yet to be resolved, though thinking tasks on the website will help you explore your own feelings.

To properly consider Web 2.0's impact, we must listen also to writers who do not believe user-generated content necessarily improves the noösphere's quality. This returns us to Thompson (2008: pp. 127–9): more forcefully still Keen's *The Cult of the Amateur* (2007). Both find in Web 2.0, and the values underlying it, a substantial threat to informational quality. For them, Web 2.0 is a technological expression of a reduction in the value of objective knowledge. Thompson (2008: p. 18) quotes:

> ...one of the slogans of that citadel of counterknowledge, the Church of Scientology: "If it's true for you, it's true".

On this relativistic philosophy (see Chapter 2), Thompson lays the blame for the erosion of the value of objective knowledge in much modern public debate. It is this relativism, rather than scientifically-proven evidence, which supports several of the forms of counterknowledge against which Thompson rails. None are supported by objectively valued forms of proof, but all are widely believed nonetheless, often by those whose educational attainment is above average.

Thompson explains these phenomena by pointing to four connected trends in the recent history of knowledge production. First, as noted, there is the spread of ICT, the greater availability of information, ease of publication, and emergence of microcultures (Thompson uses examples such as the online microculture created by sufferers of chronic fatigue syndrome). Second, there is the increased power of the information industries, and thus a market for counterknowledge even when it is known to be untrue. Thompson draws attention, for example, to the marketing campaign behind Gavin Menzies' *1421* despite the lack of objective value in the work (2008: pp. 113–6). Third, he suggests that traditional sources of authoritative knowledge – churches, education, politicians and science – have, for one reason or another, lost credibility. Fourth, Thompson blames the intellectual movement that is postmodernism, its promotion of relativism and multiculturalism rather than objectivity, and a resultant aversion in some academics towards criticising certain forms of counterknowledge (like afrocentrism or Muslim creationism) for fear of appearing racist.

All are important, but the first two have already been covered. Let us think about the last two in more detail, however. I do not want to criticise Thompson's book as such: it is far too good a polemic. Having access to work like this, and the way of thinking that it represents, is a vital weapon in any arsenal against information obesity at the personal level. But it can only be a *part* of such an arsenal. Asserting the value of objective knowledge is important: but we may *know* that the sugary cake should be avoided, yet many other psychological factors turn us towards it. And it would be an austere world if objective value was all that mattered: which is precisely why issues of credibility and subjectivity are important.

It is easy to mock some of the consequences of postmodernism, particularly from the "common sense" stance that Thompson exhibits (and which is mimicked in right-wing newspapers across the world). When it leads to "politically correct" absurdities postmodernism's value may seem questionable. But we must not mock or dismiss something without looking carefully at the reasons why it exists. Postmodernism is an intellectual current which has been developing for some time, and gained strength in the French-speaking world in the 1960s and 1970s. I must here be brief (see the reading list, and also Chapter 7) but, broadly, postmodernists:

> ...claim that technologies such as computers and media, new forms of knowledge, and changes in the socioeconomic system are producing... increased cultural fragmentation, changes in the experience of space and time, and new modes of experience... postmodern theory provides a critique of... the modern belief that theory mirrors reality, taking instead "perspectivist" and "relativist" positions that theories at best provide partial perspectives on their objects... (Best and Kellner, 1991: pp. 1–4).

None of those are easy ideas (something characteristic of this kind of social theory), but in brief, what postmodernism is saying is that it is exactly the search for objective truth which, pushed too far, causes precisely the social problems it seeks to eradicate. This is a contradiction at the heart of the Enlightenment project (see Chapter 7). Aggressive claims to "truth" in fact lead to unfreedom, as once those claims are turned into values, theories and ways of thinking and thereby become embedded into the infrastructure, any dissent is directly and indirectly repressed. Environmental conditions stop being amenable to the spread of alternative ways of thinking.

Postmodernism actually provides ammunition for those who want us to take up a critical, questioning stance towards any stated "truth".

What Thompson is concerned about is that such a stance could be targeted at, say, Darwinism just as much as at, say, afrocentric history. Others criticise postmodernism on the grounds of its being "neo-conservative" (see Habermas, 1991; Callinicos, 1989); that because it is unwilling to criticise *any* position, by default, values and ideas currently in positions of strength will be those which persist. Again, we can now see connections between this criticism, the points made earlier by Avis about activity theory (its tendency to avoid addressing "primary tensions" in a system) and the way in which values become reinforced by being embedded into an infrastructure.

Postmodernism drew strength from the linguistic analyses of writers like Saussure, Wittgenstein and Bakhtin. I find the latter to be the most accessible of the three (and recommend Bakhtin, 1986 and Morson and Emerson, 1990 as useful reading). Bakhtin's analyses of how language and communication were actually *used* showed that interpretations of any utterance must vary between individuals. Indeed, without such variance, there would be no *creativity*. Bakhtin says (1981: pp. 291–2):

> ...languages do not *exclude* each other, but rather intersect with each other in many different ways.... [languages] are specific points of view on the world, forms for conceptualising the world in words... each characterised by its own objects, meanings and values. As such they may all be juxtaposed to one another, contradict one another and be interrelated dialogically. As such they encounter one another and co-exist in the consciousness of real people.... these languages live a real life, they struggle and evolve in an environment of social heteroglossia [from the Greek meaning "different tongues"].

He means here more than just the English language, the Russian language and so on. Each age group, professional group, community and so on has its own way of using words. If I speak the word "Ward" to a hospital cleaner, they will probably assume I mean the place where they perform their daily tasks. If I speak it to a fellow Brighton & Hove Albion FC fan it will probably be taken as a reference to Peter Ward, a famous ex-player of the 1970s. Though little cross-fertilisation could occur between these two usages, it is through sharing and developing understandings of each other's utterances, and investigating how they differ in subtle but important ways, that *mutual problem solving* occurs, and conflicts are creatively resolved without the imposition of force by either party. By doing so, ways of using language may change, and conditions set which will alter ways of working and thinking in the future (and to which the "literate" person, however that is defined, must adapt). Thus, the noösphere evolves, and communication becomes an essential aspect of life in a democratic society (I return to this point in Part 3). But if the "one best" solution to a problem has already been determined "from above", by scientists or managers who then do not enter into debate with those affected by these decisions, no mutual, reciprocal and creative understanding of a *particular* situation can develop.

It is not that there would be no creativity in a world where objective value was paramount; the scientific project itself is, of course, a fundamentally creative one. But not all scientific knowledge is valuable at a personal level. Bakhtin gives support to the idea that there are "personalised" forms of knowledge which are nothing to do with "truth" but which remain fundamentally valuable to the knower. I have already mentioned the movie *Contact* (in Chapter 1): here is some dialogue from it. Palmer (a priest) is arguing with Ellie (an atheist astrophysicist) that her trust in science cannot explain the whole of her reality:

> *Palmer*: Your Dad, did you love him? [Ellie's father died when she was young.]
>
> *Ellie*: Yes.
>
> *Palmer*: Prove it.

Thompson rightly expresses his frustration when highly educated people believe in crystal healing, Scientology, alien abduction and so on. But this is powerful dialogue because Ellie has no answer here. I doubt anyone would, and even if they tried, their "proof" would not reside in the sort of objectively valuable, falsifiable knowledge which Thompson (and scientific method) revere.

Subjectively valuable insights and feelings are as likely to lead to new creative understandings of a situation as are objectively valuable scientific statements. They can forcefully motivate activity and creative engagement with the world, and in highly positive ways. Aesthetics – the appreciation of beauty – is another, one scientists use themselves to describe the elegant way the cosmos is constructed, and as inspiring their love of science and the search for objective truth (e.g. Johnson, 2000; Feynman, 1998). Closer to home, beauty inspires politics: for example, around a road or residential development which may be "objectively proven" to be beneficial to a town's economy but not its aesthetics or general environmental quality. Can a value be put on transcendent moments such as watching the birth of one's first child? Or watching one's team score the crucial goal in the last seconds of the play-offs? And if these cannot be "valued" does that make them "meaning-less"?

Thompson would doubtless respond that it is not his intention to dismiss this kind of thing, but rather to draw attention to the dangers posed when the axiom "if it's true for you it's true" spreads into not just popular discourse, but economic decisions. And he is right to do this. (See p. 22 where he draws the distinction between a position of faith, and one of counterknowledge.) But nevertheless this nugget of relativism, these moments of unprovability, will always remain in our communicative exchanges. This is what makes something like *Counterknowledge* no less troublesome, in combating information obesity, than any other strategy seeking to distinguish between "good" and "bad" information *from the top*. What we need is not to be hectored by someone like Thompson. His being right is not the point. What we actually need is an *educational* strategy that allows us to distinguish for ourselves what "good" and "bad" mean – and thus filter against these criteria. And this educational strategy must be one that prevents us simply accepting that "if it's true for me it's true" – which will return us into all the problems of relativism that currently exist – but which turns us into critical consumers of information.

This is a crucial point for my argument, but nevertheless, risks leading us round in circles (a phenomenon not unconnected to the difficulties many find in using social theories like this). The only way out is to recognise that subjective value is not the same as critical attention. It is the job of Chapter 7 to explore this idea in depth, but some initial moves should be made here.

Even objective statements need critical attention. For example, Thompson's criticisms of aromatherapy (2008: p. 76) are brief and rather half-hearted compared to the other "counterknowledge" he attacks. In fact there have been published, peer-reviewed papers in academic journals which suggest the usefulness of certain plant oils for the treatment of both external and internal ailments, combined with the therapeutic value of massage[1] – which, in combination, are how

---

[1] For example: Eccles *et al.* (1988) describe how menthols can decongest nasal passages; interestingly, they suggest this is only true of certain menthols, which challenges the idea that aromatherapy's effectiveness is based only on scent. Hasson *et al.* (2004) conducted a randomised clinical trial on the effects of massage compared to non-manipulative "mental relaxation", and observed clear positive effects of massage while the treatment was underway, although longer-term effects were inconclusive.

aromatherapists treat patients. These points do not make Thompson "wrong" and aromatherapy (or me) "right", but they are grounds on which to be critical about one particular page in his book. Any such claim can be investigated with time, indeed, such investigations are exactly what drive scientific enquiry. But of course time and the other intellectual and financial resources required are not always easy to secure.

Credibility is a strong influence over whether counterknowledge (or any knowledge) is accepted. Credibility is a mixture of expertise and trustworthiness, and has been said to be more important than the "objective" quality of information when judging how communications are received (see King, in Kahn and Baume, 2003: p. 104). The Ancient Greeks gave the art of *rhetoric* – persuasion through technique – high value in their democratic society. Politicians, propagandists and advertisers continue to employ it to secure attention and acceptance for their utterances. Lawyers often counter the testimony of expert witnesses not by attacking their statements, but their position, qualifications, and credibility (a technique frequently used in the "McLibel" trial: see Vidal, 1997: p. 120 for instance). Anyone who believes themselves to be deeply involved and concerned with something will question the credibility of those whose information contradicts what they think to be right: for instance, those trying to stop the closure of a local school, post office or other community facility will not look on the pronouncements of those who "objectively" insist it must be closed as being credible.

From where, then, does counterknowledge's credibility stem? I can see two possibilities. First, the scientific establishment has done itself no PR favours through past association with high-profile failures such as Thalidomide. More significantly, governments frequently exercise power by rejecting even their own scientists' advice on policy[2]. Whether or not these are "rogue" elements or unfortunate mistakes in scientific,

---

Furlan *et al.* (2002) undertook a meta-review of the literature on massage and lower back pain and concluded that massage was beneficial for sufferers. Finally, Bassett *et al.* (1990) conducted a randomised trial and concluded that tea tree oil (*Melaleuca alternifolia*) had measurable positive effects on the treatment of acne, with fewer side effects than a lotion of benzoylperoxide. None of this should be extrapolated into a belief that, say, burning lavender oil in one's bedroom each night will prevent cancer: but it does suggest that certain treatments offered by aromatherapists have clinical value of the sort which medical science accepts as proven.

[2] As I wrote this chapter, the UK government ignored a report, years in the preparation, by its own scientific advisors and reimposed restrictions on cannabis use which were relaxed several years previously. See also the discussion of nuclear power planning inquries in Kemp (1985) and Chapter 9 below.

objective value-making (to be corrected by better research conducted later), in such high-profile cases, coupled with the distortions of the publishing industry, it is little wonder that credibility can be largely a matter of opinion.

However, perhaps the credibility of counterknowledge is also partly down to its use of narrative. Many of Thompson's examples are *stories*, often with romantic appeal (lost civilisations, evil government conspiracies, etc.). Knight's excellent review of "conspiracy culture" (2000) draws attention to the same point. And it is interesting and significant that the credibility of romantic teaching stems from the fact that many *adults* have not really got far beyond the romantic stage in their intellectual development (Egan, 1990: p. 178). Hence the appeal of things like human interest stories in the news, rather than factual analysis (Egan, 1990: p. 161). The appeal of "celebrity culture" – particularly for advertisers – is an offshoot of this.

Nevertheless, as Egan argues, these difficulties arise not because the two traditions – reason and imagination if you like – are at odds, but instead through failing to see that they complement each other. Romantic understanding can easily collapse into "whimsy, sentimentality, weak mysticism, and high-sounding vacuousness taking the proper place of reason" (Egan, 1990: p. 173). But if the instrumental, objective value of knowledge is emphasised too strongly, or a community's ability to intersubjectively make knowledge from what it experiences (and embed these new understandings into the environment on which they depend) is corrupted by economics, politically manipulated or simply ignored by a government which supposedly represents it – to what can individuals or communities turn?

Counterknowledge may be dangerous. But so is objective knowledge, if inappropriately applied. These points, again, do not discredit Thompson's book. In fact, they reinforce his arguments. One should never read only one opinion on any issue. To *educate* oneself about something requires investigating different points of view, analysis, and synthesis. The trouble is that the instrumental point of view encourages the idea that there is always "one right answer" to a question. And if this "one right answer" is then embedded into the organisations and even the languagues which govern our lives, the conditions so created will no longer be amenable to alternative solutions.

The key strategy involved in making links between "rationality" and "romantic understanding" is, for Egan (1990: pp. 143–4), the *critical reflection on claims to objectivity*. This makes explicit what had been implicit, investigating all claims with reference to the "technical resources to aid thinking" (Egan, 1990: p. 2) which include scientific method but which must also include subjective and intersubjective methods as well. These constitute *filters* for the information around us, and in principle help us combat information obesity by selecting only what is healthy, and which will nurture and sustain the communities and environments in which we are embedded.

The difficulty is, how to move away from a "one size fits all" approach to information education and towards a more critical approach *without* collapsing into exactly the kind of relativism and counterknowledge that Thompson rightly castigates. To explore this more deeply we need to move on to talk about computer and information literacy, the subject of the next chapter. I will give the final word in this chapter to James Boyle (in Hess and Ostrom, 2007: p. 132) who says that this question is:

> ...fundamental to the division between the progressive and the populist impulses.... The progressive notes the dangers of collective irrationality, of lack of understanding, of availability cascades that violently skew perceptions of risk and benefit. He puts faith in the expertise of technocratic specialists working for the public interest, but isolated from public pressure and hubbub. The populist, by contrast, is skeptical of claims that restrict knowledge, decision making, or power to an elite group. He sees the experts as being subject to their own versions of narrowness and prejudice, their own cascades. Most sensible people acknowledge that each of these perspectives on the world has important truths to offer. The question is where the balance is to be drawn....

Boyle writes from a perspective that is fundamentally optimistic about the effects of giving greatly increased access to information to the "ordinary" person. He definitely takes the view that we live in a time of information abundance, not overload. His argument (Boyle in Hess and Ostrom, 2007: p. 133) is that "we do not *know* the benefits and costs that wider access to cultural and scholarly material could bring". I completely agree; and it is the task of the remainder of this book to establish how individuals and communities can empower *themselves* through realising that the noösphere can, in principle, be seen as a resource now more abundant and fertile than at any previous point in human history.

6

Computer and information literacy

Once they start offering courses, you know the field is dead.
Stephen Fry, *Making History*

This chapter explores education's response to the changes ICT has wrought on our environments. In line with the previous chapter I term these "computer literacy" and "information literacy". The latter term is now in common use, but the former is used more for convenience's sake, and I do not claim it has definitive status in the field.

Many books exist which deal both with the specific content of computer literacy education (e.g. Kennewell *et al.*, 2003), and with the use of ICT in other subjects from the primary school (McFarlane, 1997) through to university education (Laurillard, 2002). This reflects a long-standing issue. Should ICT be a subject in its own right ("computer studies", in earlier parlance) or something that seeps into all other subjects? This question has never been properly resolved (see the chapters by Watson and Cox in Passey and Samways, 1997). In any case, it is impossible to review every initiative from the last 40 years. I stress then that this is not intended as a history of computer and information literacy; instead I selectively focus on certain initiatives as examples of different approaches, illuminating them with the help of the environmental model and assessing their contribution to information obesity – for better or worse. I want to show how a great deal of computer and information literacy education struggles to incorporate the two types of value identified as important at the end of Part 1 – objective and intersubjective/community value – and instead promotes mainly relativist and subjective means for countering perceived defects in how learners exploit ICT and information. It is then the task of Part 3 to explain, in more detail, why we must get beyond these limited approaches.

The typical educational policy response to ICT is based on economic arguments. Worldwide, the case is made that individuals and workforces must improve skill levels to remain competitive. It is further argued that computer literacy is a significant part of this portfolio; perhaps the most significant at this time. Where skills are lacking in individuals or the workforce, responsibility is often laid at the door of the education system, cast as outdated, unwilling, or unprepared for the challenge of educating the workforce of an information society. What follows is a representative selection of quotes illustrating this view. First, from 1982, Fred Williams (in Robins and Webster, p. 1987: 108):

> Our schools, with their assembly line instruction and even their bells, are a holdover from the industrial age... Yet we are depending on them to train our youngsters for life in a clearly developing postindustrial era of high technologies.

In 1985, his namesake Shirley Williams MP said (Beynon and Mackay, 1992: p. 129):

> The ability of the education system to match the needs of the information society for highly educated people has now become the main determinant of a country's employment prospects.

Graham Day, chief executive of Rover (Robins and Webster, 1987: p. 109):

> ...current educational methods and policies "are not producing the stream of managerial talent which business and industry currently requires...".

Fast forward to 2005, and an unidentified US project manager (Zeller, 2005: 2):

> People want to ensure that colleges are actually preparing students for the future, the future being an information society.

Finally, the Partnership for 21st Century Skills (2004: 1) warns of the competitive threat from emerging Asian "tigers":

> Americans cannot be complacent about improving the quality of education while competitors around the world are focusing on preparing students for the demands of this century.

With such pressures in favour of change, and a belief that the benefits of computer literacy education are manifest, why is the field characterised by "missed opportunities" (Capel, 1992; an excellent review of the first 20 years of computer literacy education in the UK[1])?

From the early 1960s, as reported by the British Computer Society in 1974 (see Capel, 1992: p. 39): "any introduction of computing techniques into schools was partly stimulated by the growing career potential in the computer industry". Teaching computing was therefore oriented to producing programmers, engineers and other computer professionals. In a subsidiary way it was also recognised that computers could help develop mathematicians and scientists, but again, the orientation was towards training specialists. Computer use was frequently restricted to mathematics lessons and/or mathematically-gifted pupils. Despite ongoing research into the way computers could be used to deliver teaching, particularly in the USA[2], computers were not cheap or accessible enough for them realistically to be used in teaching humanities or arts subjects. At this time, number-crunching, and simple programming in the BASIC language, were what computers were best at (see the example of the Sinclair ZX Spectrum, below). There was no convenient e-mail or Internet, office programs such as Lotus Notes were only just emerging, and Microsoft's era of domination (and resultant standardisation) was half a generation away.

Computer literacy education was therefore restricted by the existing educational infrastructure. Qualified ICT teachers could not simply materialise, they had to be trained, and that needed both an organised system of training, and agreement on how relevant qualifications could be accredited. Mathematics and science graduates would have typically been "good with computers" because they would have been more likely

---

[1] This chapter does have a bias towards the history of ICT skills education as played out in the UK setting. I ask non-UK readers to forgive this stance but I believe the UK case is at least a representative one. Links are provided on the website to resources and thinking tasks which will enable readers to explore the experience of their own countries.

[2] The development of the PLATO system at the University of Illinois from the 1950s is a fascinating story. It shows that many of the "educational technologies" we assume to be fairly recent developments, like chat rooms and online quizzes, were first explored using PLATO over 40 years ago. It is also a good example of the instrumental approach. The search for something like PLATO was a direct response to the "GI Bill" which entitled veterans to college education, and other factors which contributed to a big rise in student numbers after World War II. The rise made it viable to seek technological solutions to the problem of managing the education of more students without there being an equivaluent rise in funding. (See van Meer, 2003.) All of this is relevant to the use of ICT in education but to keep this chapter manageable I do not discuss it in detail.

than social studies graduates to have used them at university. When computers could be afforded, it made economic sense to install them in the teaching spaces used by these teachers. It would therefore have been difficult for a teacher in another subject, however enthusiastic they were, to access, explore and develop their own understanding of what ICT could do in their classroom. Wellington's paper on computer studies teacher training (1984) highlights this; he observes that in 1982 there were as few as 26 trainee teachers in the whole of England and Wales who were specialising in computer studies.

However, even early in the subject's history, it was recognised that "computer literacy" should include more than technical skills. The BCS (see above) recognised that as computers provoked changes in society, they were relevant to social studies curricula. One attempt to introduce study of the social and organisational conditions into which ICT emerges was *informatics*. Innovators such as Langefors and Longworth (Capel, 1992: pp. 50–4):

> ...developed a course based on the study of information rather than the computer... The pupil should be less concerned with how the computer works and more interested in establishing it as a tool for manipulating information (a view which has been developed throughout the 1980s and now established within the National Curriculum).

However:

> Although Longworth's course was probably one of the most notable departures from what could be described as mainstream computer appreciation, it never gained wide currency. The course was wide-ranging, cutting across subject boundaries.... This seemed to testify to the strength of a traditionally subject-based curriculum... which was able to resist pressures to break down barriers between subjects...

Capel (1992: pp. 49–50) reports that 1970s maths and science teachers found discussion of ICT's potential social implications to be "woolly"; meanwhile, social science teachers were reluctant to get involved in what they considered a science subject. This is not to say informatics did not emerge as a subject, but once it did, it put up its own barriers between itself and other subjects. As McGarr explains (in press), resistance to diffusing computer literacy skills throughout the Irish curriculum came from informatics teachers, concerned about eroding the status of their own specialism.

Though informatics seems to prefigure information literacy (see below), it can easily turn into what amounts to the study of the design of sociotechnical systems. This has its uses. For computer professionals such as systems analysts, it is an important part of the portfolio of skills required in such a job. But as a result, informatics is no more likely to result in a *critical* view of ICT than is learning programming[3]. What this word means here can be illustrated by comparing it with US initiatives (described in Jonassen *et al.*, 2003: pp. 123–4) to implement "critical [TV] viewing curricula" in the 1970s:

> ...to ensure that elementary and junior high school students (especially) did not just watch TV, they monitored it.... Most of these critical viewing curricula taught children how television and television production work, the components of entertainment television stories, the purpose of commercials and how to view their claims critically and become informed consumers, how their lives differed from television characters', that television violence should not be imitated and how to get the most from television news programming...

Nowadays we would probably call this *media literacy*, and the term is significant. It was believed that such underlying critical knowledge about a medium is what really indicated "literacy" in that medium, not just the skills needed to operate and consume it (which in TV's case, as noted in Chapter 4, are instilled in us without the need for formal education). However, a sign of the relative priorities here is that "only a small minority of children have ever been exposed to these critical viewing curricula..." (Jonassen *et al.*, 2003). In fact the existence of "media studies" is often considered evidence that teaching has gone soft or overly liberal, draining resources and students away from more important science and engineering work[4].

---

[3] The field of participatory design (see Bijker, 1989; Schuler and Namioka, 1993) acknowledges this point, though only partly; it is discussed further in Chapter 11.

[4] See *http://education.guardian.co.uk/chooseadegree/story/0,,1864452,00.html* (last accessed 23 Jun 2008) which reports a 2006 announcement from Cambridge University that qualifications in Media Studies will no longer impress admissions tutors. Also, the report says: "This month ministers complained that there are more students taking media studies at A-level than there are taking physics". Whatever one thinks about the relative value of these subjects, this serves well to illustrate governmental values: mediated (note the word) by the writer of the report (Francis Beckett, 4 September 2006).

This has been just a sketch of the earliest forms of computer literacy education, but they reflect long-standing institutional difficulties in defining what ICT skills education should be, and tensions resulting from external pressures to produce learners with specific skills; a lack of resources and/or trained personnel; and internal institutional factors such as the way education is organised around disciplines and the inflexibility of teaching space. But countercases from the same period do exist, and I want now to present two. One is anecdotal, drawn from my experiences in the 1980s in the UK. The other was documented in *Science* by Nevison (1976) and concerns the policy at Dartmouth College in the US in the 1970s.

I started secondary school in the UK in 1980, around the time that the first cheap home computers came on the market. These were produced by small companies and to many readers their names may mean nothing, but to people (especially men) of a certain age, names such as the Commodore 64, Dragon 32 and Sinclair ZX Spectrum will evoke memories of rickety hardware, non-existent graphical user interfaces and blocky graphics. (On the website is a short film made in homage to the Spectrum, showing how primitive it now seems; the film also makes some points about *empowerment* which will be repeated below.) They retailed, in real terms, for around the same as a lower-end laptop does today, so at the time remained beyond the reach of many families, but nevertheless were the first really accessible home computers.

Also on the website are copies of advertisements for these products – four from 1983 and one from 1980 (all from *The Times*). Some of the claims are comical now (the Dragon's "truly massive 32K of memory" would hold a two-page Word file), but they remain interesting historical documents, particularly regarding how these consumer goods were marketed. Educational motivations come to the fore, sometimes quite explicitly: for instance, the ZX Spectrum advert dated 13 July 1983 reads:

> The Government's "Micros in Primaries" scheme is introducing more and more microcomputers to Britain's 27,000 primary schools. All of these schools are offered subsidised computer packages based on three approved computers – the BBC Model B, Research Machines' 480Z and the Sinclair ZX Spectrum.
>
> The trouble is, that even though the computers are subsidised, there are likely to be more children than computers – which means that each child gets only limited time to use the computer. The solution, of course, is to buy one of the approved computers and

carry on the good work at home. By far the cheapest of these computers is the Sinclair ZX Spectrum.

Several things are apparent from this extract. First, only certain models are "approved". (Software written for a Spectrum would not work on a BBC, nor any other model, even if written in the same BASIC language.) There is an implication that time spent at a computer, regardless of how it is used, is a good thing, worth investing in; also the idea that the investment will supplement school resources.

The Commodore Vic 20 advert lists its applications in an order that was presumably calculated to appeal to *The Times*' readership. Note, however, the enthusiastic comment at the end, which betrays another principal marketing point:

> The VIC 20 has educational programs for all ages (spelling, physics, arithmetic etc.) plus music, typing, chess and home accounts. There are special programs like Robert Carrier's menu planner and BBC "Mastermind", and not forgetting, of course, lots and lots of wonderful arcade games.

Did I play games on my home computer? Yes, but here we start to get to the point. No home computer these days would be advertised, at least outside the specialist press, with copy like this:

> The ZX80 cuts away computer jargon and mystique. It takes you straight into BASIC, the most common, easy to use fundamental computer language. You simply take it out of its box, plug it into your TV, switch it on at the mains – and start. With the manual in your hand, you'll be running programs in an hour. Within a week, you'll be writing complex programs of your own, with confidence and competence.

As the film on the website shows, though games were certainly part of this culture, so was *writing* them (and other applications). BASIC, the language built into the computers mentioned here, is maligned and now obsolete, but it did introduce me and others of my generation to the notion that the computer could be *instructed*; and that this was a *creative act*. By the time I left school in 1985 I had acquired enough knowledge to have written my own games (selling a few copies of one) – and enough enthusiasm to study for another 2 years, gain a Computer Studies qualification, and get a job as a programmer. (University came later, but I won't bore you any further.) In that respect, I suppose, computer studies education had the desired effect. I became a "computer professional", and the education I received as a teenager directly contributed to my subsequent career.

However, there is an important caveat, which is the point of this story. Until starting technical college in September 1985, I *never once* used a computer in a classroom. All of my "ICT education" was informal, arising through self exploration of computing books and magazines and from collaboration with peers who shared my interest. It was in school where most of my computer knowledge was shared and communicated, but not in classrooms. There was a definite group of "computer kids" around, and yes, in later times we would have been "the geeks" but regardless of reputation it was a highly active *informal* learning community based around a shared interest, not only in games playing but in BASIC programming, and sharing our enthusiasm for both. This was also supported by a community-based computer club organised by volunteers. Many contemporaries attended this club along with adults whose own private enthusiasms drove their participation. Around 20–30 of us met once a fortnight. (All were male, I recall.) It was at one of these club nights, in about 1983, that I logged onto the Internet for the first time, though I only remember this with hindsight. (We networked through a modem hooked up to a coin-operated payphone!)

As I said, this is anecdotal, and I cannot draw objective conclusions about the effect this informal learning had on my use of ICT, both at the time and in my future life[5]. Nevertheless it's an example of how people motivated to learn will find ways of doing so – and of gathering together with others to do so – in ways that do not involve formal educational institutions, qualifications and fees. This happens all the time. Teenagers gather in a mate's garage to jam on cheap guitars, learning how to play and write songs. Others spend weekends riding horses, or playing football. All show how the *community* provides resources we can use to learn, and motivate ourselves to learn.

This less formal, community-based approach to ICT education has been recorded within institutions. Nevison (1976) describes how the prestigious Dartmouth College helped its staff (faculty, in US terminology) and students engage with ICT. I find this article fascinating

---

[5] You might like to look at the questionnaire on the website, which is a start at collecting data that may help answer the question of whether these technologies made any difference to their users.

as it paints a picture of technology use in higher education that seems decades ahead of its time. In his summary, Nevison writes:

> Ten years ago one could have argued over whether undergraduates would really have much use for computing in their liberal arts studies. One could have wondered whether there were many subjects where a conscientious instructor could make significant use of a computer program. One could scoff at the possibility that a liberal arts college would regularly graduate classes where more than 90 percent of its members had used a computer. One could have raised a skeptical eyebrow at anyone rash enough to suggest that a person interested in a liberal education should learn how to write a computer program....

Those questions are pertinent enough now, but the projects he describes took place in the early 1970s! Nevison is discussing a situation in which these skills are not just taught to people but thoroughly embedded into curricula, across all subjects. He also asserts that this has happened without direct management or "training":

> The growth of computing among the students and faculty at Dartmouth has been organic. It has proceeded at an unhurried pace where students and faculty learn to program largely on their own.

> A new instructor at Dartmouth will find computing all around him. At a faculty meeting about half of those attending will have used computing and almost one-quarter will have included it in their teaching in the last year.

Again, how happy would a manager be nowadays to report such figures! You might think I am over-stating the case: after all, every teacher and student will now use computing at some point. But Nevison is talking of more than low-level use, such as using e-mail and chat, browsing the World-Wide Web and using Word and maybe Excel occasionally. He is talking about significant and relatively technical applications of computing technology in teaching, and to labour the point he's writing in 1976. And this has not happened through managerial decree, but "organically", through people exploring this technology for themselves and developing applications that solve educational problems in individual working lives.

So where did we go from there?

"Social impact" approaches to computer literacy implicitly criticise the idea that literacy can develop through learning to program (e.g. Senn Breivik and Gee, 2006: pp. xii–xiv). It is true that programming has firm roots in instrumental rationality. But there remains a *creative* element. Programs are created to solve problems the user faces. This can be empowering, particularly for the young, as McFarlane says (1997: pp. 10–11):

> The fact that the computer behaves differently when the user does something can create a powerfully motivating response. In a child, used to a world where things are largely beyond her control and whose attempts at new things are usually only met with at best partial success, the reactions of the computer may elicit wonder, excitement and a rare feeling of empowerment.

Computer literacy education as defined from the 1990s on retained this idea of "instructing" the computer to perform certain tasks. But the creative, problem-solving aspect is often lost. Instead the aim is to produce "effective users": which no longer necessarily means "active" users. What was once a limiting but more active definition of computer literacy – being able to write a computer program – has been changed in a way which makes it more accessible, but simultaneously, less active.

The classic example of this approach is the European Computer Driving License (ECDL). The first heading of one ECDL course book which I downloaded in 2006[6] asks, "What is Excel?", which is a fair question with which to begin. The next few lines are (bullets in original):

- Excel 2003 is the spreadsheet and data analysis program in Office 2003. It combines incredible power with ease of use, giving both professionals and occasional users the features they need. Excel 2003 is designed in such a way that you can use it as a basic spreadsheet program, and learn more advanced skills as you need to.

---

[6] From *http://www.cheltenhamcourseware.com*. In spring 2008 I looked again at their materials for Excel 2007 and there have been some changes in wording, but the basic structure and message of the pack is the same. The fairest thing to do is to check for yourself: use the thinking tasks on the website to do this.

Using Excel as a Spreadsheet

- A basic spreadsheet is comprised of a table of values, some of which are calculated by formulas and functions. Excel 2003 can check your formulas and help you define functions using wizards.

- With a computer-based spreadsheet, you can change a particular data value in the spreadsheet and all the values that are affected by the change are recalculated. To take full advantage of this feature, you should use formulas and functions instead of numbers where possible.

The definitions are recursive, closed. The course exists because learners want to use Excel. No mention is made of *why* someone may wish to use this technology (even instrumentally, that is, explaining that it can make keeping numerical records more efficient and reliable). The ECDL cares not what people use the technology for; just that they learn to use it. Likewise, its features are simply *there*; formulas and functions exist and "should be used".

It is highly unlikely that the ECDL will help anyone develop a critical, adaptable relationship with ICT. We should be fair, and observe that form follows function. Most learners on the ECDL are there for instrumental reasons (MacKeogh, 2003: p. 16). That is implied when the only motivation suggested – twice – in the first paragraph is *need*. There are advantages to having a standardised qualification, accepted across most of the world, indicating the holder has reached a level of competency with a range of basic ICT techniques. But in an environment where this sort of thing forms a substantial part of the educational response to ICT, it is unsurprising that the quality of society's informational resources continues to degrade.

This argument has been made before (Reffell and Whitworth, 2002; Garson, 2000; McFarlane, 1997). Why do we often see a failure to meet organisational and personal learning needs in a dynamic, rapidly changing environment "when the specific is transient and the abstract is that which must carry the learner through a lifetime of education and re-education" (Garson, 2000: p. 192)? In other words, why are so many resources still devoted to teaching "button-pushing" skills instead of a wider, creative, critical approach to the use of computers, many successful examples of which exist?

There are two reasons that can be proposed. Firstly, technical skills like those taught by the ECDL will go out of date when the software is upgraded. The courses for Excel 2003 and Excel 2007 are not the same. This is a substantial money-earner for the training companies and publishing houses which subsist through providing continual revisions of their own products, just as the manipulation of fashion trends is for the clothing industry: it is "planned obsolescence", a way of persuading customers to buy new products before they may otherwise choose to. Second, I have already discussed how creativity is not something that the whole of a workforce is required to manifest. The ECDL delivers skills required not by ICT's active users, but rather its passive consumers, cogs in the sociotechnical machine, given little choice as to what technology they will be trained in.

Robins and Webster, in their review of the UK situation, describe how the Thatcher government greatly strengthened the link between education, "enterprise" (connected firmly to industry and commerce, as opposed to, say, public service work, political activism, etc.) and ICT. For example, they quote (1987: p. 1) a Department of Trade and Industry statement:

> Where young people are regularly using technology to enter, use and manipulate information at school, they will be better placed to help industry and commerce to compete effectively.

But in an infrastructure based around the enclosure, rather than dispersal, of informational resources, this does not necessarily mean that everyone will "help industry and commerce compete" through applying the same *kind* of technological skills. Capel wrote (1992: p. 56):

> All countries need to spread technological knowledge in order to maintain and improve their productivity. This then requires changes in education and work which can help to create new relations between specialists and non-specialists. However, in a society characterised by systematic inequalities there are also counter-pressures to restrict that knowledge and control the form it takes...

Robins and Webster say, "the discourse of 'computer literacy' embellishes and simultaneously clouds the real issue on the government's agenda: *work* literacy" (1987: p. 125), and summarise the situation thus (p. 184):

> The striking lack of skills in the workforce originates not in the inabilities of the people, but in the fact that modern industry requires little of its operatives, and advanced technologies, in their conception, design and application, are a major cause of this.

Something like the ECDL, which reduces ICT use to a series of steps which can be performed regardless of the context, removes the need to think about one's activity. Reaching for the "approved" tool can be done, semi-automatically, without needing to think about whether it is the best way of doing a job. Or rather, the decision that it *is* "the best" has already been taken, embedded into the technological tools accessible within an activity system. Users are not encouraged to develop the skills needed to cope with software that is not on the "approved" list even if they could access it. This is the social shaping of technology applied not only to the machine but to the social frameworks and educational practices which surround it, locking the technology into the wider infrastructure and storing information in our environment about what is approved and what is not, allowing some forms of thinking to flourish but not others.

What of schools, however? The picture is not quite so gloomy here, but there are still danger signs. For the next few pages I draw primarily on the UK situation: again I encourage use of the website's thinking tasks to help explore your own environment.

When Robins and Webster wrote their critique, a National Curriculum had been discussed in the UK, but not enacted. Now, however, all schools have a statutory requirement to "make judgements on the 'appropriate use' of Information Technology in every context" (McFarlane, 1997: preface). What follows is only a summary discussion of the UK National Curriculum (NC) in ICT. For the full definition of all the programmes of study see *http://www.nc.uk.net*[7].

On the surface the UK NC uses more positive, creative terminology than the ECDL syllabus. As Kennewell says (Kennewell *et al.*, 2003: pp. 21–3):

> Progression in ICT demands that pupils develop greater autonomy and confidence in their selection and use of information sources and tools. They are expected to develop into discerning users of ICT, with increasing awareness of the benefits and limitations of the software they use. They become able to present their ideas in an increasing variety of ways with a developing sense of audience. They use ICT

---

[7] The UK has introduced a new secondary curriculum, to be rolled out from 2008–2011. I return to this in Chapter 12 as it makes interesting points about the connections between schools and the local community. However, as this is not intended to be a critique of the UK situation, but rather the use of it as a representative example of a state education policy, I do not discuss these new developments in detail, here or later on. They will need to be attended to by anyone working in the UK, of course.

based models of growing complexity for increasingly complex lines of enquiry involving progressively greater decision making and personal autonomy. Their ability to evaluate their own work grows, and they become progressively more able to discuss and appreciate social, economic, political, legal, ethical and moral issues...

ICT capability thus involves more than the secure knowledge and understanding of a wide range of ICT skills, techniques, processes and strategies. It also includes the disposition to construct ICT solutions to problems that are appropriate to the context and are based on knowledge of the opportunities and limitations offered by the systems available.

In summary (Kennewell *et al.*, 2003: p. 35):

progression to more advanced courses in ICT requires a more formal, systematic approach to problem solving.

These skills are (p. 177) "not expressed in terms of specific ICT techniques" but "higher order skills" such as planning, decision making, monitoring and evaluating outcomes. All these developments seem positive. Yet in their preface (xiv), Kennewell and his colleagues observe that in 2002, ICT was highlighted by the UK's school inspectorate as "the least well-taught subject in the curriculum".

We have already noted that ICT has not had time to develop intellectually in the same way as subjects like physics, or literature, which have established pedagogical roots and institutionalised teacher training. While many new entrants into the profession will now have some level of ICT skills, and training programmes are available for more established teachers, there can be obstacles in the way of teachers' being able to take up these opportunities, like lack of time or resources. For professionals, admitting to a need for re-training can be a risky experience. Tanner (in Kennewell *et al.*, 2003: p. 183) says:

...for many teachers the introduction of ICT to their teaching represents a threat to their professional standing. Most teachers are already operating successfully according to their own standards and to the norms of their school. To ask them to change their pedagogy to accommodate ICT is to ask them to take a risk.

Also, while average homes would not contain apparatus suitable for a large-scale chemistry experiment, they may well contain ICT resources which are superior to those at school; either technologically more advanced, and/or through lower learner-per-computer ratios. Nor, probably, will pupils be allowed to play on a Playstation or use MSN, Facebook or other social networking tools while at school, yet these are already integrated into the way they relate to ICT at home and with their friends. The home and school environments therefore have ICT integrated into them in different ways. (See also Selwyn, 1998 who makes similar points regarding ICT use in higher education.)

I could say things are little changed from the 1980s, where I and my co-learners discovered home PCs and exchanged the results of this interaction through informal networks. Many would see this as a criticism and considered with reference to the huge amount of resources poured into ICT in the last 25 years, it probably is. But we might also see it as supporting the claim – for which there is considerable justification – that we should *never* rely on the school system to provide a complete educational experience. Despite the efforts of individual teachers, many of whom perform heroics on a daily basis, there will *always* be a role for community-based, informal learning networks in developing a critical awareness of our environment and the resources within it. I will return to this argument in Chapter 12, as one of the key elements in combating information obesity.

Pupil autonomy is "not the dominant characteristic of secondary education" (Tanner, in Kennewell *et al.*, 2003: p. 11), and despite the potential of the Internet to free pupils from the "controlled learning environment provided by schools" (Tanner, in Kennewell *et al.*, 2003), learner behaviour is often quite rigorously controlled by National Curricula and associated assessment regimes. Assessment is a significant means by which values can be embedded into education: assessment strategies usually make very clear statements about what is to be valued (graded highly) and what not. Anyone who has worked as a teacher or lecturer will agree that it is not always easy to persuade learners to do things that they feel will not contribute towards their final mark. While it's unfair to say this is true 100% of the time, *strategic learning* is something every learner does at some time or another – not least because it is a useful step in information filtering. Making it known what sort of knowledge or experience will be rewarded in the final examination is therefore a powerful way of shaping learner behaviour[8]. Yet despite these

---

[8] On the website are links to websites of UK examination boards such as *http://www.ocr.org.uk, http://www.aqa.org.uk, http://www.edexcel.org.uk, http://www.wjec.co.uk*, as well as thinking tasks through which you can explore these schemes of work and think about how they may affect learning conducted in their name.

systemic biases against informally-developed knowledge, community-based networks for the construction and accreditation of knowledge will always have a *complementary* role to play alongside the formal education system. The school/home/community relationship in fact reflects the objective/subjective/intersubjective levels of value formation, and each is therefore a place in which solutions to information obesity can potentially be found.

I want to propose another reason why formal ICT teaching of the kind described and promoted by Kennewell *et al.* is relatively unsuccessful. Unfortunately, though their book is a useful guide for the trainee teacher, it is presented with no sense of criticism nor romance. No theory of ICT is ever mentioned, nor theories of teaching, except some brief references to constructivism and pupil- versus learner-centred teaching (2003: pp. 40–1). For a book directed mainly at specialist teachers of ICT this is a significant gap, though it would matter even if the audience were teachers just wanting to use more ICT in their own subjects. It is also, I'm afraid, not an inspiring book. I doubt that it will enthuse anyone to teach this subject with verve and passion. If such words seem out of place in teaching ICT as opposed to, say, English or Chemistry: surely that's the problem? I doubt there is a single pedagogical suggestion in here that would be replicated in Egan's *Romantic Understanding*. The two works are almost polar opposites in terms of how they define good teaching. I will take up this line of criticism again in Chapter 10.

Another reason computer literacy education is difficult is the ubiquitous nature of the technology itself. Loveless says (in McFarlane, 1997: p. 141):

> The images and expectations of ICT that are held in our society are wide ranging and powerful, both extending and constraining people's experience and teachers need to consider how these are reflected and acknowledged in classroom practice.

This power stems from the increasing penetration of ICT into the everyday lives of "digital natives", embedded into environments at a level that is not fully to the forefront of consciousness. It is harder to reflect on what is familiar to us than what is new and unexpected. There may be ways to stimulate a critical approach, however, and do so within what is demanded by most National Curricula. Inspiration can be found in Jonassen *et al.*'s discussion of the use of TV in education (2003: pp. 125–6). They observe that using TV in education is difficult because:

Children too often watch television to fill time or avoid more cognitively challenging activities. In order for television to foster learning, learners have to have a reason for watching it. They should be seeking answers or confirming hunches, either about themselves or about some problem that is presented on the television program...

But this kind of self reflection and/or problem solving is hard to awaken. Television uses a presentational manner proven to reduce levels of brain activity. We watch TV passively, almost hypnotically: and "leisure television viewing habits appear to be impossible to discard when the content is educational...".

A proposed educational solution, however, then follows:

More effectively, let students produce video rather than watch television. Producing television programming will engage them in active, meaningful learning because they are solving design problems.... television technology is a powerful learning tool when students are critical users and producers, rather than consumers.... Video production requires the application of a variety of research, organisation, visualisation, and interpretation skills...

Video and other media production require problem solving: to do them well requires critical attention to not just the medium's technological aspects but its politics, history and culture. Even the act of editing helps show students how the TV industry can manipulate "reality" and have people, for example, appear to answer questions they were not asked. Elsewhere in Jonassen *et al.* examples emerge of the use of this approach in teaching ICT. One is built around WebQuests, in which the teacher sets an information search task, a kind of "treasure hunt" through the World-Wide Web. (For more, see the website.) Jonassen *et al.* observe that such an activity can be completed mechanically, students seeking the "right answer" without giving thought as to how it was reached: a kind of sat nav approach to web navigation. But if students are asked to *design their own* WebQuest, they really have to think about what is out there to be found, what it means, how it can be reached: in short, what its value is.

Linking the activity of information production with the community stock of information leads us towards the sort of project described in my introduction: high school children researching a community-level issue like obesity. Here, we see information resources and technological interfaces working together to potentially empower a community seeking a solution to a problem. This kind of engagement with information is one constituent of *social capital* and shows a possible way that education with ICT can regenerate the noösphere at the community level, and contribute towards decolonisation. I return to this idea in Chapter 11.

Yet for all that the multiple and interrelated literacies involved with ICT – and the need for links between community, school and the home – are recognised, there remain institutional "holes" into which worthy efforts continually fall. Consider the experience of Garnett whose "Six ICT literacies" (2008) were developed in the 1990s as a direct response to the UK government's "National Grid for Learning" project, a massive investment in getting the Internet into UK schools. Garnett's model is one of the few attempts to explicitly recognise the interdependencies between various literacies. For him, these six literacies encompass:

- Technical literacies – computer literacy (here defined as "simple technical competence with a computer") and ICT literacy (using a computer to access web-based resources and to communicate with others through e-mail).

- Underpinning literacies – information literacy (see below) and system literacy (developing in students an understanding of how the web worked, and thus improving their effective use of bandwidth).

- Composite literacies – e-learning literacy (the ability to identify learning goals as well as find, contribute to and moderate learning discussion groups) and e-government literacy (a direct response to the UK government's initiatives to put official documents online, thus risking an intensified digital divide: this literacy would encourage learners to "understand the structure of government online as it would affect their rights as citizens").

Yet once again, the institutionalised structures of education mitigated against such a broad-brush approach. As Garnett reflects:

> The operational under funding of UK online centres meant that revenue was always a problem. So centres needed to identify revenue streams which usually, but not always, came from Community Learning budgets. This structured learning into existing funding structures for learning. As a consequence newly thought out strategies like the Six ICT Literacies were not supported as they would require separate funding. ICT skills became synonymous with ECDL as there was both funding available and it was also about developing a European standard for ICT employability skills....

Like experienced generals in a new war we use the technological solutions that worked last time… whilst the need for ICT Skills was identified what this meant in practical terms was never thought through. The Treasury-driven underfunding of the revenue dimension of UK Online centres meant that, in the main they turned to existing funding structures to fund learning. So the first new educational institutions of the 21st-century, which were entirely ICT-based, were offered funding if they operated on 20th-century learning models and taught traditional basic skills.

It is necessary now to properly discuss *information literacy*. This has secured considerable official backing in the last few years and may finally prove a means by which education for information management can find for itself an institutional location. Once again I remind readers that this book is intended not as a detailed "how-to" guide but as a summary investigation of developments over time, reflecting on them with reference to the environmental model. There are many books and resources on information literacy (hereafter, IL) that analyse how it can and should be taught. I refer to some in this chapter and others (particularly online resources) on the website. However, the website does, as usual, contain practical "thinking tasks" which will help those of you unfamiliar with the idea of IL appreciate what it is and why it is needed. You can then explore the more detailed resources on your own.

What is IL? At one level it can be defined fairly simply. The American Library Association (1989) say that:

> …to be information literate, a person must be able to recognise when information is needed and have the ability to locate, evaluate and use effectively the needed information.

The next question is *why*. As Bush noted, technology has improved our ability to publish and produce information, but not necessarily to manage, filter, select and organise it. But this is more than just a skill useful in the workplace or laboratory. IL:

> …is described in the Alexandria Proclamation of 2005 as essential for individuals to achieve personal, social, occupational and educational goals. IL skills are necessary for people to be effective lifelong learners and to contribute to knowledge societies. This is why IL was endorsed by UNESCO's Information for All Programme (IFAP) as a basic human right. (Catts and Lau, 2008: p. 9)

Let us not underestimate the significance of this last statement. It says not just that *some* people should become information literate, but that *all* people should – and that as a basic right, their capacity to do so should be protected and guaranteed. Without doing so, they cannot contribute to society, nor adapt to changing environments (the basic point of "lifelong learning"). Catts and Lau (2008: pp. 9–11) go on to say that IL skills are essential contributors to: national development; health and wellbeing; standards in the education sector; work and economic activity; and civic society (these, especially the latter, will be expanded on below). They also say (2008: p. 13):

> The essential difference between ICT skills and IL is illustrated by the distinction that can be made between receiving and transmitting information using ICT and the process of transforming information to create new knowledge (IL) before transmitting the new information.

The information literate person is not just a conduit of information, but is actively using it and enhancing it, for their own benefit. IL, in principle, provides "a framework of knowledge construction that fosters *independent* learning (the foundation of lifelong learning...)" (Andretta, 2007: p. 3, emphasis added).

Declarations such as these define IL as more than just another ICT skill. They give it the status accorded to "simple" literacy in earlier times – an essential foundation of learning. These are bold claims, and not made only by narrowly-defined interest groups. UNESCO – via the Prague Declaration of 2003 (Senn Breivik and Gee, 2006: Appendix E) and Catts and Lau (2008) – directly promote IL, linking it to the egalitarian development of the information society and meeting the UN's Millennium Development Goals. IL therefore claims for itself a significance that requires, in response, critical analysis of its claims. That is the task of the remainder of this chapter.

The Association of College and Research Libraries (ACRL, 2000) proposed the following influential definition of IL. The information literate person is someone who:

- determines the nature and extent of the information needed;
- accesses needed information effectively and efficiently;
- evaluates information and its sources critically and incorporates selected information into their knowledge base and a value system;
- uses information effectively to accomplish a specific purpose;

- understands many of the economic, legal and social issues surrounding the use of information and uses information ethically and legally.

What we have here is IL broken down into a series of steps to be followed by those with information needs. The Cambridgeshire Schools Library Service provide another definition, which shows the stages even more clearly, along with questions that the learner should ask at each stage (McFarlane, 1997: p. 164):

- What do I need to do? (Formulate and analyse need.)
- Where could I go? (Identify and appraise likely sources.)
- How could I get the information? (Trace and locate individual sources.)
- Which resources shall I use? (Examine, select and reject individual resources.)
- How shall I use the resources? (Interrogate resources.)
- What shall I make a record of? (Record and store information.)
- Have I got the information I need? (Interpret, analyse, synthesise and evaluate.)
- How should I present it? (Present and communicate.)
- What have I achieved? (Evaluate.)

These are not the only definitions of IL – Markless and Streatfield (2007) present others such as the "Seven Pillars of Information Literacy" and the "Big Blue Model" – but all tend to describe the process as a series of steps like this. What each amounts to is a *procedure* for conducting an information search in an environment where securing access to (large amounts of) relevant information is taken as a given. Prior to the information-abundant era, as noted, the educational environment acted as a filter, guiding learners to the information needed to solve an educational problem. Now, where more information is in the ambient environment, the onus is moved more to the learner, to determine filters for themselves, rather than expecting a teacher to do it in advance.

Immediately, issues arise with these definitions. Describing IL as a series of steps does not have to imply a strictly linear sequence (McFarlane, 1997: p. 165), but it may well be taken as such. What may then go missing is the idea of *iteration*. A search may not be successful first time. Or, once it has been evaluated, that may suggest better sources were available, established either through judgments of effectiveness, or perhaps through discussion with other learners, sharing experience and pooling search results. From this *communication* may arise new understandings, perhaps even further problems that in turn require information to solve. But such iteration is not easy to embed into learning. First, because of pressures of time. Second, learners, whether adult or child, may become discouraged by unfavourable results, and not see the need to change basic elements of their searching strategy to be successful. (See Chapter 11 on problem-based learning for some discussion of how to overcome these blockages.)

It may be that students do not have the prior knowledge required to critically evaluate an information source. This may be due to the complexity of the subject matter. Even well-educated people may struggle to keep up with technical debates outside their own field, even if they have a lay interest. When faced by any difficult question, even the most information literate learner still needs a *teacher* to guide them through the complexities. This becomes even more true when divisions in a field of knowledge are based not only on scientific differences but are complicated by the overt manipulation of opinion. For instance, faced by a manipulatively racist site (see the thinking task and discussion on the website), will a learner have the intellectual detachment to recognise how the site achieves its aims? Especially if they are young and at least half-inclined to be strategic thanks to *Big Brother* being due on TV and thus limited time to find yet another site on Martin Luther King then condense it into a 500-word paper? These pressures are, in fact, exactly what are exploited by the creators of material such as this: it is ambitious to expect learners to expose them on their own.

Who, then, should facilitate IL? Who is the "learned friend" helping students identify an information need, explaining the complexities of a subject where necessary, and guiding the learner through the search?

IL has been strongly influenced by the idea that it is the province of librarians. Bodies such as the American Library Association and the Association of College and Research Libraries have been prime movers in establishing IL (see Rockman, 2004: pp. 4–6). Patricia Senn Breivik, chair of the ALA's Presidential Committee on IL in 1989, entitled her book with E. Gordon Gee (2006) *Higher Education in the Internet Age*; but the subtitle is clear about which wing of HE is considered most significant: "Libraries Creating a Strategic Edge". Jacobson (in Rockman, 2004: p. 138) says:

> Before the term *information literacy* became current, *library instruction*, or *bibliographic instruction*, was the label given to the instruction that librarians provided.

Librarians clearly have a vital role in information management. They have a head start due to their technical knowledge of information handling, and ethical values long embedded in their profession, such as equality and free access. However, the library is not necessarily the ideal institutional location for IL. Libraries, particularly public ones, are under pressure, faced by declining funding that is itself a reaction to the increased availability of information online. Roszak (1994, Chapter 9) made this point and others have done so since, even while seeking to reassert libraries' importance in the Internet age (e.g. Rockman, 2004; and many others).

Historically, the library has taken a passive role in information management. It serves as an agent between publisher and user, an organiser and preserver of information, and (perhaps as a result of its passivity), occupies a position of integrity and credibility within the educational system (Pradt Lougee, in Hess and Ostrom, 2007: pp. 321–6). But the instrumental returns from libraries are hard to quantify. How would a library's "success" be measured? If on borrowings, or footfall; even if either could be maximised in the Internet age, this might retard the environmental quality of a library (who would frequent one where all the books were out and which was noisy and busy?). If on the quality of work produced by its users: how could the library's direct contribution be measured? It is therefore difficult to connect the value of the library to other instrumental motivations driving education in the present time. Libraries still have advocates, of course, sometimes forceful ones; writers like Senn Breivik and Gee (2006) do a good job of promoting the library's contribution in any case. But the budgetary situation, and the "audit culture", mean that any widespread allocation of teaching responsibilities to libraries is unlikely, either in schools, universities, or (via the public library system) society as a whole. (It should be noted that initiatives such as "Library 2.0" – see Miller, 2006 – are addressing some of these challenges and trying to give the library a more active role in the information age.)

Instrumental rationality's tendency to emphasise quantifiable returns may have other effects on IL education. For education institutions, criteria of success vis-à-vis information management may include measures such as the quantity of information resources available, levels of IL training provided to staff and students, and perhaps external inspection (cf. Senn Breivik and Gee, 2006: p. 14). Individuals may then also have their "IL skills" examined through measures of "competence" (Cameron, in Rockman, 2004), indicators (Catts and Lau, 2008), rubrics and so on. Like all indicators, these may well be a valuable resource for guiding practitioners, but there are both practical and strategic problems with using them. IL could become just another "hoop" to jump through, something else to stick on the e-portfolio, recorded and used as another form of information filter by employers and the like. And if that comes to pass then students will inevitably treat it very strategically. They will, most likely, want to know what the "right answer" is, to ensure that their record of achievement is unblemished. Universities may become judged on the IL scores of their graduates, and gradually, the achievement of high IL detached from the *learning* it is supposed to support. It may become just another strategic indicator, a rote-learned, quantified set of competencies which we can measure, then castigate those who do not have them (courses, or individuals) as "to blame" for not promoting the "right" set of skills.

If this seems an unfair extrapolation of current trends then remember that IL is emerging into an education system that, as noted, is no longer solely built on the presumption that empowered, flexible learners are its primary product. Recall Robins and Webster's criticisms (1987: p. 181) that "the process of technological innovation this century has been one which has brought about a reduction in the performance skills of the bulk of workers". Very little in the "stepwise" definitions of IL suggests something which requires creativity; rather, it has the feeling of a performative or routine response to information overload, a piece of social engineering even.

This is most apparent when IL is touted as the best response to plagiarism, considered a significant threat to the validity of education in the Internet age; particularly amongst university students, though prominent writers and academics have been discredited for using others' work without citation[9], and "even the UN Security Council has begun to use [anti-plagiarism] technology to ensure the originality of commissioned reports" (Senn Breivik and Gee, 2006: p. 149). IL initiatives such as those of California State:

> place a high premium on helping students to learn correctly how to represent the language, thoughts and ideas of others... how properly to cite sources, how to understand and respect copyright laws and intellectual property rights... and how to avoid unethical behaviour (Rockman, quoted in Senn Breivik and Gee, 2006: p. 150).

---

[9] In the week I wrote this chapter, Dr Raj Persaud, long a fixture in the UK media, was branded a plagiarist: see *http://news.bbc.co.uk/1/hi/health/7452877.stm* (last accessed 19 June 2008).

However, might this be another case of a simple solution being proposed to a complex problem? Most students I know are already paranoid about inadvertent plagiarism, and I believe that few incidences of plagiarism are truly pre-meditated. They can also be avoided by better assessment design. On my degree, all assessments involve the students either submitting a draft of work-in-progress, or a project proposal, prior to the principal submission, and/or working on projects that are specific to them, such as writing reflective learning journals, assessing practice in their own school or workplace, or creating websites or other software designed to solve specific educational problems. Plagiarism is not impossible in such circumstances, but it is a lot more difficult than when students are given a question such as "Assess whether Britain's policy of appeasement contributed to Hitler's invasion of Czechoslovakia", an essay which has probably been written thousands of times before, and in any case could easily be written by a third party.

McFarlane (1997: pp. 115–6) also points out that the rise in plagiarism may be a result of the increasing separation between teachers and learners, whether in large universities or elsewhere. Someone who sees a student only as one face amongst hundreds of others is likely to be unfamiliar with their writing style, level of English, and subject knowledge. When marking their papers, how does the teacher know whether it is typical of that student? However, through deeper involvement with the student *as a learner*, communicating with them on a regular basis, coming to know their personality, style and competence, and seeing many pieces of work instead of just one; plagiarism will not only leap out of a page if it happens, but may be less likely in the first place, thanks to greater personal respect and understanding.

Nothing in these last two paragraphs is the direct result of IL, but that is the point. Plagiarism occurs because of a complex set of organisational and institutional factors connected to the increasing commercialisation of education, bad practice by educators, their employers and students, and information obesity. Not only lecturers and students, but parents, the wider educational community and the consumers of the end-products of education (employers) need to look more closely at *why* plagiarism happens[10]. It is this kind of critical debate, about the wider impact of ICT on how we make knowledge, which is needed to combat information obesity: but which for reasons that I am concerned with throughout this book, happens so rarely.

---

[10] In early Key Stages of the UK National Curriculum, copying-and-pasting off the Internet is actively encouraged in younger learners (see Parkinson, in Kennewell *et al.*, 2003: p. 159).

That critique of plagiarism policy distracted me from the main strand of my argument, which was the role of libraries in IL instruction. There is another way in which the emphasis on libraries in IL is significant, and I want to spend a few pages dealing with it.

The basic point is that librarians are not subject specialists, but information retrieval specialists. Because of the values embedded into their profession, they cannot help with the creation of *new* knowledge. That is what teachers do. One needs a base of existing knowledge in order to synthesise and create new knowledge from found information. But as Egan says (1990: p. 237):

> Knowing where to find knowledge and "learning how to learn" have their clear educational values, but they become enemies of education if they are used as justifications for reducing the amounts of knowledge that students should memorize; the mind and imagination can do nothing with the library of knowledge one knows how to access when "needed".

His emphasis on memorisation may seem old-fashioned now, even unpopular, but goes some way to suggesting why examinations remain prevalent[11]. Kohr writes (1993: pp. 94–5) that if intervals between examinations are long, requiring students to keep knowledge in their head for a year or perhaps even longer:

> ...you have to retain the totality of the subject for so long that it usually stays put for life.

However when intervals between examinations (or other assessments) are short:

> Examinations are so frequent, every three to four weeks, that an increasing number of students treat knowledge like hot coal, to be dropped, lest severe damage be done, as soon as the examination is over.

It is when things are *retained* in the mind that new information has a better chance of being evaluated properly. The prior knowledge one

---

[11] There are other benefits to examinations. It is the one form of assessment where the marker can be almost completely sure that they are reading the students' own, original work. This alone will probably ensure a continued role for examinations in 21st century education despite the stress they cause.

needs to use to construct new knowledge from information retrieved must, by definition, already be there. This is what allows the knower to better criticise the found information. But if all that matters is "retrieval", this may promote the assumption that knowledge does not need to be in the head any more, as it can all be found "out there". This alone should give pause for thought for anyone who thinks IL is the solution to all information obesity problems. Good food nourishes the body – bad food just passes through and does very little on the way. Focusing only on information retrieval not only does not combat information obesity, it may even be a fundamental cause of it. Information is *not* knowledge: it is the sum total of the "symbolic codes" in which we store knowledge, but without it being *worked* on by individual minds (with or without the help of others) – and this process takes time and effort – it will not become knowledge in those minds.

Egan links these ideas with the notion that IL is the quintessential "transferable skill" for the information society (1990: p. 46):

> One of the stranger, and I think educationally destructive, currents in educational discourse during the later 20th century has been the suggestion that one can achieve some of the finest fruits of learning without actually having to do the learning. This is often connected with the claim that knowledge is doubling every *x* number of years and so it is pointless to try to teach a great deal of particular knowledge.... These observations then commonly lead to the conclusion that we should rather focus on teaching generic thinking skills. Thus instead of students tediously learning a great deal of factual material, they can instead acquire the skills that will enable them to recognise problems and know where to go to find whatever particular knowledge they need to solve them.

The idea that all one needs to do to learn about something is to retrieve information that has already been created by others is actually no more than the old behaviourist approach to education reconstructed for the Internet age. Students are again being treated as "empty vessels", minds ready to be filled with the expert's pronouncements, only now, the role of expert is delegated largely to the authors of web-based material. Even if students are expected to select from a menu of expert pronouncements – or rather, identify what is "expert" by picking through a heap of other stuff, much of which will be trash – their own responsibility and capacity for constructing knowledge is diminished.

I may seem to have been rather critical of IL. Let me say then that I consider IL to be a very important element of practical strategies to combat information obesity. The guidelines that the principal authors provide (and if the preceding chapter has not served to indicate who these are, see the annotated reading list) form the basis of the teaching strategies developed in Part 4 of this book.

I have also taken a rather limited view of the topic, which again I must blame mainly on a lack of space. Some authors, particularly Christine Bruce (1997; see also Bruce and Edwards, 2007), have developed a more rounded view, recognising *degrees* of IL running from a purely technical approach (with learners expected to mechanically work through the various steps without conscious reflection on why), through recognising its role in individual knowledge-building, up to a wisdom-based conception of IL, in which the learner is being information literate if they are *applying learning to help solve environmental problems in the community* (Bruce and Edwards, 2007: p. 51). This fits perfectly with the environmental model of information, and will therefore be returned to in Part 4.

But that model also requires us to see the whole environment as an information storage medium. Our absorption of information does not always happen consciously, as the result of an active learning process. Our reactions to information – even our need for it in the first place – are not always placed to the forefront of our consciousness. Possibilities for the use of information are as much embedded into the technologies and organisations that structure our lives as they are into formal learning situations. It is here where I believe most IL theory and practice is currently lacking. I want to show that people are *not* mentally and cognitively free to define their own information needs, and will not necessarily see the tensions between what they need in order to make meaning in a given environmental situation, and what the constraints are on their doing so. These points need further elaboration, and that is the task of Part 3 of this book.

In summary, this chapter has tried to show how social shaping can apply to the sociotechnical frameworks and activity systems that support a technology, as well as just to the "machine" part of the technology. The values which control the development of that technology set conditions in which certain ways of thinking (both thinking *about* the technology, and thinking *with the help of* the technology) are more suited than others. Alternative modes of organising the creation of knowledge may arise at certain times and in certain places; the "Dartmouth" model is one at the level of a university, and my experiences with the Spectrum may have constituted one at the level of a school and community. But such approaches are now discouraged, through monitoring and evaluation processes which accredit through more instrumental criteria such as financial returns and exam results, and disregard the *inter*subjective value the alternative methods may have had for the learners.

The tendency in ICT and information education at the present time is to emphasise the economic and instrumental value of ICT to organisations and society, and use subjective value as the basis of the strategies learners are expected to develop as they are turned, by the educational system, into resources for these organisations and society. I suggest that in combination, these tendencies are very dangerous for our future creativity, and therefore, the health of our communities and their informational environments. The value of both *objective* and *intersubjective* knowledge in this area are frequently overlooked. Little attention is paid to knowledge, even when developed through sound principles of scientific method, that has over the years warned of the educational dangers of such an approach; and the value of informal, community-based, intersubjective understandings of ICT is almost completely discounted by most educational policy, despite the rhetoric of governments.

I can only repeat warnings made by others, to which I have frequently referred throughout Part 2. ICT absorbs enormous amounts of the education sector's financial resources, used not just as a teaching tool but for administration, strategy-setting and marketing as well (Senn Breivik and Gee, 2006). Education risks becoming obese on this technology just as the military sector has become, consuming resources to little effect. This is quite in opposition to the idea that ICT should allow its users to do more with less: to become more prpoductive, in other words. At the same time, ICT remains something that can liberate at the individual level, free a mind from a fixation on current possibilities and allow creative solutions to be developed. Is this a paradox? Or an indication that we have an educational system in which the creative development of the individual mind is no longer a priority? What can we do about it if the latter turns out to be true?

This contradiction has lain beneath the argument of this chapter. Yet both sides of the fence are agreed on one thing: ICT education is often poor, whether from the instrumental point of view, concerned with the effective use of large investments, or from the more individualist and community-based view which believes it the role of the education system to develop critical, self-empowering and active citizens. The fact that these warnings have been repeatedly made, to little effect, must now itself become the subject of critical enquiry, and is what I will now go on to investigate.

Part 3:
Critical theory

Critical social science

If we want to sustain – and perhaps even survive – the technological project then we must confront, rather than repress... its dark side. (Robins and Webster, 1987: p. 252)

When studying education, we are engaged in *social science*, regardless of whether the educational problem faced is, say, in engineering or chemistry[1]. Therefore, appreciating the foundations of social science is vital. It helps us better understand the term "critical" which has occurred throughout this book – critical TV viewing, critically evaluating information in an IL framework, etc – but is not always fully explained. Can a consistent definition be found? Can that break the tension between ways of thinking that are overly objective, overly subjective, or purely economic, each of which, in different ways, degrade the long-term quality of informational resources?

Much of this chapter[2] is based on Fay (1975) and work by Habermas. Both describe how instrumental rationality devalues intersubjectivity and the communities based around it. Each helps show how the quality of our informational resources is – or rather, in the modern age, is not – sustained through education and participation.

Let us start with the idea of *the Enlightenment*. This is a summary term for the transition from the mediaeval era into the modern, scientific age, driven both by great thinkers like Da Vinci, Descartes and Galileo,

---

[1] Carr (2007) objects to calling education a "modern social science", preferring to term it a *practical science*, along lines suggested long ago by Aristotle. For him, social science is instrumental and prescriptive, neglecting the experience of practitioners. In some ways I agree but as I will be developing my own critique of social science here, this distinction, while useful, is not a challenge to the argument of this chapter.

[2] Some of which has already appeared in Whitworth (2007a).

and by the democratic revolutions which first occurred in 18th century France and the USA. Broadly, the Enlightenment:

> ...championed reason as the source of progress in knowledge and society.... Reason was deemed competent to discover adequate theoretical and practical norms upon which systems of thought and action could be built and society could be restructured (Best and Kellner, 1991: p. 2).

These "theoretical and practical norms" were contrasted with older bases for society such as religion, myth, absolute monarchy and so on[3]. They form the basis of objective systems of value, defending reason and truth in the face of distortions like tyranny and counterknowledge.

Enlightenment principles were not only applied to the study of "nature" (astronomy, chemistry etc.), but society. Tyranny was no longer accepted as a rational means of control, but chaos, its polar opposite – a war of "all against all", in Hobbes' words – was equally feared. August Comte was among the first to apply Enlightenment methods, already used in mathematics and the sciences, to the task of establishing laws explaining the relationship between different parts of society (Burrell and Morgan, 1979: p. 42). Thus was formed the discipline of sociology.

Comte followed the decrees of *positivism*, characterised by:

- objectivity through the application of scientific method;
- the privileging of these forms of value over others such as subjectivity, philosophical speculation, bargaining and so on;
- a will to control.

The last indicates that laws of social interaction (or anything else) were not sought for their own sake but in order that understanding environmental processes could lead to mastery over that environment. Events could be predicted, and controlling strategies employed if desired. Taylorism/ Fordism is a classic example of positivism, as are some forms of ICT education. More detail could be given, but largely, I've already covered the necessary ground: see Fay (1975) and Burrell and Morgan (1979).

---

[3] Of course, history is more complicated than that. The Enlightenment was at least partly provoked by Europeans, particularly in Italy, absorbing science and philosophy from Arab and Hindu scholars. The Arabs, in turn, built on the work of ancient Greeks: while further east, the Hindu, Chinese and Japanese civilisations are all of long standing and sophistication. The "Enlightenment", as such, is thus mainly a European phenomenon.

Problems with positivism's rigorous application have already been discussed – such as its reducing workers to components in a machine, or devaluing subjective motivations like love and aesthetics. Fay wants, additionally, to show that positivism is contradictory even just as theory. Positivism promotes methods of organising society that Fay terms *policy science*. These involve engineering organisations, communities and social relationships to reach certain ends or prevent certain occurrences. For example, to tackle crime, policy science develops formal laws (and procedures to be followed when amending or applying them), creates organisations such as the police, judiciary and prisons, and attempts social engineering through schools or the media. None are specifically undesirable, but they do neglect the individual causes of lawbreaking, hence, can sometimes be applied indiscriminately. Also, the *need* for a given law will often go unquestioned: it is its successful *application* with which policy science is concerned.

According to Fay, what this means in practice is individuals are treated only as the passive recipient of policies designed and implemented by "experts". Taken to its extreme, this destroys the principle of intersubjective value, and as a result is deeply undemocratic. Policy science may be concerned with determining the "best" means to reach a given end (such as rises in GDP, better exam results, or whatever is considered valuable), but these ends – and the criteria on which the "best" means is to be judged – are not themselves open to negotiation. The subjects of policy science decisions are not meant to agree to these policies, just to submit to them, as their usefulness has already been decided upon. Ultimately, then, policy science is:

> ...an attempt to eliminate politics as we know it, overcoming its limitations and uncertainties by replacing it with a form of social engineering analogous to the applied physical sciences... objective answers established through the rational use of evidence and technique will replace opinion and rhetoric and persuasion, and social life will be thereby redeemed from the uninformed guesses and purely subjective life-preferences of politicians and thus transformed into a rational enterprise (Fay, 1975: pp. 27–8).

A society based on such principles would not be an inclusive society (Fay, 1975: p. 26):

> ...it would simply not be possible for non-scientists to determine the worth of the policy scientist's decision, just as it is inconceivable

that non-engineers could participate in decisions as to how best to construct a bridge or programme the directional rockets on a spaceship.

Is this unfair? Perhaps. With engineering and other problems where safety was an issue, many would think it justified that scientists were left to get on with it. This is the basis of Thompson's polemic against counterknowledge, one that he casts firmly as a defence of Enlightenment values. Also, the existence of democratic checks and balances which counter this ideal – themselves Enlightenment principles – must also be noted. Nevertheless there are observable tendencies towards this kind of exclusion in many of our democratic societies in the present day (some of which are discussed in Chapter 8). You can use the thinking tasks on the website to develop your own ideas here.

Where the contradiction lies is in embedding policy scientific ideals into our governing institutions, and these institutions' desire for information literate citizens. If problems are identified by individuals and/or communities which give rise to an information need; if these individual or community actors then find, evaluate and filter the needed information; where, in a society governed by exclusionary policy science, could they then *apply and use* that information? Or will they, at best, be acting as information-gathering agents for policy scientists who will subsequently take control?

Carr and Kemmis (1986: Chapter 2) discuss positivism's effects with more specific reference to education. They observe that positivism was originally intended to liberate our minds from the shackles of dogmatism and myth (Carr and Kemmis, 1986: p. 61). But, like Fay, they observe that instead, the ability to *use* the insights of positivism is not granted to all. The knowledge-building task that is educational research is not encouraged in teachers (let alone learners, who are just as subject to its effects). Instead, a policy scientific education leaves teachers in a role of "passive conformity" (p. 70):

...expected to adapt and implement educational decisions made on the basis of scientific knowledge... [but] not themselves participate in the decision making process...

The trouble is that, as Carr and Kemmis explain in detail (1986: Chapter 4; see also Carr, 2007), education is an innately practical activity. What teachers and students face when entering a learning environment is not wholly predictable in advance. Conversational exchanges will take place in this space that, like all communication, will be full of ambiguities, failures of understanding, and consequently, constant description and redescription of positions (Laurillard, 2002). All teachers must possess some kind of theory of education, even if they are not consciously aware of it[4]: a theory here meaning, at least, "some knowledge of the situation [learning environment] in which they are operating and some idea of what it is that needs to be done [reaching the goals of the lesson in that environment]" (Carr and Kemmis, 1986: p. 113). But the idea that these theories can *successfully and fully* be developed in a policy scientific environment which is *different* from the classroom in question – e.g., a government department, the educational research establishment, or the developers of a piece of educational software – is, for Carr and Kemmis, highly dubious (p. 115). It is not that these educational stakeholders have nothing to say, but nor is anyone claiming that positivism is value-less. Rather, their theories, values, ways of thinking and – most importantly – the technologies and organisations into which they are embedded become *resources* for teachers. In order to be effective, teachers should ideally be constantly selecting these resources, based on the self recognition of their needs and discussion with colleagues; analysis of the resources (theories, technologies, etc.) available; and the effective use of these resources once selected. In short, they should be information literate.

But positivism accords little or no status to subjectivity. The policy scientific approach to the educational problems caused by ICT is to recognise and analyse "skills deficits" and their negative economic effects, to design new programmes of training, buy equipment to deliver it, pass new laws[5] and measure success according to "checklists" of achievement, exam results and other quantitative criteria. IL was originally intended to surpass this limited approach, but as we saw, there are signs that it too may be reduced to a set of "rubrics" or "skills" that a qualification (like the ECDL) might indicate one possesses, but which gives little idea about how to use these skills in new and unexpected situations, and thus to creatively work with the information one gathers, filters and evaluates. Positivism would turn us all into information processing machines, working on the assembly lines of the information society, uncreative, mechanical, following procedures designed by others and not expected to question what we know. If this sounds unfair, remember Wenger's

---

[4] That anything can be held in the mind beneath conscious awareness is very significant but we will leave it to one side for now: it will be returned to in Chapter 9.

[5] In the UK, thanks to the National Curriculum, it is a legal requirement for schools to teach ICT.

insurance claims processors, or workers in call centres who can respond to customer enquiries only by reading from a script. This is why the rise of the service society does not promote community, or a more fulfilling and caring society. Instead it reduces these human-human and community relationships to things that can be engineered, made more efficient, *dehumanised* and technical. One *can* mechanise "a relation between persons" (Bell, 1976: p. 155, in Robins and Webster, 1989: p. 19). A mechanical response to information abundance, reaching for the IL "script", is no more likely to lead to empowerment and the building of knowledge than is any other semi-automatic response.

If positivist social science can provide only limited insights into what goes on in educational situations, and in society more widely, what else is there? The next step in the evolution of social science is *interpretivism*. This has as long a history as positivism, but was subordinate to it in the late 19th and early 20th centuries. Following the work of theorists mentioned earlier, like Bakhtin, it experienced a revival.

For interpretivists, reality cannot be defined objectively, through the discovery and application of natural laws. Truth, meaning and reality itself are subjectively created in individual minds as new information interacts with existing subjective perceptions, knowledge and values. There is not one truth to discover but a multitude; no "one best" solution to a problem. Political and social interactions do not have one convergent end point, but divergent ones (Arendt, 1958). The "value-free" nature of positivism and scientific method "cannot tell us what goals we ought to pursue, what direction policy ought to take, what values ought to be promoted" (Fay, 1975: p. 23); these can only be developed by people, drawing on their subjective responses to the world, and communicating and reaching agreement about the values driving their lives. (See the website where thinking tasks help illuminate these ideas through practical examples.)

Interpretivism helps improve our understanding of *postmodernism* – mentioned in Chapter 5. Lyotard, in *The Postmodern Condition* (1984), criticises the Enlightenment project as a "metanarrative", meaning a grand plan for the evolution of society. Despite claims that it is "value free", Lyotard points out (1984: p. 28) how the impartiality of science has been corrupted; manipulated by authorities in charge of the organisations, laws and so on which apply policy scientific judgments and secure public consent to them to prop up the existing order. What is claimed to be an *objective* basis for policy science is in fact intersubjective and exclusionary. Limits are placed on what counts as "valid" or "valuable" knowledge, or activity, in fields such as politics, education, technology, even art and architecture. Subjectivity is devalued completely, but so is intersubjectivity, as people or communities whose values do not match those of the powerful (minorities, say, or those living in the path of an airport runway) are denied a voice. There is restricted access to decision-making spaces, and even to information on which decisions are based, information that may prove useful to these communities in working out their *own* solutions to problems.

This access is more and more controlled by technology:

> In the computer age, the question of knowledge is now more than ever a question of government (Lyotard, 1984: p. 9)

...although Lyotard recognises, as do many other writers on ICT, that this could work both ways (Lyotard, 1984: p. 67):

> ...the computerisation of society... could become the "dream" instrument for controlling and regulating the market system, extended to include knowledge itself and governed exclusively by the performativity principle [that is, instrumental rationality].... But it could also aid groups... by supplying them with the information they usually lack for making knowledgeable decisions.

Postmodernism plays itself out in a variety of fields, but generally stresses individual participation and activity, in order to decisively break with Enlightenment thought and institutions. Ephemerality and dynamism are valued over permanence and stability, as these challenge embedded values, bringing to the surface assumptions which underlie the status quo. (See also Chapter 9 and Chapter 12.)

What, though, is postmodern knowledge? Lyotard observes that the natural sciences now suggest that predictable, stable systems are actually the exception. Most of reality is chaotic, turbulent and unpredictable (1984: pp. 53–60; also Gleick, 1988). Patterns can still be sought, and theories invented to explain them, but the role of science is equally to establish what is *in*determinable, what is *un*knowable; to assess risks arising through the interaction of variables, to understand trends and tendencies, not certainties. In the social sphere, interpretivism suggests that situations are best researched by interpreting individual actions and beliefs, and their manifestations such as texts (speeches, diaries), collective action and cultural phenomena (e.g. social movements, fashion). Positivism uses these too of course, but instead of scientific analysis, the interpretivist research method is akin to *learning* about the subjects' context or environment. An:

> ...interpretivist social science thereby increases the possibility of communication between those who come into contact with the accounts of such a science and those whom it studies (Fay, 1975: p. 96)

Communication takes on the role filled by control and efficiency in a positivist social science. The interpretive, or postmodern, scientist is not setting laws or discovering truth, but "telling stories" (Lyotard, 1984: p. 60), writing an ongoing, ever-changing understanding of the dynamic world around us, providing guidance for actors – intellectual resources, in other words – but not prescribing their action, nor placing limits on how these resources can be used.

Interpretivism combats the notion of prescriptive "educational science", criticised above via Carr and Kemmis. In a complex but significant passage (1986: p. 115), these authors argue that any "theory" of education must, by definition, be interpreted by teachers and other practitioners before it can be applied in an educational situation. The adequacy of these practices cannot be determined in advance, but only after the story of the application has resolved itself. The key to good teaching is not to move from theory to practice as such, but from "ignorance and habit to knowledge and reflection" (p. 116), and the role of professional development in education is not to "train" teachers in specific ways of thinking but to provide them with:

> ...the skills and resources that will enable them to reflect upon and examine critically the inadequacies of different conceptions of educational practice.

Hence what was said above, regarding the need for teachers to select from a range of educational resources available to them.

In this quote, however, appears again that word "critically". What does it mean? Let us now discuss this. There are problems that exist with interpretivism, some of which have already been raised. Interpretivism can easily become relativism: "if it's true for you it's true". Writers like Thompson would almost certainly not accept the use of the word "science" to describe interpretivist or postmodernist approaches (as Lyotard uses it), precisely because of the denial of the objective value of scientific method.

This is not just an ideological position; relativism can lead us into dangerous territory. Look again at the ACRL's definition of the information literate person as given in Chapter 5. There is no attention paid to the *nature* of the information need that stimulates the search. For example, the would-be poisoner seeking information on ricin manufacture might secure approval if they did so "efficiently" and then "incorporated the information into a value system", one that would in all likelihood devalue human life. Interpretivism can fail to examine "the conditions which give rise to the actions, rules and beliefs which it [*or the information literate person*] seeks to explicate" (Fay, 1975: p. 83).

The ACRL try to embed a safeguard into the definition. If all selection criteria are equally valid, how can it be guaranteed that relevant information will be "used [or selected]... ethically and legally", in accordance with their final bullet point? Self contradiction would arise. But even here there are complications. Values, morals and laws are noöspheric creations, therefore dynamic and subject to change – sometimes rapidly. The ability to define what is "ethical" and "legal" is a matter of power. Certain forms of communication and participation can be ignored or even criminalised; others used in undesirable ways. In the UK, for example, "anti-terror" laws have been used against peace campaigners, such as when elderly activist Walter Wolfgang was expelled from the Labour Party conference in 2005.

The ACRL's definition of IL (and similar definitions) are based on an interpretivist view of social science – that it is up to the *individual* to identify their needs and undertake the search. It does try to avoid reducing learners to information-processing machines, who react to stimuli but cannot identify needs for themselves. But here is where interpretivism gets into trouble. By focusing on the intentions and beliefs of individuals, it cannot explain unintended causes of actions (Fay, 1975: p. 85). Nor can it help us understand *structural conflict and tensions* within a society, organisation or activity system; particularly where actors in these systems are "blind" to the reasons why they believe or feel what they do, and what the primary tensions are. This is a very important point:

> An interpretive social science promises to reveal to the social actors what they and others are doing, thereby restoring communication by correcting the ideas that they have about each other and themselves. But this makes it sound as if all conflict... is generated by mistaken ideas about social reality rather than by the tensions and incompatibilities inherent in that reality itself... the intepretive model would lead people to seek to *change the way the think about what they or others are doing*, rather than provide them with a theory by

means of which they could *change what they or others are doing,* and in this way it supports the status quo (Fay, 1975: pp. 90–1).

In order to meet this requirement, Fay (p. 94) offers the idea of a *critical social science.* This retains certain elements of interpretivism, but also:

> ...recognises that a great many of the actions people perform are caused by social conditions over which they have no control.... [It] seeks to uncover those systems of social relationships which determine the actions of individuals and the unanticipated, though not accidental, consequences of these actions.

And this is not just something that describes states of affairs, but must include "an account of how these theories are translatable into action" (p. 95). People working in organisations and activity systems *learn* about the contradictions and tensions which affect their work: and then *actively participate* in adapting the systems about which they are learning (p. 102), as opposed to simply producing information as a result of their learning and then passing this to a policy scientist, manager or teacher who then prescribes the next phase of creative activity (p. 103). It is not that these "managerial" roles are irrelevant, but "there must exist a constant critical interchange between the policy expert and the actors who will be affected by... decisions" (p. 106). The relationship becomes two-way. The "expert" should understand the felt needs and values of the "actors" – the actors in turn accept the expertise of the expert, but not uncritically: the expert's decisions are opened up to public scrutiny and accountability (p. 107). (See also the next two chapters.)

This is an *evolutionary* process, constantly engaged in developing, checking and if necessary revising the values which drive activity systems, whether these be schools, universities, workplaces, community groups or a society as a whole. Critical theory "is not a static doctrine, a fully completed set of laws" (p. 109) – thus, not a "metanarrative" in Lyotard's terms. Rather, it is "corrected and reformulated as it continually confronts" (p. 109) the individuals and communities it seeks to empower. Indeed, such people would – and must – have the power to reject or modify any prescriptions made in the light of such a theory.

Ultimately, the aim of a truly *critical* IL education would be the reversal of general trends towards the exclusion of most people from participation in the debates, decisions, activities and processes of knowledge formation affecting their lives. The goal of critical learning must be to see the:

...results of evolutionarily relevant learning processes find their way into the cultural tradition, the world views, and interpretive systems of society; in the form of empirical knowledge and moral-practical insights, they comprise a kind of cognitive potential that can be drawn upon (McCarthy, 1984: pp. 254–5).

What counts as "evolutionarily relevant" is, of course, a political question. The competition for resources such as information, attention, and knowledge does not take place on a level playing field. Not all ideas have the same "cognitive potential". Let us therefore consider how these theoretical ideals may be translated into practice – particularly in an era where more and more of our learning is mediated through ICT. This is the next step towards establishing what a critical educational approach to information might involve.

Readers might be wondering why these ideas differ from values supposedly present in the principles of democracy, but which in practice are difficult to enact or justify in real situations. Is critical theory just a Utopian declaration? What *actually* can, and should, we do to make these ideals a reality? And what have they got to do with information obesity and ICT?

To help answer these questions, I will use the work of the German social theorist, Jürgen Habermas. His work, particularly his magnum opus, *The Theory of Communicative Action* (1984/1987), is one of the fullest developments of critical social science. The rest of this chapter introduces his work with reference to ideas of objective, subjective and intersubjective value. Chapter 8 and Chapter 9 then link Habermas to the environmental model of information, and show how, in practice, the forms of education which might encourage a critical view stand in opposition to the way education – and its use of technology – are typically organised.

The processes by which Enlightenment principles, intended to release humanity from tyranny and dogmatism, can themselves become tyrannical, were first thoroughly considered in the 1920s and 1930s by a group known as the "Frankfurt School". Faced with fascism on one side of Europe and Stalinism on the other, the Marxist position – that the ills of society were rooted in the ownership of property (an over-simplification, but near enough) – was no longer considered sufficient to explain the state of Europe. Instead, Horkheimer and Adorno, in their epic *Dialectic of Enlightenment* (1972), suggested that instrumental rationality – the technical, convergent approach to finding solutions – ultimately led to totalitarianism. Nazism and Stalinism were deeply irrational and mythological, but ruthlessly deployed technology and instrumental reason to perpetuate themselves. Later, in *One-Dimensional Man*, Marcuse (1964) adapted these arguments for the post-World War II consumer age, suggesting the consumerist society was "totalitarian" in the true meaning of that word. It reaches into every part of our lives, leaving no space for dissent. Should discontent arise, it can be placated with consumer products that we are educated to believe are vital and necessary: "social control is anchored in the new needs it has produced" (Marcuse, 1964: p. 9).

However, although the Frankfurt School's ideas are powerful explanations for the ills of society, they struggle to suggest ways to *change* it. The problem is that they view the modern age as being rooted in rationality, and all rationality as being instrumental. But that means they can only find alternatives in irrational forces such as art, love and anger (McCarthy's introduction to Habermas, 1984: p. xix). As we have seen, these forces can strongly motivate action and the creation of value, but because they are almost impossible to define as *rational*, they are easy to exclude from the organised processes which drive modernisation. There is thus no effective place from which to launch the *work for change* required by a critical social science. (Note that this problem also affects some accounts of the impact of ICT and technology: particularly Robins and Webster's 1987 work, which cites the *Dialectic of Enlightenment* on page 252. These authors raise awareness of the problems very well, but like the Frankfurt School, find it almost impossible to say what should be done about them.)

Instead, Habermas sought an *alternative form of rationality* – one that is not instrumental, but which also transcends subjectivity; one which can be used to validate information, communication and activity in ways other than just considering its "efficiency", economic value or usefulness to vested interests. The first volume of *The Theory of Communicative Action* proposed that rationality could also be found at the intersubjective level – what Habermas called *communicative rationality*. Communicative rationality is present in the very form and structure of language and communication. When we speak, write or otherwise communicate, we make claims as to the validity of what we are saying. If language was never rooted in such claims we would simply not be able to use it in a productive way. If we are trying to have a rational discussion with someone we assume that what they are saying is true, that it represents what they believe, and that they are using language and information in the way we expect. We also assume that our communicative partner(s) will allow us to respond in due course; that the conversation is therefore *open*, and everyone potentially affected by the outcome of the discussion can have a chance to contribute (speak *and* be heard) on an equal basis. Finally, communicative rationality assumes that the ultimate aim of the conversation is to reach an agreement or *consensus* (Habermas, 1984: p. 11). This objective, says Habermas, is the foundation of the structures and channels through which we communicate. Communicative action, therefore, can be contrasted with instrumental action, where the end goal is "success"; instead, its end goal is consensus.

None of this is necessarily self evident, nor has passed without criticism. Lyotard, for one, has dismissed the notion that "consensus" can drive activity. He says that the suggestion we can always eventually agree can be manipulated by those in power to maintain their own position (Lyotard, 1984: p. 60). But Habermas defends himself by saying that he is describing an *ideal*. We can approach, but never reach, the state of consensus. But ideals still serve as means to criticise reality's failure to live up to them (Geras, 1999). There are many limitations on actual decision making and other communicative exchanges such as pressure of time and imperfect information. Limitations can also be the result of power relations. Many distortions of communication:

> ...are not inevitable, they are artificial, and thus the illusions they promote can be overcome. Such distortions are, for example, the deceptive legitimation of great inequalities of income and wealth, the consumer ideologies inherited and generated from the organisation of capitalist productive relations, the manipulation of public ignorance in the defense of professional power, and the oppressive racial, ethnic and sexual typecasting to which vast segments of the population are subjected daily (Forester, 1985: p. 205).

Forester goes on to say (Forester, 1985):

> Habermas assesses the problems of distorted communications not only at an interpersonal level but also at the level of social and political-economic structure. In this way, he begins to fulfil the critical tasks of revealing how the citizens of advanced capitalist societies may remain not only ignorant of their own democratic political traditions, but also oblivious to their own possibilities for corrective action – as they are harangued, pacified, misled and ultimately persuaded that inequality, poverty and ill health are

either problems for which the victim is responsible or problems so "political" and "complex" that they can have nothing to say about them. Habermas argues that democratic politics or planning requires the consent that grows from processes of collective criticism, not from silence or a party line.

Compare this to the points made in the introduction regarding obesity, and how its solutions might lie in activity (not just discussion) at the *community* level. In large part, it is Habermas's intention to show how communication can be pulled away from the intersubjective level of knowledge making, and how the quality and value of informational resources, and environments as a whole, are degraded as a result. Communicative rationality gives Habermas both a *location* and the *necessary conditions* for resisting the dehumanising effects of modernisation (Calhoun, 1992: p. 1). Dehumanisation retards the ability and rights of communities and individuals to participate in decisions that affect their lives, with information (and access to it) being systematically manipulated and distorted in order to effect this. But there are practical activities which can reverse this distortion, based around: free and open communication; reaching consensus; learning through collective criticism; participation; activity; and self-guided research. To better explain what is meant here, we need to open another chapter.

The colonisation of the lifeworld

We're not trying to withhold information from you, but some information remains classified for security reasons. (Brigadier General Janis Karpinski, head of "coalition detention centres" in Iraq, 16 September 2003.)

Habermas argues that modern problems stem from the way the Enlightenment developed systems of control and regimentation, which spread throughout society. However, there are qualifications to make here. First, Habermas is not against the application of instrumental rationality as such. He recognises that it is a necessary part of activity. Communication and information alone cannot *act* in the world to bring about change. Therefore, Habermas is not suggesting that the Enlightenment project has reached a dead end, and should be somehow rejected. Rather, communicative rationality is intended to *revitalise* the Enlightenment project, rescuing it from its instrumental shackles and spreading its benefits to the maximum number of people in society. Reason is to be reformed, not abandoned.

This chapter explores why Habermas believes reason is in need of such reform. His starting point is the idea of the *lifeworld*, which is connected to the concept of the noösphere, but crucially, is not the same. I will explain what Habermas means by the idea of the lifeworld's *colonisation*, and how this causes some problems faced by learners, including information obesity. Finally, I will show how Habermas provides not just grounds to criticise the existing state of affairs, but, as noted, identifies practical activities and necessary conditions for people to develop responses to colonisation that are not based in counterknowledge, irrational expressions of anger or other emotions, but are firmly linked to rationality, information and communication.

It was by developing the ideas of *lifeworld* and *system* that Habermas broke through the dead ends of other Frankfurt School theories, which saw no place from where "rational" action could be other than instrumental, and thus controlling. The lifeworld is defined as the "reservoir of implicit knowledge" which supplies actors with "background convictions upon which they draw in the negotiation of common definitions and situations" (see Habermas, 1984: p. xxiv and pp. 335–7). The lifeworld is universal, a background for all human communication. It *has* to be so, because even if we do not share a common tongue with another person, we do at least "speak their language" in terms of having enough in common to *potentially* reach an understanding. We recognise them as people, with interests, and a language in which to express them. These interests, and other relevant concepts, might need explanation. To reach an understanding we may need to *learn* about the environment, personality, culture and other significant factors in the life of the other. Nevertheless this is potentially possible due to the lifeworld's universality (Habermas, 1987: p. 133). And the lifeworld is dynamic, constantly reproduced by communicative action, absorbing the results of learning processes which occur as people constantly interact with the environment, producing new situations, coming to mutual understandings about them, and using these understandings to help us build our individual and community identities:

> Under the functional aspects of *mutual understanding*, communicative action serves to transmit and renew cultural knowledge; under the aspect of *coordinating action*, it serves social integration and the establishment of solidarity; under the aspect of *socialisation*, communicative action serves the formation of personal identities.... The process of reproduction connects up new situations with the existing conditions of the lifeworld (Habermas, 1987: p. 137).

These factors – its being a dynamic stock of background knowledge, constantly reproduced through learning and communication, and thereby acting as a foundation for action – suggest that the lifeworld and noösphere ideas are closely related. And so they are, but with one crucial distinction. The noösphere stores information in our environment, but storage can occur through processes disconnected from reaching understanding. Rather, both informational and physical environments can be altered by instrumental rationality, which emphasises not activity *within* a given environmental context, but action that is, to at least some degree, *independent* of that context (Habermas, 1984: p. 15). The technical and social processes which communities have developed over time to adapt to and accommodate their environment can be overruled by prescriptions developed externally, "objectively".

Such processes sustain not the lifeworld, but what Habermas calls the *system*. The system is those parts of social and organisational life which have become separated out from the lifeworld over time and which are based on the principle of achieving instrumental and strategic goals rather than reaching understanding. The lifeworld and system have become "decoupled". The system is driven, or "steered", by the media of money and power, means of determining courses of action that become separated from community-based activity which may check or control them. Steering media are institutionalised in the global economic and state systems, and have developed self-sustaining, reproductive processes which are no longer connected to public debate, agreement, even democracy. Money and power thus lose their accountability to society. No one is truly *responsible* for them, no one oversees them, and communities become less and less able to influence their effects on lives and environments. This is what Habermas calls *colonisation*.

The ideal is a balance between system and lifeworld (Habermas, 1984: p. xxxi), each "subordinate to and controlled by the other"; but the system, having increased control over the society's sociotechnical base (see Chapter 9), is now highly dominant. The steering media of money and power come to substitute for reaching understanding. This has a "disintegrative" effect on the lifeworld (Habermas, 1984: pp. 341–2), breaking the links between different elements of the lifeworld like communities, education, value formation, turning information into knowledge, using these to develop identity and personality, and so on. The institutional state and monetary system, uncoupled from the values and activity of groups and individuals, no longer contributes to renewing traditions and values (Habermas, 1987: pp. 145–8). The lifeworld is "cut down more and more to one subsystem amongst others" (Habermas, 1987: p. 154). Economic and political action can thereby "be co-ordinated without the constant necessity for complex and risky negotiation and processes of common will formation" (Goldblatt, 1996: p. 117).

It can hopefully be seen how the notion of colonisation serves as a summary explanation for developments to which I, and others, have already referred. For example, Robins and Webster (1987: p. 34) tell the tale in their own words:

> ...the most significant feature of the development of advanced capitalism and the nation state has been their endeavour to integrate diverse areas of life into domains over which they have

control. Drawing in and extending into once exempted activities, corporate capitalism and state agencies typically have achieved a greater management of social relationships, have increasingly "scripted" roles and encounters, at the same time as they have advanced their criteria as those most appropriate for conducting affairs. This process should be seen as the rationalisation of control in pursuit of particular interests.

And information – its "gathering, scrutiny and dissemination" – is wholly bound up with this process (Robins and Webster, 1987). Robins and Webster therefore directly link colonisation to the social shaping of technology, meaning (as in Chapter 3 and elsewhere) not just the actual machinery of ICT but the educational and organisational practices which wrap computers and people together in sociotechnical systems.

Examples of this can be drawn from many fields. I mention only three, which between them show how corporate and state control over information extends into technology development; infrastructural planning; and education.

The instrumental orientation of business organisations extends, as we have seen, to controls placed on the creativity and innovation of employees. From a business perspective there are justifications here. When someone is financially compensated for their time and skills, it makes little business sense for their activity to be spent on work from which the business will not benefit. However, what is *economically* rational may retard the exchange of information throughout a business sector. It also makes the business parasitic on the creativity of others, taking from the lifeworld but giving nothing back. A recent story in the online magazine *The Register* refers to these processes with reference to open source tools such as Linux[1]. It observes that the pool of code and knowledge represented by an open source application is becoming harder to maintain due to restrictions placed on the activity of employees, even when their companies are actively using applications produced in this way. Indeed, by placing restrictions on the work of their developers, they are in fact increasing their own development costs, without evidence that they subsequently benefit commercially from this control. A decision that is strategic, therefore – retaining control over the creativity of employees – turns out to be not only not communicatively rational, but not even instrumentally (economically) rational.

---

[1] See *http://www.regdeveloper.co.uk/2008/04/08/open_source_user_participation/* (last accessed 16 June 2008).

An equivalent would be a university placing restrictions on what its employees (academics) could add to the common stock of knowledge, through publication. No university – yet – would do such a thing, but many spin-off companies and other innovators in various sectors do restrict the dissemination of knowledge developed "in house", hedging it with intellectual property rights. Copyright, patents and digital rights management are economically rational, but "chill" the *lawful* exchange of information, damaging the "openness necessary to accelerate the progress of technical knowledge" and enhance the understanding of environmental threats, whether these be challenges to a market sector, environmental problems or terrorism (Kranich, in Hess and Ostrom, 2007: pp. 90–1). However, no business would suggest that their employees remain ignorant of work undertaken elsewhere, whether in academia or (when available in some form) a competitor. Plus, the skills which these employees possess in the first place will have been developed, at least in part, within the formal education sector and the freely-available information accessed within, and then turned into knowledge through learning processes designed and facilitated by teachers. So though restrictions on the creativity and activity of employees in any business are economically rational, they can be seen as a form of enclosure. Businesses engaging in them are taking freely from the noösphere but limiting their contributions back to it.

The second example shows how governments restrict and manipulate information, regardless of democratic safeguards that supposedly exist to prevent this.

The institutionalised activity that is the public planning process is usually considered a way to assert democratic control over developments that have significant environmental impact. But Kemp (1985) suggests that the public inquiry system's origins (in the UK) in the Enclosure Acts of the 19th century, as well as the general tendency towards colonisation and control of major projects by government, has instead turned public inquiries into symbolic procedures which actually further the agendas of the powerful. Basically, they make the process of enclosure more effective, rather than democratically checked. He examines particularly the case of THORP (the Thermal Oxide Reprocessing Plant, at Sellafield, Cumbria) but similar processes were seen at other public inquiries around this time into nuclear plants and the building of major roads (Tyme, 1978). For instance, those in favour of building nuclear plants were often allowed to claim immunity from cross-examination under the Official Secrets Act. Justice Parker, who led the THORP inquiry, announced "that any evidence of the unsatisfactory economic performance of THORP need not count against the proposal... [but] evidence of financial advantage would count in favour" (Kemp, 1985: p. 192). The overarching government policy in favour of nuclear power (or roadbuilding) was not open to discussion, thus skewing the criteria by which the plans could be evaluated. (Aufheben (1998: p. 103), discussing roadbuilding, also observe that cars remain "the pre-eminent consumer product", their design, advertising, selling, taxing and refuelling raising far more money for the system than public transport.) All in all, though the public inquiry process *potentially* leads to democratic control and consensus-formation over large infrastructural projects and/or environmental change, in practice, the outcomes are not only not communicatively rational, they are not even "objective" in the legal sense: "they are manipulated to further the interests of both state and capital" (Kemp, 1985: p. 177).

The third and final example at this stage is "instrumental progressivism", an educational ideology described by Robins and Webster (1987: pp. 207–25)[2] and, again, implicated in the social shaping of technology. This is particularly significant as it arguably forms the basis for educational policy across much of the world. Robins and Webster link instrumental progressivism directly to the requirements of the corporate sector and its influence over educational policy. The objective is "education for flexibility", and "contracts in which students assume responsibility for their own development", but this is not intended to empower learners to act autonomously in public community life. Rather, these skills are oriented "to the world of business and industry": it is education "for flexible production" (Robins and Webster, 1987: pp. 204–5).

What initially seems a paradox is that this "new instrumentalism is in fact rooted in progressive educational traditions" (p. 207): child-centred pedagogy, for instance, the use of experiential learning and a focus on general skills for learning rather than tightly-bound disciplines. But when combined with the audit culture and a will to control, instrumental progressivism amounts to an attempt to break the *traditional* educational establishment and its basis in long-established and only partially integrated schools of knowledge. It would then be replaced, not with community-based or individualised ways of accrediting and, thus, valuing learning, but criteria set, and controlled, from within the government and clients in business and industry; in other words, the

---

[2] If any of these seem less worthwhile as examples because of their age, look at the thinking tasks on the website, through which you can explore examples of colonisation with reference to your own context.

system. What counts as valid (and thus valued) practice is no longer under the control of individual teachers, but prescribed from above.

Along the way, there is a *market* created for educational management services: thus money comes to steer education policy as well as power. Software can be designed that deliver standardised curricula and help manage educational organisations. Profiling students, or keeping records of assessment, become major industries. This *information* is collected not only to make educational management more efficient, but as a permanent record of achievement. Roles are allocated by the market depending on whether students "tick the boxes": not just subjects studied, and grades, but the skills they acquired, the personality they exhibited at school, and the extra-curricular activities they undertook. Formal assessment becomes more and more pervasive, reaching into every aspect of the educational experience. Educational initiatives such as the No Child Left Behind Act in the USA and Managing Information Across Partners (MIAP) in the UK (*http://www.miap.gov.uk*) are empirical examples of instrumental progressivism. With the latter, not only is control asserted over the learning experience, but also the accreditation of providers: informal learning, work experience provided by voluntary organisations, private training courses for adults and community work will all have to be submitted for approval to "objective" assessors who will determine whether the learning they provide is valid. Otherwise, no record of it can be kept in the database. When, later, these records of achievement are consulted by prospective employers, learning undertaken outside these approved stations will likely not be valued at all. This is a form of social shaping of the wider educational scene, through assessment and accreditation.

In an increasingly complex, technology-driven environment, programmes like these make economic and administrative sense. And the backers of projects like MIAP are not being accused of an overt assertion of power. Their behaviour is perfectly *rational* when viewed from inside the organisations within which they work. But these developments set the conditions for the future. They have arisen not through public consultation and consensus, but through applying instrumental rationality to the lifeworld's reproductive processes: in short, they are colonising. Let us move on, then, to consider why it is that Habermas believes colonisation to have such a negative impact on individual and community life.

Colonisation, first, gives rise to a *passive* relationship to steering media: and thus to the technologies, organisations, procedures, information and so on produced by these media. Habermas identified four roles which individuals can fill with respect to the economic and administrative systems (Habermas, 1987; Goldblatt, 1996: p. 119). These are *consumer*, *employee*, *citizen*, and *client* (of welfare, public services etc). The first two are adopted towards the economy, the last two, the administration. Each role can be defined in an active sense. Through work, consumer demands, voting and other political activity (at national and local level), information can be passed *from* the lifeworld *to* the system, and system institutions evolve as a result. But under colonisation, each role becomes passive, and information passes only the other way (Goldblatt, 1996: pp. 118–21). "Public opinion", rather than being the starting point of democratic will-formation, becomes merely another environmental factor to be manipulated, usually *after* a decision has been taken (Habermas, 1987: p. 346). Goldblatt (1996: p. 145) points out, incidentally, how the passive form of each relationship is more likely to be found in lower-income groups, who are more likely to lack the education, access to technology, political awareness and financial independence to resist colonisation. (See Part 4 for more here.)

The state and economy "push to the fringes" anything in which alternative forms of rationality can be embodied, such as aesthetics, morality, and communication (Habermas, 1984: p. 354). As a result, the making of knowledge, and thereby, resources, by individuals and communities finds less and less *formal* support from institutions based on values other than the economic or pragmatic (that which makes money for someone or supports their existing position); or, they look to what is irrational for this support, such as forms of counterknowledge. Arguably then, colonisation encourages the spread of counterknowledge. Other reactions to it include alienation and anomie (a feeling of hopelessness); widespread cynicism; and a lack of accountability in government and business, which leads to bad and self-defeating decisions.

In their ideal states, both democracy and free markets – forms of governance – depend on:

> ...good, trustworthy information about stocks, flows, and processes within the entities being governed, as well as about the relevant external environment... Information must also be fit with decision makers' needs in terms of timing, content and form of presentation... Information must not overload the capacity of users to assimilate it (Hess and Ostrom, 2007: pp. 66–7).

As we have discussed, however, the reliability and credibility of information is challenged in many ways: overt restrictions on access; an inability to discern what is quality information through the data smog; and a lack of critical information skills in the general population. Public, informed scrutiny of important decisions is either deliberately restricted[3], or the necessary skills have atrophied. There is denial that the public is qualified to participate in decisions that affect them (see the next chapter). Thus, conditions are set in which only memes approved of by those in positions of power are reproduced in the lifeworld and, ultimately, the noösphere and the physical environment. The development of the technological and organisational infrastructure is controlled by these approved values. Activity deviating from them is marginalised at best, considered subversive or illegal at worst.

One does not have to be "left wing", or even particularly "democratic", to recognise the dangers inherent in restricting public scrutiny of decisions and the accountability of decision makers. What motivations then remain for avoiding bad decisions? How could we continue to *learn*, and adapt to new situations, if a current way of working becomes inappropriate in changed conditions, whether at an individual, community, organisational, national or global level? True rationality – in the Enlightenment tradition – involves "a readiness to learn and... openness to criticism that are the outstanding features of the scientific spirit" (Habermas, 1984: p. 62). The more we have decided for us in advance what can be accepted, and the more these decisions become embedded into the technologies and organisations through which our activity is mediated, the more the "burden of interpretation is removed from the individual" (1984: p. 71) and absorbed into a sociotechnical system, the design of which has been undertaken without widespread consultation, and the effectiveness of which may not be perpetuated under changed conditions.

This failure to maintain a critical awareness of information in the general population – and the denial of information of *quality* to those groups who may need it, but who are not backed by those with power to control access and determine the conditions under which information will be used – is not at all counterbalanced by the explosion of access produced by ICT. This is precisely Shenk's point in *Data Smog*. The notion of "information obesity" being caused by vast increases in the quantity of information but a simultaneous deterioration in quality also

---

[3] The UK government publicly announced in 2006 that they would simply repeat the distortions of the previous round of nuclear power inquiries, when Alistair Darling, then Trade Secretary, announced that local councils would "be unable to reject power plants on the grounds they were not needed" – see *http://news.bbc.co.uk/1/hi/uk_politics/5154054.stm* (last accessed 16 June 2008).

speaks directly to it. This is another of Habermas's "pathologies" (problems) caused by colonisation. There is an "overburdening of the communicative infrastructure" (Habermas, 1987: p. 395). Modern society (Habermas, 1987: p. 355) is oriented to "preventing holistic interpretations from coming into existence... *Everyday consciousness* is robbed of its power to synthesise; it becomes *fragmented*". Through such fragmentation "the conditions for a colonisation of the lifeworld are met", as diffused "local cultures" cannot be sufficiently co-ordinated. Lacking, then, any intersubjective ways of valuing and filtering information, and of then turning this information into knowledge and other resources which will be useful to them in the future, these local cultures – individuals and communities – are half-encouraged, half-forced to adopt merely a passive role with respect to the information flowing around their activity systems, and as a result, become obese on it, as has been defined throughout this book (see the end of Part 1).

Colonisation is, when properly understood, a critique of society that does not follow traditional "left–right" divisions in politics. The question is not whether the public or private sector should predominantly manage society and individual lives. Rather, Habermas recognises that democracy must allow for *individuals and communities* to participate – actively – in decisions which affect their lives. Dehumanisation arises *both* through the workings of global capital *and* the state system, which reinforce each other, to the detriment of individuals, families and communities throughout the world. When a "right winger" complains about a "nanny state" exerting too much power over private lives, and a "left winger" observes that multinational corporations can bulldoze local environments and exclude local people and businesses from any benefits, each is in fact talking about the same thing. Counterknowledge may be "anti-Enlightenment", according to Thompson: but so is any governmental or business decision that refuses to heed, or even hear, the rational arguments of communities affected by them. And as Goya observed, when reason sleeps, we produce monsters[4].

As I seem to say frequently, this has only been a sketch. Readers are urged to look both at the website and the annotated reading list for ways

---

[4] From a famous image produced in 1799, and shown on the website. There is a double meaning in the image; that it is not only the *denial* of reason which produces "monsters", but its passive, "sleep-like" acceptance, and a lack of awareness of how "reason" can turn into tyranny without constant vigilance over its potential dark side.

to further explore what is a complex and fascinating set of ideas. Let me also make a few supplementary points.

All that has been said about colonisation may seem to pull us towards familiar traps. The trends being discussed seem so pervasive, so powerful, that "resistance is futile". However, Habermas's ideas have beauty and strength because they help us see *actual* instances of decolonisation, and determine the *locations* and the *conditions* under which colonisation might be reversible.

Once colonisation is accepted as a useful general description of how modern life devalues consensus, self-guided understanding, community, creativity and learning itself; one becomes encouraged to abandon the idea that decolonisation may come from within the system's institutions. To expect sympathy for community and individual needs from the steering media of money and power is a fundamental contradiction, despite the rhetoric of "personalisation" and "consumer choice". Communities and individuals may be provided with a menu of options to choose from, but rarely have they been developed *by* the individual or community. To establish what communities can do *for themselves* takes a shift in perception, challenging the ingrained assumption that modern life is too complex to be managed any way other than by hierarchical, instrumental organisations (see Blaug, 1999a, and Chapter 9).

In principle, the lifeworld/system model allows influence to flow both ways (Habermas, 1987: p. 185; also p. 390, with specific reference to the broadcast and publishing media). Decolonising activities are not abstract or Utopian. They are a concrete series of practices based on principles of learning, participation, openness to different opinions and willingness to reach understanding: thus, *educational*. Nor is Habermas a "traditionalist", demanding we return to older and somehow "better" ways of life. He recognises the new possibilities that "media-steered subsystems" offer to society, going so far as to say they have "evolutionary value" (Habermas, 1987: p. 339). What is needed is to incorporate into them elements of "democratic countersteering" (Habermas, 1994: p. 117 and Blaug, 1999b: p. 52). This will not be straightforward: it will face resistance both internal and external (see the next chapter). But without it, there is little chance of orienting new technological and other developments towards *sustaining the environments from which we draw our resources.*

The conditions that permit decolonisation include spreading "communicative competence" through communities (Whitworth, 2007a). Communicatively-rational actors need an ability to recognise rhetoric and persuasion, and the ways in which money and power distort free and fair communication, both directly and, through being embedded into our organisations and technologies, indirectly. They need a *critical* awareness of how these processes affect themselves, their workplaces, learning environments and communities. They must not just wait for information to come to them, but actively seek it, treating information literacy proactively by developing their own information needs, rather than waiting to be told what information is required by others. And the ways in which the "effectiveness" of their activity is measured must be developed not only with reference to criteria of cost and benefit but in line with criteria developed in Chapter 2: preserving the diversity and health of their informational environments. There is a *principle of preservation* in operation here. Just as "sustainable development" is defined (by the 1987 Brundtland Report) as meeting the needs of the present without damaging the ability of future generations to meet their needs, so the principle of (democratic) preservation has been defined as being able to take communicatively-rational decisions now, without damaging the ability to take similar decisions (in a given community or organisational setting) in the future (Blaug, 1999b: pp. 125–6). This is exactly what is meant by saying that resources are things built for the future, not just harvested from the past: but when we suffer from information obesity we are not using resources effectively to create forms of knowledge and understanding that we and our communities will need in the future. Instead, we passively consume them to little subsequent effect.

Once again, idealism may be creeping in. If decolonisation is so important, and easy to define, why is it so rarely done? One answer is that it *is* being done, all across the world, in many communities: what we have is not a failure to act, but a failure to *see* when activity is already taking place. Our perception is distorted, and this itself is another effect of colonisation; we are discouraged from believing such activity is either possible, or effective if it does ever take place (Blaug, 1999a). And there are strong forces and pressures that work against decolonisation, and make it effortful, sometimes even dangerous. Organisations do not just alter the way we act, but the way we think and see the world; they work very effectively to shape the way we make knowledge, and indeed are the primary channels by which colonisation occurs. These ideas are discussed in detail in Chapter 9.

Nevertheless, Habermas's theories remain a valuable way of not just describing, but of potentially changing, the status quo. Thus, they are critical in the true sense, and in terms of the traditional "left–right" political divide – the debate between public sector and private sector control – they are effectively apolitical. This was mentioned above but let me return to it briefly. Neither Habermas nor I promote an "anti-business" agenda, for example. The *local community business* is just as valuable a part of the lifeworld as "public" or community organisations: and just as much threatened by dehumanising global capital as other parts of the community. Employment, at least in some ways, is a means by which resources can be "retrieved" from the system and put back into a community, and small business enterprises are crucial sources of innovation and creativity for the economy. The counterposition between state and corporate control of resources is not really an opposition at all (see Bollier, in Hess and Ostrom, 2007: pp. 32–3). Either form of control stands in undesirable opposition to community control, whether in practice this is asserted through active citizenship, voluntary work or local business.

Colonisation is an elegant theoretical foundation for analysing the world as we see it and recognising that within it, certain things *will never be* valued by the system. If information literacy, for example, truly *was* the solution to the system's problems, then its skilled practitioners would already be the recipients of grossly-inflated rewards – as are corporate tax lawyers, advertising executives, commodities traders, and a few entertainers in sports and the arts. All service the resource needs of the system, and as a result, are lucratively compensated. Similarly – not quite at the same level of financial reward, but with power and other benefits – the governance system rewards those in positions like the heads of quangoes, MPs, and senior civil servants.

Decolonising activity will never be so rewarded, by definition. Its rewards must be sought elsewhere; in self empowerment, in revitalising community life, in nurturing and sustaining local environments, in art, aesthetics and beauty. None are "irrational", instead all are crucial components of healthy, sustainable environments which work to spread the benefits of the Enlightenment to the *maximum* number of people, not merely to a carefully-selected, controlling and parasitic elite.

How organisations affect the way we think

"I need some information!"

"Sam, this is Information Retrieval, not Information Dispersal."
(Dialogue from the movie *Brazil*)

Those who seek to discredit "idealist" politics often invoke the "iron law of oligarchy". This term was used by Michels in *Political Parties* (1959), who observed that despite the ideal of democratic participation, in reality, power within any organisation inevitably, over time, became concentrated in a small elite: the "oligarchy" (a Greek term meaning "rule by few"). Another version of this argument is that "power corrupts".

An equally common argument is that it is inefficient, even dangerous, to give small groups power or influence in decision making:

> Almost all of us intuitively assume such [community-based] forms to be hopelessly inefficient, quite incapable of running complex activities, quite unable to co-ordinate action in such a way as to deploy, or even adequately resist, state power. At the root of this negative evaluation is the widely held belief that, if you want to win any given power struggle, if you want to survive against the others, you have to be organised (Blaug, 1999a: 35).

Blaug calls this perspective "hierarchism", the belief that things can only get done through strong, tightly-controlled organisation and management, in which roles are specifically defined and relationships of power and subordination are formalised. Hierarchism constitutes one of the most powerful *memes* that sets the conditions for other activities and ways of thinking. It:

...is so ingrained into our political culture as to severely limit the set of possible strategic and procedural solutions available to us. When an army, government, political party, radical movement, trade union, voluntary group or department meeting faces organisational difficulties, it is likely to reach for solutions which strongly express this hierarchical orientation (Blaug, 1999a).

This chapter is based mainly on Blaug's work. He explains how hierarchy has "hidden cognitive costs" and, as a result, "important implications for the prospects of a more participatory democracy" (Blaug, 2007: 24). This is crucial for finally understanding how modern life affects the way we absorb, filter and then use information. The organisations through which we mediate activity are *not* "neutral" spaces in which we are free to interpret environments, and the information stored within them, and then make new knowledge as we choose. Instead, organisations "push" ways of thinking at us, exploiting tendencies in the ways our brains process information, and as a result, prevent us seeing and/or constructing alternative ways of thinking and acting which may solve our problems and help us creatively adapt to changing circumstances. Technology, particularly ICT, has greatly enhanced the capabilities of organisations in this regard: it has also deeply embedded these capabilities into the infrastructure and thus, made these processes harder to lift into view and subjected to critical analysis and potential change.

Learning becomes a process of coming to see these "pushed" ways of thinking, and working within communities to construct alternatives. Active learners must do so in full recognition of the resistance that they will face both from the system and also internally, due to inescapable tendencies in human behaviour. Blaug accepts the notion that "power corrupts"; but what he does, and what makes his work valuable, is ask *why* it does so. And as a critical social theorist, he then asks what we can do about it.

This is the final piece of the jigsaw built through the first three parts of this book. At the end of the chapter I explain how learning can still – and must – occur in classrooms, organisations and communities which are saturated by ICT and suffering from information obesity, but how this learning needs to specifically attend to how organisations affect the way we think. The practical strategies through which this might happen are then outlined in Part 4.

The intersubjective realm is most significant in human life. We are social creatures, not to the extent of ants or termites, but certainly more than some animals, like cats. Communities and organisations clearly allow us to undertake activities which otherwise would be, if not impossible, at least more difficult. These include large-scale activities such as roadbuilding, running a business or going to the Moon, but may be smaller in scope, such as building a house, organising a theatrical production or playing competitive sports. All the latter are innately *social*, but do not necessarily have to be *formally organised*.

In addition, it is the intersubjective level at which knowledge is made. Reaching consensus on important issues is something we do all the time, through the very nature of language. Language is not completely objective: when we use the term *dog* (or *chien*, *Hund*, σκυλι or a thousand other words which refer to the canine species) it will not bring to mind exactly the same dog in the minds of hearers; this even before we consider the word as a metaphor. But nor will we start thinking of umbrellas, Michelangelo's *David*, antidisestablishmentarianism, or whatever. The word "dog" is a *sign*, and various canines are all potentially *signified* by the word; as Saussure recognised, the link between sign and signified is a social construction, but with a word like this, the link is so familiar to us that we treat it as "common sense". What makes language so potentially ambiguous, and useful as a way of imposing one way of thinking about the world rather than another, comes when we see similar social processes at work with signs such as "democracy", "freedom", "human rights", or even "work", "education" and "literacy". The ability to embed one's interpretation of these terms into a sociotechnical infrastructure is how conditions are created in which some memes and ways of thinking can prosper, and others not[1].

Despite these potential conflicts, we need institutions within which such meanings are created. Otherwise we would live in a perpetual Babel, unsure of any utterance's meaning, and thus unable to act in co-ordination with others. Habermas develops these points at the start of the second volume of *The Theory of Communicative Action*, drawing on the work of Mead and Durkheim. Institutions allow for "common responses in the community" (Habermas, 1987: p. 37). Actions are co-ordinated through direct agreement but also with reference to *values* embedded in the social system, such as morality. Violating instrumental

---

[1] A huge amount of literature exists which explores these ideas in more detail. The works of Wittgenstein and Bakhtin are particularly useful, though not easy to follow: plenty of secondary texts exist, however. For a simple and brilliant commentary on how language is used and abused to further political agendas, read George Orwell's *Politics and the English Language*: see the website and its thinking tasks.

principles may be "punished" through failing to successfully complete a task (e.g., not shoring up a roof will lead to its collapse; not advertising a play will leave it with no audience). Violating moral principles, by contrast, brings sanctions that cannot be defined in any way other than with reference to membership of a group (Habermas, 1987: p. 48). These include shame, ostracism and legal punishment, but also more subtle processes like peer pressure, conformity and socialisation, all of which constantly help us absorb notions of "acceptable" behaviour in social situations. Like other intersubjective values, these must be *shared*, thus are based on the related concepts of communication and community. (See the thinking tasks on the website for practical examples.) *Communication is what mediates between personal identities and the group, or institutional identity* (Habermas, 1987: p. 61).

What is an institution, exactly? An institution is any system by which we organise socially. Institutions have their own codes of practices, traditions, and so on, but these may not be formal. "Marriage", for example, is an institution (interpreted slightly differently around the world, though with the same basic core). Institutions act as filters, determining what can and cannot be said within them, what counts as valid or valuable inside the institution (Lyotard, 1984: p. 17). Already, then, we can see that institutions play a role in how we filter information.

The idea of an "institution" also serves as a way to bring together communities and organisations. As noted, "community" is based around ideas of sharing, as discussed with reference to the institution that is "Brighton and Hove Albion FC" (or similar clubs). But there is an organisational kernel inside the institution. The organisation that is Brighton & Hove Albion FC is that part of the institution that is *formally recognised*, and in two separate ways. First, the "team", the entity that is a member of the English Football League, competes against other teams and has its performance recorded by a set of conventions (points, goals, fan approval). It is also a legal organisation, a limited company, which pays taxes, employs workers, and records its performance in balance sheets and bank accounts. The institution therefore contains internal divisions, relationships and, possibly, tensions. Laws, regulations and performance indicators constrain and channel the (actual, and ideal) behaviour of the organisation; thereby, the values and expectations shared by the institution as a whole.

Institutions cannot be considered as merely the sum of all the activities and learning of the individuals within them (Habermas, 1987: p. 306). Instead, they have a permanence, an identity, extending beyond the individuals who make it up at any given time. In organisations, this permanence is formalised. They contain "positions", "roles", "offices" and the like into and out of which individuals can move (Weber, 1947). The activities of these holders of office are defined and constrained by job descriptions, performance criteria and reviews, not to mention salaries and other benefits that may be withdrawn if the holder of office works poorly. Chains of command are written into the organisational structure, and channels of communication formalised into procedure. While individuals, particularly those in positions of power, can still affect an organisation through asserting their own personality and values, more common is that the organisation "thinks" and "learns" *structurally*, with knowledge stored within its sociotechnical systems, often very deeply and therefore almost out of sight.

Before we analyse the consequences of this, it should of course be noted that this is not the only way to organise, even formally. Many writers, from antiquity onwards, have studied, described and enacted alternative organisational forms. Organisations can be based around charismatic or traditional authority, like a church; they can also be based around more democratic or anarchist principles, such as job rotation, decision making by consensus rather than executive decree, equality between employees, co-operative ownership, and so on. (Here see Rothschild and Whitt, 1986, amongst many others. Gastil, 1993 is a detailed investigation of a co-operative organisation and the problems it faced.) It is Blaug's (1999a) point that we often underestimate the contribution of these alternative organisational forms to our society because of the pervasiveness of hierarchism. Kropotkin, for example, cited the Royal National Lifeboat Institution (and similar institutions elsewhere), which performed regular acts of heroism without needing a management structure (1955: p. 275). Other successful examples exist in the voluntary sector and internationally, such as the postal service.

We must be careful, however. It is easy to laud alternative organisations as being more "democratic", more "empowering" for their members, while being blind to hierarchies which remain within. This was best argued by Freeman in her superb critique, "The Tyranny of Structurelessness" (1984: first distributed 1971). Even if there is no formalised division of labour, stratification – the separation of something out into layers of difference – can still occur within organisations that declare themselves "free of hierarchy". Freeman observed that in the women's movement stratification could be based around charisma, ideological "soundness", commitment and so on. Other writers (e.g. Merrick, 1996, Whitworth, 2003: 137–8) have seen similar processes at work in environmental protests, where those who were more willing to be "in the front line" (climbing trees, digging tunnels, for example) had more power to impose their interpretations of events on the group's activity: a "hierarchy of the harness", in effect. Therefore, any grouping tends to have criteria through which admission to "inner circles" – positions of influence and power – are judged. Any institution can become parochial and closed to new inputs. Tightly-drawn rules of membership can be used to exclude; and information used as part of this.

I may seem to be getting off the point, but it was worth the digression. These examples suggest that *any* institution, organisation or community has some *form* or *structure*, a structure always based around values of some kind. What is important for judging the communicative rationality of that institution (and its activity) is the question of whether these values are *open to critique and alteration from members of the community/organisation*. Remember, this is the essential feature of a critical approach to social science. It also reflects *double-loop learning* (Argyris, 1999: first mentioned back in Chapter 3) – the ability of members of an organisation to not just take decisions within an existing system of values, but if necessary, to *examine, critique, and change* those values (resources) if they are no longer appropriate to circumstance and if, as a result, they threaten the organisation's ability to take similar decisions in the future (sustainability). By definition, double-loop learning requires environmental conditions in which there is open access to alternative ways of working and thinking. (See Chapter 11.)

What Blaug does is explain why this kind of critical awareness is not always easy to secure. With informal, community organisations like social movements, the reasons are a little more complex, and discussed more in his 1999 paper than the 2007 one (see below). For formal, hierarchical organisations, however, this awareness is difficult because of the way hierarchy "assists the capture of meaning by the interests of power" (Blaug, 2007: 24). This idea is worth detailed analysis: indeed it is the core of Blaug's argument, and thus crucial for understanding the relationship between organisational form, information filtering and information obesity.

As activity theory (and related models) show, we are active *makers* of knowledge, not passive recipients of information. But this knowledge making takes place within a world saturated by information, even before considering the impact of ICT. Without filtering we would be overwhelmed by information. I have written the following elsewhere (Whitworth, 2007b: p. 211):

The world contains too many data for our limited cognitive resources. To understand sensory data, we select from what is available, usually subconsciously: "subjects are aware of that to which they are attending, but not of the selection process directing their attention" (Evans, 1989: p. 16). For example, until you think about it, it is unlikely you are conscious of the feeling of your backside against a chair. The sensory data are gathered constantly but filtered out. Without consciously registering them, they slip beneath awareness, fading into the background over which we engage in other work.

This is the problem of *cognitive load*, brilliantly illustrated by the famous film of a basketball game (see the website) in which an incongruous intruder is simply not registered by an audience *after they've been told to concentrate on something else*, namely, counting the passes during the game. (If you have never seen this film I urge you to watch it – I am always amazed by its effectiveness.) Magicians exploit it when using misdirection in their tricks.

What Blaug does (2007: 28–33) is examine more complex forms of *cognitive bias*; information filters deeply embedded into our brains and the way we organise our making of knowledge (*cognition*). These have been experimentally verified by scientists. The crucial point is that such filtering criteria *must exist prior* to the encounter with the information (Blaug, 2007: 29, via Augoustinos and Walker, 1996: pp. 169). As there are too many data, even in everyday situations, for our cognitive capacity, we cut, or filter, inputs *before* getting down to cognitive work. This ordering is vital because it shows that the information filtering process is not done consciously, as part of our cognitive work with the information: but largely unconsciously, before we get down to such work. So rather than being in the forefront of consciousness, something actively engaged in, as IL pedagogies urge us to do, we largely do it without thinking, as a preliminary stage. Now it is true that much of this filtering works on sensory input (e.g. filtering noise out at a party or in a busy street so we can listen to a conversation, read a newspaper, or the like), but Blaug's point is that there are also higher-level forms of "automation" in our filtering. These are "by-products of a cognitive apparatus that is structually oriented to selectivity and automation" (Blaug, 2007: 30).

The first example (there are illustrations of each on the website) is the *confirmation bias*:

> Numerous empirical studies show our strong tendency to seek evidence that validates our prior beliefs, and in the laboratory, we

can be readily induced to accept a hypothesis, collect data that confirms it and *fail to notice* data that suggest our hypothesis is wrong. Even when pressured with contradictory evidence, we still prefer to moderate our existing position rather than to generate a new one.... (Blaug, 2007: 31, via Evans, 1989: p. 44).

All these biases help us make our way through the world. They reduce response times and "stabilise" our views. But the confirmation bias:

...can also lead to complacency, to a loss of responsiveness, and thus to a chronic failure to learn (Blaug, 2007).

There are many examples of this. Right-wing voters read right-wing newspapers; left wingers, left-wing newspapers. Neither is commonly exposed to analyses from "the other side". Researchers write off possibly anomalous data, which may challenge their hypotheses, as "sampling error", and may even program such biases into their automated data gathering systems (it is well known that this was why the Antarctic ozone hole was not discovered until years after it first emerged). A beautiful exploration of the confirmation bias is given by Knight in *Conspiracy Culture*. He discusses how elaborate conspiracy theories can be continually "confirmed", rather than refuted, by new evidence. With the Kennedy assassination for instance, conspiracy theorists:

...claim that any new piece of information which would undermine existing theories or confirm rival ones might itself be a deliberate plant by the powers that be to lead investigators astray. Likewise the lack of evidence of a conspiracy can itself be taken as evidence of a conspiracy to deliberately withhold vital information. The infamous backyard photos of Oswald confirm that he was indeed the lone gunman? Then they must have been faked (Knight, 2000: p. 98).

Similarly, objectively valuable challenges to the belief that, say, the MMR vaccine causes autism, or the US government had prior knowledge of the 2001 attacks on New York, can be written off by "believers" as further misinformation from the establishment (Thompson, 2008). But even if we do not go so far as to use the confirmation bias to prop up counterknowledge, some information, which may be of lower (objective, subjective or intersubjective) value than others, seems more palatable because it fits comfortably into existing *cognitive schema*. Schema have been given various names; mental models, mental maps, scripts: Blaug

(2007: 30) uses "schema", so I will retain the term (from Bartlett, 1932). Schema are ways in which we organise the knowledge in our minds, they are "products of prior experience... learned and stored" (Blaug, 2007: 30). We:

> ...have schema for greeting another person, for getting into a lift, for eating a meal and, indeed, for the full range of everyday events, objects and activities. Schema function to pick out relevant, "schema-consistent" data from the rush of information we regularly confront. As such, they are pre-existing selection criteria that manage cognitive overload and enhance the capacity to solve problems (Blaug, 2007).

One can therefore see that IL strategies are themselves schema, developed by others. However, the confirmation bias makes it difficult for us to "filter in" knowledge that may require us to substantially change our cognitive schema, or develop new ones. A model of IL that does not account for the existence of confirmation biases is therefore an incomplete strategy for confronting information obesity: and confirmation is only one of the three significant cognitive biases.

The second is that of *affirmation*. Affirmation "produces false and self-flattering beliefs about our own cognitive processes" (Blaug, 2007: 31, via Evans, 1989). We tend to overestimate our own abilities and knowledge, and are over-confident about our reasoning and judgment. Using hindsight we tend to declare that our powers of prediction are better than they were ("I always said that would happen") and while we take responsibility for successes, we blame failures on others. Once again these have been proven in experiments, and are universal among human beings: except, interestingly, those suffering from depression, who tend to be the best judges of their real ability (Augoustinos and Walker, 1996: 93). There will be those who (applying the confirmation bias) have long held a somewhat negative view of other people and who may see this as justifying that cynicism. In fact, the "affirmational bias helps us join the world" (Blaug, 2007: 31), freeing us from self-imposed mental prisons, giving us confidence to act when the outcome is uncertain, and preventing us being crushed by existential angst, believing nothing that we will ever do can make a difference.

Nevertheless, it can also "impede our judgment" (Blaug, 2007) quite dramatically. We may simply fail to see when we are heading down a wrong path of thought, or activity, until it is too late. The more cognitive work we have invested in something, the less likely we are to abandon it.

We embed prior decisions into sociotechnical systems that subsequently direct our action; thus institutionalising the affirmational bias. This is a very dangerous trap for activity, possibly leading organisations into negative feedback loops, where it becomes impossible to see the basic flaws in a strategy or set of values that are leading towards disaster. Arguably, major institutional collapses, such as those of Barings Bank and Enron, have stemmed from the affirmational bias. (See the website for a more detailed discussion of that claim.)

The third and final bias discussed by Blaug is perhaps the hardest of all to resolve, which is exactly why it is so influential on our processing of information. It is the *reification* bias. Reification (a term best developed by Lukács, 1971) describes the "tendency of socially authored structures to appear as real, as external to and independent of, individuals". In the terms that I have used: it is a tendency to treat things as having objective value, a kind of "natural" existence, when in fact they are values and concepts developed intersubjectively. Arguably, as we have discussed, the whole of language is intersubjective, but reification is more easily understood as something that comes by degrees. Hierarchism, mentioned above, is an excellent example: the "need" for hierarchy is very strongly embedded in our psyche, but is an expression of value developed and promulgated mainly by those benefiting from it. Certainly there are times when hierarchical management can be useful; just as often, there are times when a more consensual approach is appropriate. Other widespread examples of the reification bias include the idea that rising GDP is the "inevitable" aim of economic policy, or that modern education must "inevitably" use more ICT than in the past. Reification can also, at least in part, account for beliefs that are less savoury (though no less damaging): that (insert name of chosen minority) are "naturally" lazy and thieving, that women are "naturally" worse managers than men, and so on. (Again, see the website.)

These biases become embedded into the sociotechnical systems which we use to organise activity. Scripts and schema are products of prior knowledge and are *stored*, thus favouring certain activities, ways of thinking, and filtering decisions. Even an information literate actor is not free to determine for themselves the grounds on which they are filtering information, particularly not as much of this may take place before they start conscious cognitive work. But these schema are not necessarily the products of the *actors'* prior knowledge and experience. Within organisations, they are as likely to have been designed by others.

Indeed this is the point of sociotechnical system design, if undertaken with reference to instrumental criteria: "processing time is reduced when incoming data are schema-consistent and… schema-inconsistent data tend to be filtered out and ignored" (Blaug, 2007: 30). Systems are designed to cope with particular inputs. Whatever is to be processed, needs first to be translated into a form the system can accept. This translation could be performed by human or machine parts of the system, but there is also the option to devolve this work out of the system; preventing particular inputs from even being considered until they have changed *themselves* into a form which the system can understand (see Bonnett, in McFarlane, 1997: p. 153). We see this all the time when we have to tick boxes on forms, regardless of whether we think this really describes our situation. This reduction of complex situations into simple summaries – a 3-year degree distilled into a certificate and classification, a complex household summarised by a postal (or ZIP) code – is one characteristic of information as a resource. Summarisation helps feed information through the systems that decide what level of credit we can have, what jobs we are suited for, what products will be marketed to us. We can also do this informally, using stereotypes; seeing "the student", "the passenger", "the claimant", "the protestor" as not individuals, still less a community, but an abstraction, an input into a system, whether university, airline, welfare office, or private security firm policing an environmental protest; in each case, exhorted to do so as efficiently as possible.

Back in Chapter 3 when I discussed activity theory I mentioned that there were two schools: CHAT, examined there, and SSTA (the sociostructural theory of activity, best elaborated on by Bedny and Harris, 2005). SSTA is more design-oriented than CHAT, and intended to be used before the fact, to establish and help analyse patterns of work in a sociotechnical system. SSTA recognises that activity – the work of the system at the highest level – can be broken down into smaller and smaller steps, as follows:

Activity → Task → Action → Operation → Function Block

For example, the activity of the team working on my course in Manchester is to run the MA. Several tasks combine to make up this activity; grading students' work, for instance. Actions which comprise this task include receiving submitted work, passing it to a marker, deciding on a grade, returning that grade to the system, and aggregating these into degree grades. Once we reach *operations*, however, things start to become performed *automatically and unconsciously* (Bedny and Harris, 2005: 134–5), and the final level (function blocks) represents the internal, mental means by which information is processed; the very lowest level of cognitive work. What is crucial here is that none of these have to be necessarily performed by *people*. The action of combining individual grades into degree grades, for example, will almost certainly now be performed by ICT (a spreadsheet), the series of operations therefore programmed into the action by the designers of Manchester's degree classification system, and in turn, resting on function blocks written by the developers of the spreadsheet program. Tools, rules and divisions of labour can mediate work in such an involved way that they effectively substitute for the subject.

The key point then is this:

> ...organisations regularly favour, rehearse, and drill certain cognitive schema *at* their participants.... The hope is that through repetition, sticks and carrots, selected schema will become automated in individual cognition. The act of influencing individual thinking here takes place beneath the awareness of the individual, for whom cognitive work is both reduced and directed. Pushed schema include criteria for the selection of information, categories of classification, interpretation and evaluation, agendas and legitimating narratives (Douglas, 1986). Hierarchic decision-making structures are themselves schema which, when reified, appear as natural and necessary, and when automated, become immune from critical examination (Blaug, 2007: 33–4).

All organisations do this to some extent. Often the process is formally designed, but it can also occur through socialisation, initiation, shared community myths and values, and other ways in which behaviour in institutions is regulated and monitored. It can happen as a result of external influence. In education, for example, National Curricula epitomise the regulation of cognition. Changing the technologies available to a system will inevitably change the schema. An organisation might purchase a new information management system or virtual learning environment. Even moving to a new office or building will subtly alter the cognitive schema which affect everyday working lives: "Because the construction of knowledge is always a situated activity, it takes place within contexts that already feature stored prior knowledge". (Blaug, 2007: 34).

The question of how we form knowledge in given environments is therefore an innately *political* question:

> To plumb the relation between individual cognition and organisational knowledge processing is thus to stumble upon an ongoing political struggle over knowledge in organisations. The

interests of power seek to control the automated heuristics [criteria] with which individuals make knowledge. It is because these heuristics occur beneath awareness that the power struggle over individual cognition in organisations is so often hidden.... In our daily organisational lives, there is an ongoing, yet concealed, struggle over the very contents of our minds (Blaug, 2007: 34).

Faced by such arguments one can start seeing manipulation everywhere, treating all managers as devious and corrupt, all information "from above" as tainted, and all attempts to make our lives easier as "colonising". However, Blaug is more subtle than this. As said at the head of this chapter, his deeper aim is to investigate not just *how* power controls our information processing and thus deflects attention from the way we are exploited, but *why*. For the belief that power inevitably corrupts is itself a reification.

"Power" is often relative (thus, intersubjective) – children and parents have power each other, in different ways – but in an organisational context, power is related to elevated status (and thus financial and other rewards) and an ability to impose one's perspective on the resolution of a problem. The organisation *within which* an individual is powerful starts to turn itself into a tool *through which* the position of power is maintained. As someone moves up an organisational hierarchy, their new responsibilities lead to a:

> ...high-status role occupant [having]... feelings in every part of the organisation, and certainly, with every part of decisions for which they have responsibility... [Hierarchy] invites the leader to confuse his own cognition with the information processing of the organisation (Blaug, 2007: 35).

This is why I said in the previous chapter that something like MIAP seems perfectly "rational" from particular organisational points of view. The sociotechnical system in which it is embedded – and in a wider, Habermasian sense, "the system" itself – has created conditions in which the micro-management of individual learning experiences is merely another informational input into the activity of the responsible government department: namely, the effective management of a nation's education system and the effective development of skills considered important in the (information) economy. But MIAP – and whether this is intended by the designers of that system is, in the end, irrelevant – simply devalues, thus fails to account for, a wide swathe of factors which have value to others within the system, the students and learning providers.

Just as a degree classification distils a wide range of experiences and knowledge into a microscopic informational space, so MIAP rejects, say, the idea of informal learning altogether by having no way of including it in its database. All learning that is to be recorded on MIAP must come from a "recognised provider". The system simply cannot accommodate it otherwise. And in turn, this will regulate the behaviour of learners, perhaps not overtly, but indirectly: strategies will ultimately be adopted that "maximise" a MIAP profile[2].

This is just one example: there are further discussions below of how these tendencies affect education. More generally, when one examines an activity system from different positions one's perspective on it changes, as when looking at a building, or painting. This is not just an issue for the "objective", external analyst of a system, though it does matter: what one is looking for in research, for example, will affect what one sees (see Chapter 11). What it also encourages is the development of "cognitive separation" (Blaug, 2007: 39) between people in different sectors of an organisation. Just as those at the head of the hierarchy may confuse their own cognition with the organisation's, so those lower down may exhibit what Blaug calls "battery cognition". This term:

> captures the sense in which this type of thinking is invisibly taken over, managed and *farmed* by the formations of power for its productive efficiency. Battery cognition is a poor stand-in for

---

[2] One thing I have not particularly mentioned is the rise of the "surveillance society". Privacy International regularly assess states' adoption of techniques such as CCTV surveillance of public space, monitoring private web browsing and book borrowing, erosion of the right to privacy, increasing demands for ID to enter even public space: their conclusions make depressing reading (see *http://www.theregister.co.uk/2007/12/31/britain_worst_privacy/* (last accessed 15 August 2008)). Surveillance is a notable and distasteful exercising of state and business power over the activities of individuals. It works on us mainly at a psychological level, as with Bentham's well-known example of the "Panopticon", a sort of idealised prison in which one warder could control the behaviour of hundreds of inmates; the inmates forced to acknowledge the *possibility* that they were being watched at all times, and thus modifying their behaviour accordingly. This idea was taken up by Foucault (1980) to show how power in our society is less likely to be overtly displayed, and instead, works on us at an unconscious level. We can now reinterpret these ideas as showing how power generally, and surveillance more specifically, seep through *all* the cognitive schema through which our activities are controlled. It is a shame to relegate this topic to a footnote, but hopefully it can be seen how the spread of the surveillance society is strongly bound up with other ideas introduced so far. By writing itself so strongly into our environment, surveillance will also surely start to affect information searching and filtering strategies: a psychological effect which cries out for proper research – but from where will the funding come? See also Stalder, 2008.

autonomy, and is certainly an example of undemocratic thinking. (Blaug, 2007: 38)

This kind of cognition is in no way empowering for individuals. Battery cognition is submerged beneath conscious awareness and directly feeds into hierarchic organisational information processing. It represents adherence to cognitive schema developed by others, and encoded into sociotechnical systems (all the more effectively now thanks to the spread of ICT): there is no critical, creative attention to the ways we work and think. It is the most significant cognitive cost of hierarchy, and is endemic through our organisations – and as a result, through the very education system that is tasked, by some, with helping us overcome information obesity.

Information obesity is a consequence of the greatly increased importance of information as a resource for 21st century organisations. This might seem an obvious link, but what Blaug does is show that the link is *direct*. People are largely *not* free to make their own knowledge, to develop for themselves the filters through which they can *individually* establish information needs, find relevant information, evaluate it and apply it in their value system. Both their working lives and personal lives, colonised by the steering media of money and power, are – in the normal state of affairs – subject to intense pressures, through which minds and habits are shaped, and automated. Worse still, when information *does* emerge which challenges these automated activities, our own cognitive processes discourage us from even seeing it: and even if we do manage to change our value system in order to incorporate these anomalies, we may find ourselves no longer comfortable inside the activity systems of which we were once part. Nor may these systems be able to change to accommodate our new, rebellious perspective. Thus, it is easier – in both the short and long term – to accept what is pushed at us, regardless of whether it damages our own or our communities' ability to maintain a healthy informational and decision-making environment in the future. Indeed, because of the way organisations affect the way we think, we may not even see the damage being caused. And so our minds grow fat and indolent, even in a time of information abundance, when all, potentially, could take what they need – and only as much as they need.

Education is complicit in this process in two ways: one internal, one external. Viewed from within, formal education (and much, though not all, informal education) takes place inside organisations that, like any other organisation, reflect divisions of labour, power relationships, cognitive separation, and the embedding of certain cognitive schema in the buildings, procedures, computer systems and regulations – that is, the technologies – which govern members' work. Educational power relationships exist most clearly between student and teacher, but also between teacher and manager, between different disciplines and their relative status, between ICT support departments and their clients, and so on.

Second, education is increasingly *controlled* through externally developed cognitive schema, which become embedded into regulations such as assessment (now of providers, rather than students, e.g. government inspections, quality assurance procedures), accreditation of learning, and so on. Adherence to these schema is enforced, or rewarded, through the steering media of money and power: the award of grants, of influence, of status: even the very right to be called a "school" or "university" or "training provider". This, like other forms of social control, is ever more deeply embedded into ICT and the systems which are developed and distributed for the management of education and learning: administrative software, course management systems, search engines: as well as non-computing rubrics, definitions (like those of IL), standardised curricula and so on. The *ecology of resources* (Luckin, 2008) available to learners and teachers alike becomes increasingly externally-determined, rather than produced and reproduced by the learning community itself.

Throughout this environment, there *are* alternatives to be found. In the classroom itself, many have noted the impact that cognitive separation can have on the making of meaning, and consequently, have developed strategies such as *critical pedagogy* (see, particularly, Freire, 1972, Shor, 1996 and Mezirow, 1990) and *action research* (Carr and Kemmis, 1986, Reason and Bradbury, 2001). With ICT, alternatives could potentially arise from more collaborative, flexible "Web 2.0" technologies and open source systems. All could help form sites of resistance to pushed cognitive schema, places which permitted critical examination of received information, of the ways we are encouraged to filter it and existing ways of thinking which affect – at an individual and community level – the transformation of information into knowledge and technological resources. All these alternatives need closer examination, a job undertaken in Part 4.

In a more general sense we can also recognise that our *cultures* are what help turn our "native mental powers" – the universal ways that we process information, hard-wired into our brains by millennia of evolution – into "very distinct forms" which are useful in particular situations (Egan, 1990: pp. 2–3). A culture is basically the "range of sense-making capacities available to us" (Egan: p. 198); it is a "conditioning context which evokes, stimulates, and develops particular human potentials in particular ways" (p. 199). This recognises the vital role that different communities play in creating these "sense-making capacities". Communities are what give the vastness of the world a human scale. They are vital elements of information filtering. To become *educated* means "to maximise our acquisition of the range of sense-making capacities" (p. 198); increasing the diversity of our own personal "ecology of resources", permitting us to select from a variety of strategies when we are faced by problems. Such a view can also inform a critical pedagogy to combat information obesity, and is also discussed in Part 4.

Simultaneously, however, the idea stands in opposition to organisational pressures on our minds, which seek "one best" way of thinking and acting, even when the rhetoric is in favour of flexibility and personal choice. A critical education cannot possibly have its form determined by others. Instead:

> ...while evidence for our recurrent compliance with power is overwhelming, there are elements of battery cognition that can be hauled up into consciousness, properly evaluated and changed. We can learn, update schema in the light of new information, question hierarchy and reorganise.... Crucial to such learning is the educational experience of participation itself. (Blaug, 2007: 40–1)

One effect of colonisation is to provoke the development of social movements and other community-level political activities that, in turn, help constitute the instutional *location* for decolonising activity. Such community-level activities seek: "the revaluation of the particular, the natural, the provincial, of social spaces that are small enough to be familiar ..." (Habermas, 1987: p. 395). They are working to defend "the reproductive processes of the lifeworld" (Goldblatt, 1996: p. 126). Hierarchism and colonisation are self reinforcing, in that the former discourages us from believing that complex social situations *of which we are a part* can and should be self managed; instead, we resign ourselves to increased control over our schools, societies, communities, and all the other places in which problem solving can take place with reference to consensually-agreed criteria rather than instrumentality. It is true that there are "trade offs" between democracy and effectiveness, between the time it takes to learn to *democratically* manage the conflicts that seep into any institution (whether formally organised or not), and the dynamic nature of the environment, in which decisions must often be taken immediately, without the luxury of reaching consensus around them. But that is why the work of organising is an ongoing process, one to which we are constantly adjusting; constantly *learning about*. Being aware of the existence of cognitive biases, and the way organisations and technologies affect and mould the way we think, is an essential first step in becoming *vigilant* (Blaug, 1999a) over these effects. Educational techniques which do not allow for the way organisations affect the way we think cannot, by definition, help people develop *new* perspectives, to learn about how to bring about change when it is required; and thus, to be critical, to retrieve our community and individual lives from the dehumanising effects of colonisation and to retrieve our minds from the indolence caused by information obesity.

Let us now go on to discuss what teachers and learners alike can do in practice to empower themselves within the modern day environment, as described thus far.

Part 4:
Combating information obesity

Information obesity and romantic understanding

> The aim would be to make the familiar strange, by sharing the human purposes that stimulated human energy and ingenuity...
> (Egan, 1990: p. 218)

The symptoms of information obesity were presented at the end of Part 1, but Parts 2 and 3 have subsequently shown that it is not caused directly by technology, but the way we organise information production and consumption in our society. These lead to the frequent failure of filtering strategies to meet personal needs, and thus decrease the quality of information received, and retard our ability to transform that information into knowledge and resources useful to us (and our communities) in the future. Nevertheless, though we embed the organisation of information production and consumption into technology, and thus into our environments, technology can potentially be "rewritten" by users who organise their activity in different, communicatively-rational ways. Through doing so, they construct filters for information that are self defined and validated at the individual level and – importantly, as this avoids relativism and counterknowledge – the community level. Such activity stands in opposition to filtering strategies pushed at individuals by organisations whether through hierarchy and battery cognition, or the unconscious acceptance of values as can happen in non-hierarchical organisations. It is therefore a form of resistance to these "pushed" filters.

The idea that a communicatively-rational approach to learning can *reduce the amount* of information we must absorb (or filter out) is a false assumption. But I suggest that such an approach can *increase the quality* of the information that makes it through our filters. This is "quality" measured in a specific way: information that can be understood *and then applied* within a community setting, a process that sustains the "ecology of resources" which that community can use in the future. Metaphorically, it represents a move from the "overload" or "smog" model to an "abundance" view, and thereby, a new equilibrium between our minds, our communities, our environments, and the increasingly dynamic noösphere.

The environmental model of information supports a position – a critique of organisation – which views information obesity as caused by mismatches between filtering processes in the lifeworld and those promoted by the system. Cognitive biases work to promote information obesity at the individual level, and teaching strategies must account directly for these biases. But organisations also exploit cognitive biases to colonise our information processing. We become passive information consumers: either seduced into consuming increasing amounts of irrelevant and low-quality information because this makes money (directly, for information industries, or indirectly, because our patterns of consumption themselves become information about us which has value); or having the fruits of our learning colonised because of the organisational roles we play. We are vulnerable to these processes because we lack collective understanding of the ways sociotechnical systems influence us; learning to see these effects is an educational act.

However, the environmental model is not just useful as a critique. It shows that any educational activity *transforms*, in some way, the ecology of resources that learners will subsequently exploit in the future. It is for this reason that *any* technology can potentially be "rewritten". This can move in either direction along the system/lifeworld axis: a technology with democratic potentials can be colonised, one driven mainly by steering media can be decolonised and subjected to more democratic forms of control. As Darwin, Dawkins and Vernadsky all recognised, all environments are transformed by many small changes which often cancel each other out but which may, potentially, spark system-wide change.

There is a great diversity of these environments. Any community – its social networks, the technologies and other resources they use, and the understandings they share – comprises a unique context. Similarities between contexts allow consensus to potentially emerge, but for this to happen, differences must also be understood. This too is a learning process, and occurs every time that activity, based on values developed through membership of one community, interacts with a different environment. Colonisation encourages ignorance of difference. Instrumental strategies are developed "objectively", and can override local environmental conditions. This damages, or at least skews, the available informational resources and thus influences what can take place in that environment in the future. Communicative action, by contrast, works *with* the resources in a given environment, sustaining them so that the ability to take communicatively rational decisions in the future is not damaged (Blaug's *principle of preservation*). And when different environments interact, the results are governed by learning and reaching understanding – not the use of force to get one's way, the distortion of the interaction by steering media, or the unconscious application of cognitive schema pushed at us by organisations.

Part 4 of this book discusses practical strategies that may help in this project. Nothing which appears within is a prescription. Remember Fay's point. Critical social science should not make prescriptions. Rather, individuals should be empowered to construct their own responses to situations they face in work, education or community life. But it is useful sometimes to supply guidance, to present resources such as stories, insights, beliefs and objectively-valuable hypotheses produced by others. Such informational resources are public goods, which may enrich environments by being introduced in appropriate ways.

These are the general areas of educational practice that I think are important:

- constructivist and romantic approaches to education, focused specifically on technology (the remainder of this chapter);
- promoting critical thinking in both learners and educators (Chapter 11);
- breaking down barriers between teachers, students and parents and using strategies such as service learning and informal learning to integrate educational locations more closely with local communities (Chapter 12).

Chapter 13 then presents three brief examples. More guidance can also be found on the website.

Teaching such as the ECDL, and even some approaches to information literacy, if they imply a simple replacement of the all-knowing teacher with the all-knowing computer or all-knowing Internet, tend towards a behaviourist approach to education. Behaviourism, while rarely present in a pure form, assumes that "learning" has occurred once a learner is able to apply the correct response to a given stimulus. This may be the right answer to a question; or the right response to a problem situation, such as knowing that one should instruct Excel in a particular sequence to summarise July's budget. These procedures are assumed to have objective value. What matters is the learner's ability to enact them when required.

The limitations of this approach, particularly in teaching ICT, have already been discussed. They amount to "sat nav teaching"; one may well get the job done through following instructions, but will have no idea how one got there. (See the anecdote about my Flash training course on the website.) The values inherent in the instructions are not open to scrutiny. The result may be passive acceptance of the "correct" way of thinking, which is not just a communicative problem but also potentially an instrumental one, as there will be no way to respond creatively if conditions temporarily or permanently change, and a different response is required. Or, there will be, at best, failure to see the relevance of the teaching; at worst, rejection and alienation in learners.

Guidance on how to instruct a computer – which buttons to press, if you like – will always form a part of ICT education. But this technical, procedural knowledge can be enriched in one of two ways. First, there can be an increase in the *depth* of "cognitive penetration" of the computer. Second, the techniques can be enfolded in an educational environment which helps learners construct an understanding of ICT as something embedded into that local environment: as a resource which has been developed over time, but which can also be rewritten by their use of it.

To an extent, cognitive penetration of ICT can be deepened by the sort of computer literacy education prescribed to schools through means such as the UK's National Curriculum. Exhortations to "teach word processing, not Word" – more, to explain that there are times when one's writing needs might be better served by web design, desktop publishing or other text handling applications – are examples of such an approach, and few writers on computer literacy education publicly say that less is required. This is the kind of teaching which allows students to construct the sort of well-grounded knowledge about ICT's technical capabilities that allows them to cope with upgrades to the software, and ultimately, to be information literate, selecting from resources according to their needs. However, despite considerable support for such teaching, both in academia and government, it remains the case that a prime global standard of computer "competency" – the ECDL – does not incorporate these values. And we have already noted that much other ICT teaching is low quality for various institutional reasons (lack of resources, lack of teacher training) and because of a failure to consider what romantic understanding can offer. The latter point will be expanded on below; the others dealt with in the next two chapters.

The educational value, especially, but not only, for children, of learning that the computer is something that can be *instructed* could be reasserted. Papert's promotion of LOGO is done for these reasons (1980). But now, in the environmental model, this can be connected to the idea of renewing the ecology of resources. Hence there is a production and dissemination element to learning about the computer. Producing and publishing a website might be one step, intended not just as a way for learners to demonstrate skills, but of approaching a *design problem*, fitting work into (or challenging, if appropriate) the conventions and culture of the medium, and thereby learning how to effectively *communicate* using ICT. Students could be encouraged to produce content that is not just on a random subject but on something relevant to them as an individual, group or community: a political issue, a shared community activity, a guide to a local environmental resource valued by the learners (a beauty spot, a building, a skate park). See Chapter 13 for an example.

Using "Web 2.0" resources such as wikis, blogs and social networking sites can allow learners to participate, and collaborate, in producing informational resources. These are valuable opportunities. But they alone do not amount to investigating the sociotechnical structures that underpin these tools. Exploiting these opportunities can, without such investigation, result in the negative corollary of increased participation in the public sphere – a deterioration in quality. First, published information must accord with objective measures of quality, like meeting accessibility and usability guidelines. Students must understand that common production tools (like Dreamweaver) are not programmed to automatically incorporate these values, and they need the technical knowledge to select a different tool from the ecology if necessary – better still, to correct the code "by hand". Similarly, certain social, cultural and economic values underpin many Web 2.0 sites, which can nowadays be considered design tools. Students should be encouraged to analyse the way that a resource like Wikipedia or Facebook has been shaped, and research differences between them. Here, for instance, they might consider the merits of allowing "anyone" to edit Wikipedia, and discover the (mostly unmentioned) role of the volunteers who are engaged in a constant supervision of updates to repair vandalism and indicate where an entry is in need of referencing. Learners might also consider the consequences of Facebook asserting certain usage rights over material placed there[1].

Incorporating into this inquiry a *transformative* element expands the idea of learner-generated content into learner-generated *contexts* (see *http://www.learnergeneratedcontexts.net/* (last acccessed 15 August 2008)). Learners do not have to just accept the ICT configuration with which they are presented and the sociotechnical systems that produced

---

[1] See *http://www.facebook.com/home.php#/terms.php* (last accessed 1 July 2008).

those configurations. They can be active (co-)constructors of the technological parameters of an environment. This does not have to go so far as to involve all students in computer programming, though interested and adept learners could be encouraged to participate in this involved way. At the very least, familiarising learners with open source software development will show that ICT resources can be constructed collaboratively, and one does not have to be a programmer to share insights developed through using ICT environments in a forum like *http://moodle.org*, thus helping to validate the knowledge and technology being constructed by this community. Knowing how to maintain one's own technological environment – how to upgrade an installation if necessary, keep it safe from viruses and other intrusions, locate and install useful freeware – is a sensible skill to possess in the information age; and just one of many ways in which the health and sustainability of informational environments can be improved. Learning about the wider context through which ICT is produced, and gaining experience about this through participation, also requires considering the negative side of ICT. Problems with "open systems", trolling, phishing, safety online etc. cannot be ignored, but need *discussing*, and coping strategies analysed and selected by individuals and groups according to their needs. These many possibilities spread through the range of computer literacy education.

However, the organisational contexts into which many learners will graduate – which, as consumers of educational products and powerful influences in the modern world, have considerable influence over educational outcomes – are often not places in which they are expected to demonstrate flexibility and self generation of context. Here we see the contrast between the *cognitive penetration* of technology – *all* users able to embed their values into the technologies they use – and the *cognitive separation* which characterises many organisations. This produces exclusionary sociotechnical systems in which users do not have the abilities to – and are not expected to – understand, and thus co-construct. This applies at all levels up to the major judicial and policy decisions that shape the ICT infrastructure. The human rights violation that is widespread and compulsory surveillance of all citizens by governments; attempts to institute alternative networks in which the principle of "net neutrality" no longer applies[2]; these decisions are also remote from public scrutiny, but their impact on our everyday lives can

[2] E.g. *http://www.theregister.co.uk/2007/06/22/bush_government_net_neutrality/* (last accessed 24 August 2008).

and must be at least revealed, with reference to objectively valuable academic research into their effects, wherever possible.

All the above asserts the value of *creativity* in understanding new technological possibilities. Levine's justification for involving his students in the creation of "public goods using the new digital media" was that "...we hope that their direct experiences with creativity will make them skilled and independent judges of the policies that govern the new media" (in Hess and Ostrom, 2007: pp. 254–5). It is through *use* that technologies can be rewritten. Active use – meaning, not just using tools assigned beforehand, but selecting appropriate ones from a wider ecology of resources – and information production, on terms that as far as possible are developed by the learners rather than assigned to them, are essential teaching strategies. Without them, education cannot hope to produce even the kind of "active users" sought by the system – and certainly not the genuinely active user who can put their skills, and these other tools, to use in sustaining the lifeworld.

From 1999–2005, I worked at the University of Leeds, UK, on a programme called ACOM. This stood for "Computing for All" and, basically, delivered computer literacy education to undergraduates. Our students were drawn from all other subject areas. Though, formally, we worked under the School of Computing, the backgrounds of most ACOM staff were non-technical: we came from other disciplines such as physics, the history of science or (in my case) politics. Over time (mainly prior to my arrival), ACOM developed a mode of teaching that was narrative-led, based around developing not just technical skills in students, but a wider understanding of the place of ICT in their studies and in society generally. The question was not just what ICT could do, but what it could do *for individuals*. We wrote a couple of papers about our efforts, one by Reffell and Whitworth (2002) and another by me alone (Whitworth, 2005), which you can read, in full, on the website. With each, I hope you can see the similarities between what we suggested then, and the strategies described above.

At that time I had not read Egan's *Romantic Understanding*, but with hindsight I can see the similarities between his approach and what ACOM did. I recount it here for two reasons. First, to suggest that we managed to substantially incorporate the use of the teaching device that is the *narrative* to help students construct their own image of how ICT could help them, a story that would be different for each student. We used these stories to show how technology had been socially shaped, how this process influenced what was possible with ICT, and how the use of ICT would in turn shape future environments. (See the excerpt from a course handbook on the website.) Second, I bring up the story as another instance of my using the narrative device in this book, which is itself an informational resource. I have used story and history here for the same reasons as in ACOM, but also to personalise the account, to show you how I am also full of subjective perspectives and values, and to illuminate how my beliefs are influenced by them as well as by my understanding of the other thinkers I have used as resources, like Vernadsky, Egan, Habermas and Blaug. In a story like the one about me and the Sinclair ZX Spectrum – described both in these pages and through the film on the website, two ways of using information to communicate a similar message – both motivations combine. My intention is to show how different educational relationships to ICT were *possible* – not necessarily "better", and certainly not objectively proven to be a more worthwhile way of engaging with ICT. But by making you aware of the possibility, I have provided resources you could draw on in the future to make your own assessment of the role of ICT in your life.

This kind of approach, in teaching ICT, has been suggested before, of course, but there is no harm in reasserting its value. Beyond our ACOM papers, the chapter by Cunningham (in McFarlane, 2007: pp. 63–77) outlines it well, and complements Egan's more general suggestions. Cunningham (p. 71) points out that a knowledge of history teaches students "to be aware of, and how to recognise, the evidence of the past in their own environment", and is contributed to by the study of artefacts. These insights support the wider project that is humanities teaching, which (p. 65):

> ...seek[s] to understand aspects of the society and environment in which... [we] live, from the immediate family and local neighbourhood to the international and global context of human and physical geography. All are characterised by questions of value as well as of fact....

Study of the wider social impact of a technology will always lag behind the introduction of the technology itself; but rather than waiting for enlightenment to come down to them from the (positivist) social science establishment, students could study the impact of ICT on *their own* social beings. As with other ubiquitous technologies, such study lifts the object into conscious awareness, "making the familiar strange" (see this chapter's header quote) and therefore an object for rational inquiry. What, then, is the impact of Facebook, or MSN, or CCTV surveillance, or the mobile phone, or other aspects of our technological environment on learners personally: on how they work, study, socialise, and, especially, filter information?

To properly answer such questions requires critical thinking and reflection, skills that are far from widespread in teachers or learners: the next chapter goes into more detail here. But with younger children, or others for whom embedding critical reflection into the learning environment is, for one reason or another, inappropriate, incorporating the romantic element into teaching may help. As well as the narrative historical approach, Egan suggests other strategies to stimulate the interest of learners and help them construct knowledge. Egan believes that mathematics, science and technology should all be taught not by starting with abstract classification systems and logical schemes but through *stories*:

> ...the technical manipulations of... these areas, that can seem so stark and meaningless to students, can be given a human and meaningful context by showing each new manipulation in the lives and purposes and social activities of its initial inventors (Egan, 1990: p. 243).

Experts could be brought in to classes to unpick these otherwise familiar technologies, and convey a sense of wonder about how they work (Egan, 1990: p. 228), helping regain some cognitive penetration of the technology, rather than separation. Adults and children alike would doubtless have many questions about how these technologies worked and (at a more sophisticated level) what values and knowledge went into their development. Levine reminds us (in Hess and Ostrom, 2007: p. 252) that:

> The early web had the feel of a commons – in part – because one could always see how a site had been constructed and freely imitate its technical features. These features were public goods.

Subsequent developments, however, have increasingly concealed these features, and thus the technology's history. Work with experts in the field, self exploration, or the guidance of a skilled teacher, can help learners lift these values back into conscious awareness.

This may seem a lot to ask of teachers who already treat the technological sphere with trepidation. Egan says (1990: pp. 166–7):

> Students' imaginations tend to be more readily engaged by materials that are organised and presented so that they not only convey information but also involve students affectively or emotionally.... Obviously teachers can best stimulate imagination by first identifying what they themselves find affectively engaging about the topic at hand. Indeed, this seems to me a first essential. If teachers cannot locate in themselves an affective response to the material, then they have little hope of being able to engage students in it.

Improving the quality of teaching ICT is not, however, just a matter of exhorting teachers to do so. There are many institutional blocks on this kind of teaching. Lack of resources for ICT education, and a shallow institutional support framework, is part of the problem but more intransigent is the impact of colonisation. All these issues can, however, be potentially addressed by moving beyond just a romantic, narrative-based approach and into one which incorporates the idea of *transformative learning*. This better reflects the influence of critical social science – and, crucially, starts to break down the barriers between learners and teachers, both of whom can start to co-construct the technological informational filters which are embedded into their environments. This is the subject of the next chapter.

From problem-based learning to transformative learning

> No one can attain to truth by himself. Only by laying stone on stone with the co-operation of all, by the millions of generations from our forefather Adam to our own times, is that temple reared... Bazdéev in *War and Peace* (Book V, Chapter II)

The desired destination is education to inspire critical thinking in both learners and teachers, but this is not easy achieve thanks to mitigating factors (for all these see Mezirow, 1990):

- The mind develops in stages, and critical thinking represents a later stage in intellectual development. Children cannot be expected to have reached this stage, nor even all adults.

- Questioning basic assumptions has psychological and organisational risks. Both our individual and our organisational cognitive structures therefore work to retard the need for it.

- As a result of both the previous points, the intellectual structures in most people's minds, created by prior experiences of education, are underprepared for the demands of critical thinking.

However, there are steps that can be made towards full critical enquiry. It is this chapter's task to describe them. As ever, space is limited; I draw here particularly on Jonassen *et al.* (2003); Carr and Kemmis (1986); Mezirow (1990) and Kahn and Baume (2003). Other resources can be found on the website.

The first step is into *problem-based learning* (hereafter, PBL). Here, the production of information, and the use of ICT, is not an end-in-itself. Rather, information and technology are part of the ecology of resources which learners use to solve a problem. Thus, these resources are potentially transformed through addressing the problem. I have already mentioned, in Chapter 6, that production work in media such as video, the World-Wide Web, student-created WebQuests and so on (work of the sort called for in the previous chapter), involves addressing *design problems*. In a wider sense, PBL embraces the idea of *research*, and covers a great number of educational "bases" (Jonassen *et al.*, 2003: p. 54). Whitebread (in McFarlane, 1997: p. 17) says that PBL:

> ...is a complex intellectual process involving the co-ordination of a range of demanding and interrelated skills. These skills include:
>
> - understanding and representing the problem (including identifying what kinds of information are relevant to its solution);
> - gathering and organising relevant information;
> - constructing and managing a plan of action, or a strategy;
> - reasoning, hypothesis-testing and decision-making;
> - using various problem-solving tools.

The potential role of ICT should be apparent, but it is also clear that information and ICT are not *all*-important. The ICT element of a problem solution would be only a part of a wider sociotechnical system that included students (individually, or in groups), teachers, and the problem environment itself, as solutions could not be properly evaluated without being tested somehow. PBL is complex because of the need to appreciate the problem environment as dynamic, changed by the process of addressing the problem. It requires an ability to plan ahead, itself a complex skill that requires the building of mental models of a situation (Whitebread, in McFarlane, 1997: p. 22), and the integration of existing knowledge with new situations (p. 25). All in all, problem solving is one of the intellectual skills with which learners are now expected to graduate from school or college, and thus be prepared for the information society (p. 37). As the US Partnership for 21st Century Skills document (2004: 12) suggests; in the dynamic modern environment, one needs the skills of "knowing what to do when you don't know what to do": not just following instructions then, but solving problems.

"Problems" come in many forms, and the role of information and technology in solving, or at least understanding, the problem varies accordingly. Jonassen *et al.* (2003: pp. 21–4) list 11 types (the examples are mostly theirs, but some are mine):

- logical problems (the Tower of Hanoi);

- algorithmic problems (solving an algebraic equation);

- story problems (like a logic or algorithmic problem, but obscured by a story, e.g. "a train leaves York at 80 mph while 60 miles away another leaves in the opposite direction at 40 mph..." etc.);

- decision-making problems (which usually have a known, limited number of solutions, such as "Which health plan should we select?");

- troubleshooting problems (what's gone wrong with this system? The assumption is that once the problem is found, there will only be one possible solution; "If the problem is this, do that");

- diagnosis/solution problems (similar, but the efficacy of the proposed solution is not necessarily clear: e.g. a medical diagnosis);

- tactical/strategic performance problems (real-time, complex decision making without time to stop and analyse – flying a plane, playing quarterback, etc.);

- case/systems analysis problems (where it is not even clear whether there is a problem; commonly found in professional situations and requiring complex analysis from several fields of study);

- design problems (how to design a product, a graphic work, a computer interface; there are, in principle, an infinity of possible solutions and the problem lies in finding one that meets various criteria simultaneously, fitting into the physical and social constraints of the environment for which it is designed);

- dilemmas (ethical, political or moral problems in which there is likely no solution acceptable to everyone).

Clearly there is a wide range and we cannot say that PBL is a clearly defined teaching strategy. For some, particularly towards the top, information in the strictest sense is not required, but mostly, information is a vital resource for problem solvers. What is needed is a way of filtering potentially useful information, with filtering strategies developed according to the specific problem context. Only with the logic, algorithmic and story problems is there a sense that all relevant information is supplied in advance. With the rest, relevant information must be *found*, and *valued*, then *put to use* to solve the problem. This is clearly the territory of IL.

PBL can be approached in a relatively instrumental way, with learners asked to find the "best" solution, measured in terms of efficiency, cost and so on. Judgment would be passed on both the efficiency of the final solution, and the process through which it was reached. This sort of problem solving has its uses, of course. But if it is the *only* type of PBL to which learners are exposed, there can be no development of critical thinking in students – an argument that develops directly from the principle of critical social science.

At the very least, there should be an *iterative* aspect to PBL. Even with convergent problems, the "right" solution may not be found first time. The good problem solver would ideally evaluate their experience and use the knowledge gained to try once more for the optimum solution. But many problems have divergent solutions. In a dynamic environment, no solution can be assumed to be a permanent one. Problems in the social sphere are what Kitchener and King (in Mezirow, 1990) call *ill structured*. They create conditions of *ambiguity* within organisations in which decision making is often not a matter of systematic analysis and objective justification, but of bargaining, negotiation and oversight, when a solution is found even though no decision has really been taken about it. (See March and Olsen, 1976. They observe, incidentally, that because of the nature of their core activity – teaching and learning – education organisations are particularly prone to ambiguity.) There should be continual review of the solution's effectiveness; this is single-loop learning, and accords with the suggestions of Habermas (1993), that agreements reached through a communicatively-rational process must continuously be justified. *Double*-loop learning would also evaluate the *process* through which the solution was reached, questioning the basic assumptions that drove the search for a problem solution, the values, ways of thinking, technological tools and other information filters which came into play. Any defects found in the activity system would, ideally, then be rectified by a redesign. Were that redesign to be undertaken from "above" or "outside" the system, it would risk being colonising, but were the redesign undertaken by those who were within the system – who were learning about the processes by which they were constructing new knowledge, and designing new information processing systems as they did so – this would be communicatively rational. System redesign in this case may lead to changes in the technologies being used: this would accord with notions of learner-generated contexts, as proposed in the previous chapter. It may also result in pressures to democratise decision making whether within the group or in other communities with which the group or its members interact. It would, in short, be critical.

This sort of problem solving is known as *action learning*, and I will return to it shortly. Beforehand, it must be observed that PBL is demanding for both learners and teachers, more so than other kinds of learning (though it is a valid argument that it is precisely because of these added demands that it is more likely to produce higher-quality resources: see the second example in Chapter 13). The more advanced and critical forms may not be appropriate for children, or even adults who have not reached a particular stage in developing the "tools for thinking" which reside in their minds or communities. Kitchener and King (1981: see also their chapter in Mezirow, 1990) describe seven stages of judgment, from the "what I see is true" stage in very young children, through an acknowledgement that other people may see different truths (including the concept of *authority*, that one can be told what is true); through stages of uncertainty, recognition that knowledge can be context-based, and finally, where learners understand that knowledge can be constructed through a process of critical inquiry. Kitchener and King's research suggested that:

> ...the majority [of learners] did not typically use reasoning higher than Stage Four prior to age 24. In other words, educators should not assume that younger students can either understand or emulate what Dewey described as reflective thinking.

Contrasting perspectives on a problem can be confusing for learners. Anyone encountering a problem for the first time will need guidance about its origins and, possibly, the more general field in which the problem is located (e.g. engineering, economics, town planning). If the filtering strategies used, suggested or imposed by "authorities" in the field are to be critically evaluated, these higher forms of understanding provide more effective intellectual tools with which to do so, but they are not immediately available to everyone, even the otherwise well-educated.

Indeed, Kirschner *et al.* (2006) provocatively argue that without adequate guidance from teachers, PBL might end up retarding learning, not promoting it. Teachers, too, must be flexible. The role of the teacher in such project or research work is not fixed. It may be that learners need help forming an initial goal or even seeing the problem. Learners may lack metacognitive skills such as note-taking and listening, which are essential resources for problem solving (McFarlane, 1997: p. 116). Some situations will require learners to read relevant literature, gather data or agree on the next course of action. The steps involved will not be the same each time as they will depend on both the problem and the learners;

both on their initial state and then, as problem and learners encounter each other, on how the resources in the environment evolve. This is, in effect, the principle of *scaffolding*, helping move learners from their current state into the "zone of proximal development" (Vygotsky, 1978): what it needs is a flexible environment, in which there are a range of informational and technological resources from which both learners and teachers can select as appropriate.

Amongst these resources is patience, for it can be frustrating, particularly (but not only) for children, to have even one failed attempt at reaching a solution. Going back and starting again, particularly if there is a need to revise basic procedures, can be dispiriting. Learners may struggle to even define the first steps to be taken, and see the whole problem as simply too large. In real-life problems, solutions may be demanded before there has been the time to review and restart. Nevertheless, Whitebread (in McFarlane, 1997), and the first example in Chapter 13 below, suggest that even fairly complex problem-solving tasks can be given to – and constructed by – relatively young learners. Such tasks also fit comfortably within the typical National Curriculum, and/or help instil in learners the kind of flexible, creative thinking often demanded by government and industry.

This last point, however, immediately reminds us of the organisational and institutional restrictions which apply to education: its colonisation, in other words. The filters we apply and the infrastructure from which we select our resources have, largely, been imposed, not constructed in a spirit of collaboration. Let us return to two points mentioned above, which together suggest conditions which must exist for PBL to be decolonising:

- members of an activity system should engage in double-loop learning, reviewing not only the results of decisions but the processes behind them: and, if necessary, redesigning the system from within;
- not all individuals possess the tools for thinking that complex decision making requires.

One answer to the latter problem is to value not individual PBL but *the group's*. This is central to Wenger's "Social Theory of Learning" (Wenger, 1998). Organisations, as Chapter 9 described, can perform tasks impossible for individuals, because of either their physical scale – one person cannot build a tall building, but some form of organisation and technology would allow many to do so – or because the task is innately social, e.g. it is not possible for one person to play a football match however much he runs around. But organisation also allows us to address problems that individuals cannot tackle because of their *complexity*. Of course, the recognition that we can share knowledge, values, skills and information and, thereby, address problems is the whole basis of politics, many techniques of which have been tried over the last 3,000 years, some more decolonising than others. Using organisations to address complex social problems can impose the necessary "tools for thinking" by imposing cognitive schema developed externally, and as a result (as Fay noted), negate politics. But organisations can also contain conditions in which double-loop learning can flourish.

Because of the cognitive separation to which all organisations are prone, no problem solution imposed from outside will be fully sensitive to the needs of communities and their context, unless there is active participation by the community in the solution's design, evaluation and review. This insight has historically driven the idea of *participatory design*, and in some places and times – notably Scandinavia since the 1970s – this has substantially contributed to the shaping of organisational environments, to those nations' credit (see Bjerknes *et al.*, 1987; Bijker, 1989; Schuler and Namioka, 1993). But a declared adherence to participatory design can easily collapse into mere sham "consultation", particularly if vested interests are challenged by the proposed solutions (Ehn and Kyng, in Bjerknes *et al.*, 1987: pp. 17–57). Participatory design is therefore just as subject to colonisation as other design strategies, though its existence, and the research which has been undertaken into its application, remain valuable resources for members of any organisation.

Educationalists work in environments with certain special characteristics, and what "participation" means in a school or university is therefore distinctive. Education is a highly ambiguous activity (March and Cohen, 1976). That is why, over time, educational organisations – universities, at least (schools have always been more tightly-controlled by governments) – have become structured in particular ways. They are loosely coupled (Weick, 1976), meaning that the component parts are relatively separate from each other. The "technostructure" – the parts of an organisation mandated to engage in instrumental analysis, and the design of sociotechnical solutions, which control the main body of workers (Mintzberg, 1989: p. 98) – has been historically weak. The "professional core" (academics) were therefore relatively autonomous. This underlies the principle of academic freedom, in fact. However, colonisation explains the increasing control asserted over academics' working lives across the world, whether by legal restrictions, market imperatives, or technologies. Systems such as Blackboard and, to a lesser extent (because of its open source nature), Moodle, cause certain values to be firmly embedded into learning environments in ways they could not be when all that was "on stage" was a stick of chalk and a blackboard (with a small B)[1].

Many suggest that leaving those times behind was nothing but good, and in general I agree, with one strict condition: that educational problems cannot be critically addressed if the members of the activity system cannot review the *process* through which solutions are reached. That now requires critical awareness of ICT, which permeates our schools and universities not just in classrooms but in information management, administration, budgeting and research.

I do not, necessarily, suggest a return to the "Dartmouth Model" of professional development around ICT described in Chapter 4, but I certainly hold it up as an example of a participatory approach different from that instituted in many other educational organisations. Doubtless the environment, internal and external, in which Dartmouth faculty exist in 2008 has changed, just as it has for academics everywhere else. Nevertheless, it is the argument of Wenger (1998) that this kind of work by *communities of practice* goes on under the surface of any organisation whether mandated by a technostructure or not. It is also the argument of Carr and Kemmis (1986) and other writers on action research and action learning that, for good professional practice in education, it *must* take place. The role of professional development in education, particularly in terms of how it relates to ICT and organisational information processing, is therefore worth discussing in more detail.

"Professionalism" involves continuous updates of the information filtering strategies applied both by individual professionals and their associations. This is the whole point of Continuing Professional Development (CPD). No one would want to be treated by a surgeon who had not kept current with developments in their field since graduating in 1986. No one wants their new house pulling down because it failed to meet environmental planning regulations. And no one, I imagine, would want to be taught by someone unfamiliar with recent literature in their subject. Increasingly this last group of professionals – professional educators – are also being urged to change their teaching techniques in view of the opportunities arising from new ICTs.

---

[1] Having said that, the architecture of teaching space is definitely an example of embedding into the environment ideas of what education should be. The design of the typical lecture theatre is a powerful constraint on the kind of teaching and learning that can comfortably take place within it.

It is the argument of Carr and Kemmis (1986) that CPD for educators cannot depend only on objective insights from the "educational science" establishment. These have value, as does any other kind of objectively developed solution – but only as a *potential* resource in the ecology, from which teachers should select according to their needs and the educational problem they need to solve. Such problems range through the scale listed above (except perhaps the first three). It is through such selection that teachers develop implicit theories of how they do their job. This is the intention of action learning, which requires teachers to:

> ...understand and formulate problems through continual cycles of action (implementation of some sort) and reflection on, and in, action (to use terminology developed by Schön[2]...). In this way, people identify their practical reasoning and begin to build personal theories of action. (Mezirow, 1990: p. 43).

These personal theories of action then serve as filtering criteria. But developing these criteria also occurs at the group level. Groups can collectively scrutinise the assumptions that underpin their activity system(s), and thereby address issues of larger scale and complexity than individuals, such as the design of ICT. Through such enquiry, learners become "social environmentalists" (Mezirow, in Welton, 1995: p. 60), collectively maintaing and nurturing the ecology of resources from which they can draw in future activity. Teachers thereby develop "critical communities of enquirers into teaching" (Carr and Kemmis, 1986: p. 40). Indeed, for Carr and Kemmis, this *set of values and the processes that maintain them* are the defining characteristics of professionalism in education: as distinct from other credentials like qualifications, government-granted licenses to teach, and so on (see Mezirow, 1990: p. 363).

In CPD, as with other forms of learning in the information society, there is less a need to focus on retrieving information, but more on filtering, understanding, adapting and communicating it. Information literacy is as important a skill in CPD as anywhere else; so is becoming an "active user" of ICT, not a passive consumer whether at an individual, community or whole-institution level. CPD activities must therefore reflect on the contribution of ICT and other forms of information filtering to the activities of participants. This links with concerns to improve "knowledge management" and, thereby, organisational effectiveness

---

[2] See his book *The Reflective Practitioner* (1991), which I do not refer to in any detail but which is well worth reading.

(e.g. Senn Breivik and Gee, 2006: p. 119*ff*). This is a concern which can be easily colonised, but at the same time, communities of practice can use these enquiries to improve their own understanding of the environment, in a decolonising way. They can enquire not just into their practice, but into the assumptions that underlie the practice, and how these have become embedded into the informational resources they use[3].

In an otherwise good book, the chapter by Fallows and Bhanot (Kahn and Baume, 2003: pp. 116–27) is a disappointment, and for me sums up how far behind we are with instilling the critical enquiry of ICT into educational CPD. Throughout the chapter, ICT is taken as a given, a technologically-determined change sweeping through HE to which teachers must respond. It is the staff developer's role to "'walk the talk' in support of the initiative" (Kahn and Baume, 2003: p. 124): they may be

> ...called upon to act as champion in support of an ICT-based strategy; again the emphasis must be on the educational capabilities of the system (what it will offer) rather than the technical (how to do it) aspects (p. 125).

What, however, of the question *why*? What of the sense that *staff* may change ICT strategy, and ICT itself, through their use and subsequent understanding of it? Both are necessary questions if there is to be an *ongoing* assessment of the contribution of ICT to individual working lives, communities of practice, and the organisation at the strategic level (though here the impact of ICT on staff, while clearly a variable for consideration, will more likely be addressed by social engineering). There is certainly little in Fallows and Bhanot relevant to the ultimate goal of CPD: *transformative learning* (see Mezirow, 1990). Transformative learning represents a continuous culture of enquiry by members of an activity system into their own work. Problems are investigated, solutions designed and implemented, evaluations made and lessons learnt in an

---

[3] The products of action research (one process, but not the only one, involved in action learning) are often published. Journals such as the *British Journal of Educational Technology* frequently contain papers which discuss the effects of ICT in teaching using enquiries undertaken by teachers into their professional practice. This act of publication is one way of contributing insights to the store of knowledge, but such insights still have to be re-justified in other contexts, to which they may not be appropriate. This is why action research, as a method for gaining understanding about the world, struggles to achieve the kind of objective value that would give it the status of "science". Action research is rarely falsifiable, for example: a key principle of scientific method. Nevertheless, action research is a valuable tool for any educator, and further reading is suggested: particularly Carr and Kemmis (1986) and Reason and Bradbury (2001). See also the website.

ongoing cycle. Transformative learning can be guided by teachers, whether these be trained facilitators, members of the community with expertise in certain specific areas, or outside experts: but this is best undertaken if these guides are themselves "role models" of self reflection and communicative rationality (not hand-picked "champions" of a singular, system perspective). Transformative learning:

> ...is not a private affair involving information processing; it is interactive and intersubjective from start to finish. (Mezirow, 1990: p. 364)

And from Mezirow again (p. 375):

> Learning is grounded in the very nature of human communication. Becoming reflective of the content, process and especially the premises of one's prior learning is central to cognition for survival in modern societies. It is the way we control our experiences rather than be controlled by them.

I suggest it is also the way we control our technologies too: thereby, our information filtering strategies, and thus combat information obesity in professional life.

Precisely because it is about facilitating changes in practice and altering ways of thinking and understanding (Kahn and Baume, 2003: pp. 10–11), staff development is a contested idea. What "development" means to an individual teacher, or a community of practice, will differ from what it means to a technostructure which has bought a new £500,000 course management system and wants a return on this investment. A great deal of "staff development" takes place in education, but as Fallows and Bhanot exemplify, much is system-led. More decolonising activities tend to be left to informal communities of practice and/or take place "under the radar" of the institution, as individuals make constant, ongoing adjustments to their working practice (see Chapter 13, and also the idea of "hidden learning environments": du Boulay *et al.*, 2007: 26).

This is not to dismiss such activity. Although it cannot be truly transformative, transformation can never happen without the:

> ...nine-tenths of the iceberg – unseen by the traveller... those critical elements of organisational learning that inform preparation,

implementation and review of transformative change cycles (Roche, in Kahn and Baume, 2003: p. 172)

But because of the challenge transformation poses to existing organisational structures, only rarely are formal institutional spaces created with conditions in which "critical elements of organisational learning" can flourish. This is exactly why participatory design efforts so often fall short and/or collapse into sham consultations. Cognitive separation is thereby maintained within the organisation. Individuals and small communities of practice can remain cocooned in a kind of microculture, "robbed of the power to synthesise" (Habermas, 1987: p. 355).

Dissemination – the transfer of new insights – implies implementation and change, if it is not to be just a passive "scattering" of information which will, in all likelihood, be filtered out by others as irrelevant (see King, in Kahn and Baume, 2003: pp. 96–115). But dissemination of solutions is not something the education sector is historically good at. Mavin and Cavaleri called higher education "the last place to find organisational learning" (2004: 287). Writers on educational management, like Bates (2000), also bemoan it with a sense of frustration. Yet when we look at the institutional constraints placed on organisational learning in education, it is not surprising. Lack of resources, lack of training, constraints like National Curricula, and a fundamental parochialism in education (partly explained by its sensitivity to context; see the next chapter) all work against disseminating solutions through the community. In that respect, the colonisation of educational practice is quite far advanced. Yet even on its own terms, there is a system-level recognition that the use of ICT throughout education is poor, and information obesity is now widespread, suggested by the lack of creativity and flexibility in the products of education. But this criticism is one the system *must direct at itself* – yet any system based on the principles of instrumental rationality finds double-loop learning impossible by definition. If the appeal to develop a transformative learning model around ICT and information filters is not to lead into a dead end similar to that faced by earlier critical theorists, it is therefore necessary to make one further step into the lifeworld – and break down the barriers between the role of "teacher" and the other members of the community. That is the subject of the next chapter.

Connecting learners and teachers to the community

"Let's put it on the Internet!"
"No, we have to reach people whose opinions actually matter!".
(From *The Simpsons*)

Formal education has traditionally been relatively contained. The standard model is of a group of learners in a particular space with one (or at most two or three) teachers: the "class", in other words. One "goes to" school or university, traditionally spending a considerable amount of time there, to the exclusion of other work.

This stereotype, however, has never been accurate; if there are barriers around "formal" education, they are relatively permeable ones. CPD, discussed in the last chapter, shows that formal learning can take place throughout a working life. Adult education and part-time post- or undergraduate students have always formed a considerable percentage of the overall student population. Even full-time undergraduates are likely to be studying and working simultaneously.

On top of these trends, ICT gives easy access to images, sounds, opinions, beliefs and events happening elsewhere, anywhere, all of which could penetrate the classroom. Many problems are global in scale, requiring value shifts and legal frameworks that may come to affect literally every living person. The globalised nature of the information society and its economy result in calls for yet more "literacies" or "skills" which are considered appropriate for this new non-parochial stage, and more concerns that the next generation of students risk missing out because education is not up to the task[1]. Yet "the class" remains our standard model of education.

---

[1] Literally on the morning I first typed this page the following headline appeared: "*Call for better 'global literacy*: A large slice of England's children may be left 'globally illiterate'

In some ways the formal education system may be waking up to the usefulness of the world beyond the classroom walls. Starting with the 2006 Education Act and now with the release of a new secondary curriculum in 2008, UK education law has begun to recognise the value of out-of-school learning (or what Baker *et al.* (2001) call *shadow education*), coupled with a more flexible approach to the curriculum and greater use of project work. As Lepkowska writes in a *Guardian* special supplement on this issue (17 June 2008):

> Self-awareness by young people of how they learn best will be crucial to the success of the government's agenda of personalising education. A major development in this agenda will be the introduction of the revised secondary curriculum from this September [2008], which will place every subject in the context of its relevance to young people's lives. Teachers will be given greater flexibility about how they teach, and they will need to tailor teaching, as well as track progress and set targets for individual pupils. More curriculum time will be devoted to learning activities outside the school gates. For students, there will be increased opportunities to research and write projects as part of their formal qualifications.... The new [age] 14–19 diplomas will include work experience and practical strands of achievement, as well as academic.

There are some encouraging promises here. At the same time, UK-based teachers and other stakeholders may view this against the background of drastic cuts in funding for adult education and developments like MIAP which appear to be doing their best to "formalise informal education" by simultaneously encouraging students to go "outside the school gates" for learning but then making it very clear which sort of "outside" learning is approved of and which is not. But as this is not meant to be a book about the UK situation, I should move on. (See the conclusion, however.)

What this brief discussion does suggest is that there has always been some kind of recognition of the role of *civil society* in education and indeed vice versa. Civil society is that part of the environment which is fuelled by social capital. In an organisational sense it is made up of community groups, sports clubs, charities, babysitting circles, groups of

---

because schools are not educating them about the wider world, a charity claims...". See *http://news.bbc.co.uk/1/hi/education/7488417.stm* (last accesed 4 July 2008).

friends and the many other associations that make up our community lives but which are not profit-driven nor, often, formally constituted in law (though this requirement is increasingly asserted by the system). It is clear that any educational strategy which makes claims to be holistic – and the environmental model clearly does promote a holistic view – must account for what informal learning and civil society can offer. I discuss two main consequences in this chapter:

- they can increase the skill set available to both teachers and learners;
- they can connect places of learning, teachers and learners back to the local community and help renew social capital and informational resources drawn on by that community: they thus give rise to *active citizenship*.

In the previous chapter I mentioned Wenger's "Social Theory of Learning" which suggested that groups of learners could be more than the sum of their parts. If certain ways of thinking, information storage and processing, activity and decision making are not possible for individuals acting alone, they can still be manifested in communities. This idea supports the argument of this chapter, and indeed the whole principle of organisation. The *history* of organisation, however, is the history of society itself, characterised by an imbalance between the principles of instrumental rationality and of communicative rationality. The reach of instrumentality has extended inappropriately into the lifeworld. One organisational consequence of this is hierarchism, and one of the real-world results of hierarchism is a way of designing organisations that draws clear boundaries around divisions of labour, and the rules which define how different roles can act; and can therefore access and filter the information they need to perform their tasks.

This tendency to put roles, information and activity into specific compartments affects how we organise education, as much as other activities. Teachers' and students' roles are defined legally, and culturally, meaning that assumptions about the role affect our understanding of what should – and does – occur in an educational setting. In other words, these expectations are information filters, based largely on the reification bias. There is also a power relationship built into any educational environment in which student performance is formally assessed, whether teacher-over-student (if the teacher assigns grades directly), and/or, through the examination and qualification system, system-over-student and system-over-teacher. Around these divisions and tensions there develop separate cognitive cultures in education, in which "information" and "technology" acquire different meanings and uses: differences between teachers and students, between home and school, between education, the workplace and community life.

For some time, this has been seen considered an educational problem:

> Years ago, John Dewey commented on the dangers of a complex society that relies on schools and classrooms to convey essential knowledge and tools to its youth:
>
> > "As societies become more complex in structure and resources, the need for formal teaching and learning increases. As formal teaching and training grows, there's a danger of creating an undesirable split between the experience gained in direct association and what is acquired in school...."
>
> The schism between real world experience and school learning is a serious concern. (Jonassen *et al.*, 2003: p. 70).

Jonassen *et al.* (p. 71) give an example of how we have come to define education in different and often incompatible ways across this divide:

> In the real world, when people need to learn something, they usually do not remove themselves from their normal situations and force themselves into sterile rooms to listen to lectures on formal principles about what they are doing. Rather, they tend to form work groups (practice communities), assign roles, teach and support each other, and develop identities that are defined by the roles they play in support of the group.

In school and university, however, collaboration is often discouraged: at best, ways are found to assess group work that do not disadvantage the individual. In addition, the work performed in schools and universities is frequently separated from the needs of the environment outside the gates: the local community. Of course, we cannot focus teaching only on matters of local relevance (though there is a good case for the argument that *all* subjects can be seen to have some kind of local relevance, if so presented); but the local community is only infrequently recognised as a vital source of informational and technological resources for the classroom.

Jonassen *et al.* (2003: p. 70) do claim that:

> ...technologies of various kinds can serve as bridges between schools and students' outside experiences, if they are used in the right way within a supportive context.

Tanner (in Kennewell *et al.*, 2003: pp. 15–16) is more specific about how these bridges can be built, then crossed, saying that a school's ICT co-ordinator should be aware of:

> ...the curriculum outside school and the resources that exist in pupils' homes and in the community that may be used in the service of education....

And in the same book, Parkinson (p. 171) says that the ICT teacher or co-ordinator should:

> ...nurture links between the home and the school, helping parents in homes with computers to develop the ICT knowledge of their children and supporting those who do not have a computer by ensuring that useful information is available about the resources in the community or provided by the school out of normal hours. Consider: (1) workshop evenings for parents; (2) after-school or lunchtime computer clubs; (3) producing a regular ICT newsletter giving news of what sorts of things the pupils are doing, achievements, news of updates of the school website, links with other schools, useful websites etc.

All are useful suggestions, though neither author quite sees that the relationship between school, home and the community is a two-way one. As well as asking how home- and community-based resources can service the school, we must also consider how the resources developed in the formal education sector can be used in the service of home and the community. (See also the Blacksburg Electronic Village project: Cohill and Kavanaugh, 1997.)

An example of this reciprocity would come through accepting the likelihood that, at least in affluent countries, the technical quality of ICT in most homes will always outstrip schools' (because of the pupil-computer ratio if nothing else). And, there will be pupils in any class who are as proficient with ICT as their teachers (McFarlane, 1997: p. 2): often in a general sense, and certainly with applications which pupils use frequently. Teachers who lack technical skills:

> ...can often be taught by the gurus in class who seem to know the answer to every question. The community thus is strengthened by its interdependencies – the teacher needs the class "techno-geeks",

just as the students need the direction and support of the teacher (Jonassen *et al.*, 2003: pp. 113–4).

This is a sensible response to the proliferation of ICTs both inside and outside schools. It may also fill many teachers with a sense of unease and even horror. Certainly it is something which directly challenges perceptions of what it means to fill the role of "teacher", particularly, but not only, when teaching children. But the interdependencies exist regardless and can be exploited to the benefit of everyone. Students, even young ones, form communities of practice within organisations which help them exchange information, "beneath the radar", regarding matters of importance. One could probably assume that communities of adult and professional learners would use their networks mostly to understand what the course is asking of them and how best to pass it. School and university communities will too, but as just one current in the wealth of learning they undertake about how to fit in socially, how to pursue avenues of interest that the school did not help them with, how to become a rock star, etc. My "geek clique" in the early 1980s was a clear example of this, and was one of many such communities about the school (including others I was part of: I didn't spend *all* my free time programming the ZX Spectrum, in case you were wondering).

It is when informal learning networks are *permitted* to disseminate the results of learning into the formal educational setting that we can say that a learner-generated context exists[2]. But there is another qualification needed; a significant one. Teachers, managers, technical support staff and others with formal educational responsibilities may be averse to students being allowed to bring whatever technology they liked into a classroom and use it as they wished. What about the distraction value, for the owners or their peers? What about the risk of computer viruses? What if the pedagogical value of the technology was unproven, or dubious? What about students who cannot afford such a technological aid? What about cheating and plagiarism? What of dumbing down? Counterknowledge? (See the thinking task on the website.)

---

[2] On reading a first draft of this book, Fred Garnett, formerly of BECTa (the British Educational Technology Agency), sent me plenty of feedback, which was gratefully received. Here, it is worth quoting him directly: "Interestingly the information learning patterns developed by UK online centres and community ICT centres... were often devalued at the accreditation stage as learners had to re-enter the formal system often at the lowest level of accreditation. ECDL became ubiquitous because it could draw down funding; this was the conundrum facing all community learning, it was often innovative and motivating, but to get funding, needed to drop the very processes that gave their non-formal learning value...".

The simple answer is this, and it effectively sums up the argument of this book. The quality of resources available in an environment is put at risk whenever a technology is accepted into it *uncritically*. The assumptions that underpin that technology – and, thus, will come to underpin the information filtering strategies that exist within that environment – will enter the activity system without scrutiny. The introduction of *any* technology into an educational situation should ideally be negotiated between teachers, learners and other stakeholders (parents, technical support) in a communicatively-rational way. The technology will then be shaped as a result of this negotiation and its ongoing review. This applies both to suggestions made "from below" (as a result of action learning and experimentation by teachers, students or others) and "from above" (as a result of instrumentally-rational calculations of value).

The influence of parents as stakeholders in education is often underestimated. Few examples exist of research which has specifically considered their contribution beyond that of voting on government (and sometimes, school) policy and of paying for it through taxes, fees, and buying ICT for the home (an exception being Luckin *et al.*, 2006, who involved parents, among other stakeholders, in the design of educational systems in a participatory way). The policy in the UK, US and similar countries is to give parents a role in their children's education, but in practice, as Walker (2008) observed, there is little sense that parents are exploiting these opportunities. Walker suggested this is, at least in part, due to a lack of IL skills in parents, who do not know how to access and evaluate the information they need to make informed choices about education; and thus to *learn* how their children's experience of education will affect the family, to observe these changes, and to influence the system if these changes are considered undesirable.

Parents are disempowered by the education system just as individual teachers are, even if the boundaries around their "legitimate" roles are drawn in different ways. Nor are there national or international "unions" of parents who can pool resources, gain power, and thus have some influence over the system. Yet the *educational* role of parents is clearly paramount. Feinstein and Symons (1999) call parenting "more important than schooling". Egan (1990: p. 277) states that a "romantic" approach to education in any subject may be more suited to the individual parent (or tutor) than the organised, constrained school setting. The environments of parents and children are not the same, but at least while children live at home they are closely interrelated, with emotional connections between the members that are rarely present in other shared environments.

I am not trying to present some idealised image of all families as mutually-supportive learning communities. Clearly there are dysfunctional families, isolated or deprived children, psychological and physical abuse, and many other failures in family lives. Even "normal, happy" family life can mask power relationships and emotional problems. Assumptions about normality run deep in the infrastructure and disadvantage otherwise healthy households which do not meet these norms, or create tensions between partners, parents and children about "who should do what". The very role of the family in a colonising, globalising world is also under threat, from commercialisation; government and corporate surveillance; multiculturalism; liberalism; a menu which commentators will select from according to their cognitive biases. These are issues of great significance for the general health of our society, but it is not my place to discuss them, unfortunately. Nevertheless the influence of parents and families over education is clear.

The separation of roles, encouraged by instrumentality and hierarchism, supports Habermas's observation that everyday consciousness becomes fragmented and robbed of its power to synthesise, as well as Shenk's model of separate microcultures developing throughout society. However, almost every person is a member of *multiple* communities, and their identity therefore a composite of multiple selves, each rooted in (slightly different) community support networks. A thinking task on the website will help you explore your own situation, but to illustrate, I count myself a member of the following *principal* communities, and can think of many other secondary ones:

- my immediate and extended family, including my in-laws;
- the local Hebden Bridge community;
- a lecturer at the University of Manchester; thus, a community of fellow employees, and the community of students and staff on my degree;
- the academic community with which I am aligned (studying educational technology and the management and organisation of education);
- a wider network of friends (though these are more like many separate, small communities);
- a supporter of Brighton & Hove Albion FC;
- the community of parents who send our children to a particular school.

I am a member of all these communities all the time, even if some lie
dormant for long periods (as with friends whom I see only rarely). In
various ways, they form the narratives with which I understand my
situations and through which I filter information. But connections can
appear between them at any point, then be exploited for educational
purposes. *Empathy* with someone – and thus, with their point of view –
means the humanisation of that person, increasing the chance that we
will find solutions to problems which are mutually beneficial. Cognitive
separation discourages such empathy. It encourages us to see the teacher
as just a teacher, the student as just a number, the parent as a stereotype
("pushy", "ignorant", "to blame"). But the teacher is often also a
parent. Certainly they will have been a child, and also a student, at some
point. Both will be members of the same community in some sense, that
of the school: many teachers are also residents in the local community.
(This is less likely with universities of course, precisely because of the
transience of students; however, see the discussion of "cyber service
learning" below for an expansion of this point.)

Of course, simply declaring that there should be more links between
teachers and parents is no different from governments writing it into
policy. When they do occur, the meeting of minds and values between
parents, teachers and administrators can be fraught, even if parents'
rights to contribute to school management are formalised (see Wodak's
(1996: Chapter 3) example of an Austrian alternative school). There is
no automatic alliance to be found between teachers and parents, nor
indeed between parents and learners, who may resent what they consider
further "interference" in their lives. Parents may express dislike for
"oppressive" testing regimes which subject their children to endless
assessment, and at the same time, work desperately hard to ensure that
their child attains a high score in them, and thus later advantage.

Nevertheless, the environmental model of information; the risk of
information obesity; and the colonisation and, alternately, decolonisation
and preservation of our informational resources; each suggest the value of
communication, learning and synthesis or consensus between
communities otherwise separated from one another by colonisation and,
relatedly, by ICT and information filtering. Such connections start to be
built even when one picks up and reads a newspaper from a different
political stance than normal. They become even stronger through critical
self reflection on activity, with an orientation to reaching an
understanding, by groups normally kept apart.

This kind of collaboration is actively retarded by hierarchism and the
sociotechnical systems it constructs. When it does happen, however, it

can develop with explosive energy. It is these moments, these "outbreaks of democracy" (Blaug, 1999a), in which the full potential of transformative learning is sometimes realised.

In the developed world, political participation is in decline, at least when measured quantitatively. Voter turnout has dropped over the last half century, notably in the US and UK. Membership of political parties, churches and other organisations devoted to local community activity is also going down. In such declines, authors like Putnam (2000) see a threat to social capital and thus community cohesion. This can now be supported by the environmental model. How can a community, however defined, work to transform its own environment, and maintain the resources within it, without this kind of participation? How can it protect itself against pushed schema, imposed solutions, and ways of thinking which will threaten its sustainability as a community, without activity on its own behalf, learning about the changes it faces? Will it degenerate into a mere microculture, fragmented and isolated from other communities, thus unable to learn from them?

Arguments such as these are not intended to eulogise the community in all circumstances. Many communities can be parochial and exclusionary, sometimes in extreme ways, and contain power relationships within them that are damaging for community members. School communities can be sites for informal learning: they can also be sites for mental and physical bullying, crushing conformity, and in various ways, prevent members from learning and adjusting to the world. Nevertheless, local informational and technological resources are essential to any community. Levine (in Hess and Ostrom, 2007: p. 264) stresses the value of "associational commons with roots in geographic communities", but communities may also be "locally" bounded by a shared workplace or other non-geographical connection. In any case, the shared generation, validation, and maintenance of local resources is a vital part of community health.

Nor are communities without power in a systemic sense. Local government still exists in some form in most countries, and/or a local community has a specific representative nationally. Unfortunately (2007: 267):

> ...professionals and experts have taken over many traditional duties of citizens, from managing towns to setting educational policy to lobbying. And it is partly because many civic functions have been privatised. For example, Americans often pay companies

to provide neighborhood security or to watch their small children. All that is left for citizens to do is to complain, vote and volunteer.... Moreover, conventional volunteering tends to mean direct, face to face service that does not change policies or institutions or grant much power to those who participate.

Some countries, like the UK, have tried to instil programmes of "citizenship education" or, as it was once called, civics. Regardless of their specific content, these programmes will be subject to the same tensions as any other subject mandated by the system, and thus needing the same kind of critical attention. (See Beck, 1998, for a good analysis of citizenship education in the UK.) Within this setting, however, there would still be scope for addressing information obesity, ICT skills and environmental relevance: for instance, by adopting Jonassen *et al.*'s (2003: p. 156) suggestion that students could debate issues under discussion by the city council, resources for which activity might include video recordings of council meetings, or online information. The first example in Chapter 13 directly addresses this suggestion. Civics education can engage youth in "research of public value, using new information technology" (Levine, in Hess and Ostrom, 2007: p 248)[3]; this is a vital way that "each generation must transmit to the next a moral concern for common goods" (2007: 254).

The school (or university) would thereby reach out and build links with the community. Even democratic practice, and a collaborative, sustainable approach to PBL, can become isolated within an organisation if that organisation does not contribute to activity outside itself (Heaney and Horton, in Mezirow, 1990: p. 91). Many institutions already work in such a way, of course. Warschauer (1999: Chapter 5), for example, discusses a programme of "cyber service learning" at a community college in Hawaii. Here, the "literacy" of students was applied to producing material relevant at a community level, specifically, the relatively deprived (and ethnically diverse) community local to the college. What had to be applied were not just broad technical skills, but an understanding of the background of these communities. By connecting the community work specifically to "structured opportunities intentionally designed to promote student learning and development"

---

[3] Levine reported that many of his students suffered disillusionment after engaging in this work, becoming less optimistic about the possibility of value shifts in government than they were before. I do not believe this is any reason to protect students from such work, however.

(Jacoby, 1996: p. 5, cited in Warschauer, 1999: p. 127), both sides benefit, learning from one another, through exchanging information and activity. (See also Bruce and Bishop, 2008.)

This should not be read as a patronisation of the "local" by the "academic" community, or some kind of missionary work. In Warschauer's case, most of the students were themselves members of underprivileged communities and were able to explore their own experiences of being on that side of the divide. The principle of *emancipatory education* suggests that true community empowerment can come through links with "expert" educators, but only under certain conditions (Hall, quoted in Mezirow, 1990: p. 95):

- Emancipatory projects should be initiated at the invitation of the community for whom they are undertaken and in response to its agenda.

- Emphasis should be placed on resources indigenous to the community itself, rather than institutional resources that are beyond the control of the community and therefore foster dependence.

- From the beginning, steps should be taken to ensure community control of projects involving the educators' institution.

- Emancipatory educational activities should encourage and support full community involvement in the production of knowledge related to local goals and strategies...

Such activities also recall the work of Freire (1972).

The interconnections between IL education and local community empowerment have long been recognised, and still form part of a relatively mainstream model of liberal education, as well as human rights legislation across the world (see Senn Breivik and Gee, 2006: pp. 64–6; Catts and Lau, 2008). An emancipatory approach would additionally recognise the roles played by colonisation and information obesity, and thus require a critical IL, connected to a transformative learning process, as described in the last chapter. As empirical examples such as those of Warschauer and Levine show, this is quite possible to approach even in mainstream, relatively colonised educational settings.

Where action learning becomes most energetic, however, is when community activity emerges spontaneously, in response to tensions and contradictions evident in that community's environment. The values on which an activity system is believed to rest may be challenged in many ways; for instance, by new information or the process of learning engaged in by members, or perhaps by management or elite behaviour which contravenes stated values (e.g. management pay increases just after they have called for restraint on worker raises). These have been termed "hidden transcripts" (Scott, 1990). Around these fractures, discontent can emerge, and through being communicated, may gather momentum. This can sometimes happen explosively, becoming what Blaug calls an "outbreak of democracy". "Democracy from the participant's perspective" (Blaug, 1999b: p. 136) is a noisy, conflictual, but basically collaborative process which can, within social movements, sometimes achieve considerable pressure on social institutions. That these outbreaks are usually not approved of – in fact are frequently repressed – by government and business institutions is precisely to be expected. They are decolonising. Though they may quickly decay into infighting, exclusionary decision making, formalised (and thus self preserving) organisations, or all three (Blaug, 1999b: pp. 137–40), social movements are valid and significant sites for learning. In social movement spaces such as the 1990s anti-roadbuilding protests in the UK (Aufheben, 1998; Merrick, 1996), there was an ongoing need for information, collaboration, activity and planning, in stressful situations requiring considerable flexibility and creativity. Sustained political activism, for some, led to "burn-out" and other psychological problems, not to mention persecution from the system (or worse); but for many, the benefits were positive, such as increased confidence, social and technical skills, critical awareness and – for some – changed lives. Within social movements, values can be formed, tolerance and respect promoted, and valuable lessons learned by both individuals and communities (see McKay, 1998: there are more examples, and thinking tasks, on the website).

Bearing in mind the wide range of skills necessary to survive and stay healthy on an environmental protest camp, we might wonder why radical political activism is not more often promoted as a worthy educational strategy. There is an element of sarcasm in that statement, but it nevertheless draws attention to the same contradiction as does Egan (1990: p. 285): that the system's need for flexible, creative individuals:

> …might have been better met had they been content to expand schools' educational role and not pay them to produce peaceable patriots well prepared to supply the manpower needs of the economy.

Teachers, parents and the children themselves regularly shoulder the blame when education fails to produce a steady stream of motivated, flexible, team-oriented, creative, flexible, confident and self-disciplined learners. Teachers are out of date, parents pushy or uncaring, children uninterested, vacuous or just plain dumb. Parents and teachers have been reduced to disciplinarians, responsible for getting children into school and training them to perform educational tasks developed by the system and embedded into sociotechnical frameworks to which compliance is rewarded and challenge a threat (Apple, 1982: 113–14, via Robins and Webster, 1987: pp. 260–2). If calls for teachers, parents and learners alike to recognise common cause in revitalising the community elements of the education system are considered idealistic, then let us remember what ideals are – narrative devices that help show us how far we currently are from their attainment. As Geras suggests, however (1999), even looking towards a "Minimum Utopia", based on a culture of mutual aid and in which basic human rights were universally respected, shows us that there is still room for improvement in learning how to achieve values that are largely agreed upon:

> If we could hope to achieve merely – *merely* – a condition in which people had enough to eat, adequate water, shelter, health care, and the fundamental rights of expression, belief and assembly; and in which they were free from arbitrary imprisonment, torture, "disappearance", threat of genocide: now wouldn't *that* be something. Even to articulate the thought is to bring home how remote this possibility is.

Government, business and, yes, community actions such as surveillance; war; electoral fraud; irreversible environmental destruction; corruption; dehumanisation; racism: these have no place in a rational, progressive society, however one defines those terms. Social movements, however, can open up around these hypocrisies, and are a way in which we can at least work towards a more just and equable world at the local level. Their power as learning environments is, in fact, what makes them more effective.

I realise it is easy to sound patronising when asserting the value of social movements, particularly from my position, a middle-class professional living in an affluent English town, quite far from genuine poverty and able to freely criticise my own government without fear of arrest. I raise their example only to define them as one of many settings, across our multiple community lives, in which informal learning can occur. Most of the time, communities are engaged in far more mundane learning tasks than working out how to stop bulldozers that are heading towards them. Nevertheless, it is in such social activity that technical, social and information filtering skills can be diffused. Deprived or disadvantaged communities can be empowered, from within, or with expert, communicatively-rational help, to improve their informational skills and resources (Warschauer, 1999: Chapters 4–6), and do so with the intention of transforming their environments, even in the face of opposition and perhaps oppression from vested interests. These learning processes are happening all over the world, usually beneath the radar: hence their power. Remember that physical obesity, and poor health generally, is more likely to affect lower-income and other disdavantaged groups; general environmental quality is also lower in these communities (e.g. higher pollution, less aesthetic value). Applying this judgment to these communities' information resources is, as this book has tried to show throughout, not just a transfer of a metaphor. It is a real contribution to the lack of control that many people have over their own lives.

Information obesity is thus politically disempowering. To reverse its effects requires educational work across a wide spectrum of settings, from the formalised classroom, to the technological development process, the workplace, the local community, the family, and the social movement.

Three examples

> You know why that [solution] won't happen? Because no one will make any money from it. (Letter in the *Hebden Bridge Times* on a town car parking issue, 2008)

I have almost reached the end of the book. Before concluding, I will present three brief illustrations of how the environmental model of information, and the notion of communicative rationality, can help describe education, information and ICT in certain ways. None are intended as a prescription for activity, ideal cases or "proofs". Read them in combination with the supporting material on the website.

The first is an approach to teaching children about information and ICT that connects their study firmly to the local community, and develops an appreciation of technology as something which helps learners meet a community's informational needs, rather than something they are expected to learn for its own sake. Compare this with how something like the ECDL would introduce students to Excel, Word, SPSS, web browsing and digital photography: all potentially useful in the task. It would be appropriate for children aged around 11 – 13, but the general principles could be adapted for almost any age group.

Hebden Bridge, described in Chapter 3, attracts many visitors and is a shopping and service centre for surrounding villages. Therefore, particularly on sunny summer weekends, there is pressure on parking spaces. Recent issues of the *Hebden Bridge Times* have featured ongoing debate over what to do about this, and whose responsibility it is. Without going into too much detail, broadly, correspondents fall into three factions, each promoting a particular solution:

- *Build a new car park*. This is further subdivided into those arguing for it to be built in certain places, with or without retail or residential premises incorporated into the architecture. Others argue that the scenic qualities of the town would be damaged by such a project, and/or worry about the motivations of the property developers interested in the investment.

- *Make more effective use of what parking spaces exist.* Correspondents have observed that two large car parks belonging to local businesses sit locked, but empty, on weekends; and the market causes pressure on Wednesdays and Thursdays because it sets up on another car park. These policies could be reviewed for less financial cost than a new building.

- *Ignore the problem and promote the use of walking and public transport.* The town already has a reasonably good, regular train and bus service. Also, many parking spaces are occupied by people who have driven into town from a relatively short distance away. Looking in the longer term, at the environmental and policy changes that will surely develop in the next 10 or 20 years, some believe that promoting further car use is unsustainable.

What we have here is a *community problem* that is amenable to *community solutions*. Though matters such as public transport policy and property prices are not entirely within the control of the community, much of what could be done to relieve the parking problem – or even decide whether it is a problem at all – resides at that level. But the problem is *ill structured*. There are divergent solutions and no "one best answer" which would appease everyone. Indeed, a combination of all three may be possible.

What is needed, to investigate the problem, is *information*. Learners could reflect on this in different ways. At a subjective level they could be asked their opinions, whether they or their families have ever found parking a problem, and so on. They could share these with the class so an intersubjective opinion could form: if not a consensus then at least a measure of the strength of support for different solutions. At that point, they could be asked what other information might be valuable, which could include:

- How many parking spaces does the town currently have?
- Usage rates throughout the day and week.
- How have people travelled into town, and why?
- Public opinion: what is the support for different solutions? Would people pay more to park? Would they travel more by bus or train?

- Images: for example, showing the empty business car parks at weekends, while public spaces outside are full to capacity.

- What have other towns, faced by similar problems, done to solve them?

These are just my suggestions; learners may develop more, either initially, or after a period of information gathering and analysis. Indeed, the three solutions mentioned so far may not represent the total range of possibilities. If learners can think of others then these could be addressed too: and so the problem environment may evolve.

It could then be asked how ICT might help gather, process and communicate these various kinds of information, not to substitute for student work or thought, but to enhance it, bringing ICT into the learner-created activity system. ICT could help with:

- designing and then producing a questionnaire through which public opinion could be surveyed amongst individuals and businesses in the town centre (using Word, or a desktop publishing application);

- analysing the results of this questionnaire, producing graphs and other summary reports (Excel, SPSS);

- producing images of sites throughout the town, and including these in a report; or, perhaps, helping with data collection (digital photography and image processing);

- giving learners access to experiences from elsewhere (World-Wide Web search);

- producing a report (Word or DTP again) or a website (HTML, Dreamweaver, etc.);

- other applications may be creatively suggested – for instance, Google Earth might help locate and present data on the number of parking spaces and usage rates.

Designing the problem solution involves more than ICT, however. There is too much here for one person to do alone, so learners would have to agree divisions of labour, a timetable for the work, and final objectives or deliverables. If all that was produced was a report to be marked by a teacher then forgotten about, this is not *critical* work with ICT. Students may therefore suggest that they publish a web page, write something in the local newspaper, or attend a council meeting at which the car park issue will be being discussed, using their analysis to support a position. Local businesses might also benefit from the report (indeed, could be invited to sponsor elements of its production and dissemination).

Afterwards, students could be asked whether their opinions have changed in the light of the information gathered, and its analysis. They might be asked what they have learnt more generally about how information is valued in the local community setting, about planning procedures and public opinion formation, and about ICT, amongst other things. Nor should the issue be considered as "closed"; students could keep an eye on further correspondence in the local paper, or moves by decision makers in one direction or another, and reflect on these in an iterative cycle.

I wanted to draw a second example from the professional teaching sector, showing how staff development could be organised around principles of communicative rationality, but it did not prove easy to find a satisfactory example. This is for two reasons. First, the idea of *design for communicative rationality* is something of a paradox (Blaug, 1999b). As soon as design takes place, one is pushing cognitive schema at participants. Design will always have a role in helping create the ecology of resources, that is true: nevertheless, to declare that a designed programme for staff development is evidence of decolonisation is an awkward logical leap. Second, though action research can help professional educators adapt to what exists in their learning and working environments, most such work is situated in specific contexts, thus difficult to make relevant to a more general audience.

I therefore struggled to find an example until a morning in June 2008, when I attended an Exam Board meeting with around 15 colleagues. Let me recount what happened there, and how I reflected on it. I offer this not as "educational research" for as you will see, it is clearly not. Rather, it is an example of the kind of ongoing *and mostly unconscious* adjustments made by a typical group of education professionals in their everyday working lives. Also, though the people involved would be easy to identify, and though the matters under discussion may seem sensitive, I would expect that most university teachers could recognise themselves here: such discussions doubtless occur regularly in every university department in the world.

Exam Boards are meetings at which the award and classification of students' degrees are confirmed. Course Directors sit around a table for 2½ hours and examine spreadsheets tabulating hundreds of assessment grades. Largely, the decision as to whether students' combined grades entitle them to a pass, merit, distinction, or fail has already been made on the spreadsheet. We confirm what we see, then deal "manually" with the minority of cases that are not straightforward, usually because of mitigating circumstances of some kind.

Exam Boards are never exciting. They are also the point in our professional lives at which it is easiest to take something of great importance to a student – their degree award, based on work they have done over a long period (and which has cost them a considerable sum) – and boil it down to a few bits of information and a brief second of time, a nod to what the system is telling us about whether they have passed and how well. It is the furthest we get from treating these people as fellow human beings and instead reducing them to numbers, informational inputs into an automated system. If this seems distasteful, recognise that every educational organisation in the world will have its version of the same meeting.

A debate rose up at one point, however. If a student has failed a particular assessment, there are two ways of proceeding. The *compensated pass* method basically says, if the student's grades in other course units raise their average score above the pass mark, this can compensate for their fail. The alternative is *resubmission*, where students, however good their marks in other course units, cannot pass the degree until they have submitted work of passing standard in every part of it. Hence, they get a chance to resubmit work that has not reached that standard. (Students cannot go through their whole degree merrily getting second chances in everything: there is a limit to how often we apply these rules. Neither method will save the truly disastrous student who would fail under any system, but might help a student who for some reason has underperformed in one part of the degree.)

The question is, which should apply? Both methods, from an administrative perspective, provide satisfactory solutions for both system and student. The student is not kicked off the course merely because of one aberration in otherwise good work. The system is provided with rules that can be consistently applied. Nevertheless they are quite different methods that send out different messages about how we deal with academic standards and our attitudes towards our students and their work. This is what the debate was about.

The compensated pass method is easier for the students, and easier for us, but was believed to represent a lowering of academic standards. In effect we would be saying, "look, it doesn't matter that you didn't attain the learning objectives of this part of the degree; we'll average it out and forget about it". That said, the resubmission method is harder and riskier for the students *and* more work for us (as we have to supervise, then mark, the student's resubmission): but was believed to be more likely to maintain high academic standards.

What is maybe not apparent – and certainly no one in the meeting consciously observed, and communicated, this at the time – is the seemingly causal relationship here. The compensated pass method lowers academic standards *precisely because* it is less work for the students *and* for us. The resubmission method raises them *because* it is more work for both students and teachers. In other words, *staff* are *retaining knowledge of the students' understanding; and students are working to improve their knowledge of the subject.* Without a resubmission, less cognitive work is being undertaken by teachers and students, and more has been delegated to the system.

The debate lasted 20 minutes and, I admit, seemed tedious at the time. But though most of us, almost certainly, did not consciously know what we were doing (it only came to mind later for me, in response to a question about what I'd done at work that day), we were keeping fresh, in our community of practice, the ongoing question of where we stood on a scale that had academic integrity and quality at one end, and at the other, delegating more decision making to the system, thus lowering our cognition of the students and their cognition of their subjects. We were, in other words, debating a *value question*. And, if you are interested: we decided that we would retain the principle of resubmission.

I wondered at one point why we did not just get this decided for us, by the university. Why were we wasting our time discussing what seemed an esoteric point of order? But it was a discussion worth having because, in the end, it was an issue which reflected on our roles as professionals, and acknowledged our autonomy, and the *humanity* of the system, all its members having interests, needs and knowledge of their own. We did not do this consciously, as I said. We did not sit down, analyse the pros and cons in some objective manner, and have an organised decision-making process about it. But it was communicatively rational, and we did reach a consensus.

However, we did not encode the result into our technologies, thus fixing it in place. In future Exam Boards, we may return to the question, and debate it again, and maybe someone will say "didn't we talk this all out in June 2008?" – but the decision could be different next time. We bring back to the surface values which are often unexpressed, certainly not consciously held, nor even directly seen to have a relationship with something so simple as what to do when a box on a spreadsheet has in it a number lower than 50. But that's the way of it. It is an educational decision: a human decision, with all its fallibilities and impermanency in the face of changing circumstances. For now, it remains communicatively rational, reviewable and, therefore, sustainable. It is an instance of how we lift our relationship with information – and the *reality* that this information represents – out of the ICT which does a lot of our work, and into awareness for a brief time, reaffirming the values that drive our professional practice.

And, later, I reflected on it, thinking about what it means for my general professional identity and also the course and students for which I'm responsible. I did not engage in this reflection in any organised way, nor because I was told to, but simply because it happened, as part of my working day and also, partly, as a consequence of writing this book. And now I present it to you, a story which you can make of what you will; not some "truth" about education, communicative rationality, information obesity nor anything else: just a moment in time, with an educational message I found enlightening. Nothing in it will "prove" anything; nor is it an example of transformative learning. But these things happen every day, in workplaces around the world.

The final example is drawn from Benson *et al.* (2008), which you can read in full on the website. It shows the values in an activity system developing both through random events and conscious decision making, which both shape later system capacities. A unique configuration develops which serves as a filtering mechanism for information and activity. This system then came into conflict with a "pushed" set of values, but information was a resource in resisting (for now) this imposed change. Compared to the previous example, what occurred here was more conscious and analytical, and it also represents a form of transformative learning (as well as showing the challenges which such learning poses to "host" organisations). Because of the restrictions placed on our use of sensitive personal data, the institution has been disguised. (All information in this section comes from Benson *et al.*, 2008: 460–3.)

The Public Administration Programme (PAP) is a a fully online Masters' programme for civil servants run by Churchampton College, a medium-sized university in northern England. Its initial implementation was funded through the UKeU initiative, an attempt to develop a commercially-oriented umbrella organisation to deliver fully online courses. The development and administration of these courses was to be devolved to a variety of universities, and the whole administered through a course management system that was to be unique to the UKeU and designed by a commercial partner.

However, only a few weeks before the PAP was launched, the UKeU collapsed (an event discussed in Conole *et al.*, undated), taking the computer system with it. Negotiators managed to save the funding, however, and it was decided to keep the programme as a Churchampton degree. But they had no system to support it.

This problem was solved by drawing on the ecology of resources available to the PAP team. These did not, at the time, include an institutional CMS, but a colleague in a different department had some experience with Moodle, which he shared with them. With only a few weeks, and no financial capacity to build or buy a system of their own, Moodle was chosen through "serendipity". However, this technology had to be integrated into a set of rules, tools and divisions of labour that had already started to form around the UKeU model, which mandated a different, more controlling approach to the design of PAP.

This is an example of how technology is not a "black box", akin to the science fiction character Doctor Who's TARDIS, which materialises out of nowhere and always looks the same. The Moodle *socio*technical system that grew around PAP looks rather different from another Moodle-based system that Benson *et al.* studied, based on looser principles of experimentation and management (see below). Rules and divisions of labour are clearly different. Yet each system was stable, continuously reviewed by its members who could operate in conditions of relative autonomy – mainly because what PAP was doing was not something Churchampton as a whole had then widely engaged with. It should also be noted that PAP's relatively high level of control over its procedures (demanding standardised course templates, for instance) was justified by a belief that as the PAP students were not technologically-inclined, such an approach would lead to a more comfortable learning environment for them. This is an example of where a relatively instrumental strategy can still be *communicatively validated* by those affected by it.

Over 3 years or so, the PAP team did start to change the rules by which they worked, and the system became more flexible to accommodate these changes. They also interacted with the *http://moodle.org* community, albeit indirectly, through the use of external contractors to help with system upgrades and maintenance: nevertheless this is also a valuable form of communication, and helps contribute to the community-based nurturing of the resource that is Moodle.

But all this was threatened in 2007, when Churchampton, by now more attuned to the potential benefits (for itself) of educational technology, tried to force PAP to adopt the new Blackboard system that had been centrally purchased. It would be easy to cast this as a clear example of colonisation, even a violation of academic autonomy, or at least an overriding of it, in the face of central, system needs. But it is a more interesting and complex event than that. PAP's teaching and learning manager told Benson *et al.*:

> We got accused of being change-averse... there were also people saying, "why've we spent all that money on Blackboard when PAP are using that free [software]?" So he [the director of IT responsible for Blackboard] was having to defend his corner... We got the sales guy in first... and showed him the difference between Moodle and Blackboard and why we wanted to stay with Moodle. And he agreed, he said "Yep, you're absolutely right.... Blackboard can't compare, it just doesn't offer the same functionality"... we ended up being given a stay of execution, and that's all it is... He wants to persuade Blackboard to do what Moodle can do, so he can shift us over.

What is interesting, first, is that PAP's team members have developed an *awareness* of the benefits of the technology, and more, that this awareness forms an informational resource which they can draw on to make a – so far successful – case against the imposition of another system and the different filtering strategies and ways of thinking that it represents. But this is not a problem with Blackboard specifically. It is likely that the same thing would have happened with any alternative system, including if PAP, for whatever reason, had started with Blackboard (or the UKeU's system) and then had Moodle imposed on them. The social and technological parts of a system co-evolve. PAP could have developed a management style more akin to E-TECH, the other Moodle-based programme that Benson *et al.* studied, a more "laissez-faire" approach in which new potential solutions were always being researched and experimented with. But E-TECH, being an educational technology Masters', had environmental conditions particular to it that made such enquiry easy and possible: PAP faced other challenges which it solved in its own way. So they are not being criticised for ending up with a somewhat inflexible system. The problem lies more with Churchampton, their host organisation, which is now seeing their autonomous use of ICT as something of a challenge. So far, at least, they are being allowed to resist: I would suggest, in fact, that any healthy organisation must allow such "pockets" of innovation to flourish, in order to diversify the range of informational resources on which its various communities can draw (see the conclusion).

My suggesting it, however, is not going to make this happen: it is down to individuals and communities to undertake transformative learning for themselves; opportunities for which, as Chapter 12 described, may open up around primary or secondary tensions between parts of systems, defined at many scales.

Conclusion

...all the history of human life has been a struggle between wisdom and stupidity... the followers of wisdom have always tried to open minds; the Authority and his churches have always tried to keep them closed. (Philip Pullman, *The Amber Spyglass*, Chapter 36)

I sit here writing these words in my house in Hebden Bridge on a beautifully sunny June evening, looking at the view you can see (in its January guise) on the website. Despite the instrumental motivations behind the building of this town – exploiting the technology of the Industrial Revolution, needing to build houses cheaply – and the way these were deeply embedded in the infrastructure, the place is now *home* to me and many others. It has been changed both at the individual and community level over many years by people interacting with the technology and making it their own, instilling into it their own values over time, without this being an obvious, measurable and strategic process. And it is a fine place to live.

Over time, technology changes to meet the aspirations of its users. We cannot any longer say the clock, or the zero, retard the way we think, that there are possibilities inherent in a world without clocks or where the zero was never invented. When something becomes so deeply embedded in the infrastructure, *we* make of it and its consequences what we will. We build the environments we live in, based on decisions possibly taken a long time ago, but over time, through work, we can change our world.

The nature of information obesity, and the reasons why it is potentially damaging our lives, have been developed throughout this book, so in this conclusion I will revisit them only briefly. In fact I will return to the original metaphor, physical obesity – caused not by a glut of food but by:

- low-quality, mass-produced food;
- an unbalanced diet;

- advertising and the pressure to consume (thus making money for others);
- a lack of exercise, or more specifically, the lack of an opportunity to exercise;
- a lack of cooking or gardening (food production) expertise in many people;
- a lack of information about all the above;
- and (we must include this), a lack of self discipline.

It is best combated through multiple methods. Simply dieting is a fragile solution, which can create just as much unhappiness as what it addresses, can be colonised and turned into a commodity in its own right, and as a result, is not always a sustainable solution. However, diet *plus* exercise *plus* better quality food *plus* information and awareness *plus* community-level solutions such as safer streets: all in combination can start to contribute to a healthier environment.

Fighting information obesity is a matter of moving from an overload or smog model to an abundance model. Any resource that seems abundant may be used profligately, in ways that (for all its abundance) threaten its health in the future. This can take place on a massive scale. Real-world examples include the collapse of the North American buffalo herds or the dessication of the Aral Sea. But with effective *management*, resources can be maintained for the good of all. What information obesity does is risk taking management skills out of the hands of individuals and communities and locking them into the system, and the technologies embedded therein: now cognitively impenetrable, thanks precisely to the devaluing of critical reflection upon them.

ICT is not a direct cause of information obesity, but it nevertheless gives rise to problems that are acutely felt at this stage in human technological development. The pace of change has now outstripped the timespan of the academic research cycle. By the time funding has been applied for, research conducted, written up and then published (perhaps in a journal with a long lag time between acceptance and publication, due precisely to the increases in the volume of information), the technology under review may have long ago moved on. This is something which should worry not only academia itself, trying to stay relevant in the information society, but commentators such as Thompson, who laud the value of objective research and acknowledge that it is a time-consuming, iterative and sometimes necessarily slow process. The risk is that even this kind of objective value is losing its relevance in a world increasingly driven by the steering media of money and power, and in which subjectivity is lauded, precisely because the system knows that individuals lack real power to effect change.

The paradox of information obesity is that it is a threat to the sustainability of the organisations whose processes contribute to it. Any organisation that binds itself too tightly to one solution – one technology, one product, one way of working, one ideal – is vulnerable. Hence the importance of double-loop learning (Argyris, 1999). Where, then, can creative work on the *next* generation of educational technology be conducted? The answer is, in communities of practice, involving both students and teachers, but these communities are either increasingly marginalised, or they are decreasing in size due to the disappearance of the creative, innovatory skills within individuals which are needed to sustain them.

The role of communities of practice, and informal learning more generally, is being increasingly recognised, however, and not just among academics. The EU's *Education and Training 2010* policy document explicitly calls for the recognition of the contribution made by the informal sector[1], and the integration of this with the formal educational system. Many business and management publications promote the need to spread learning and creativity throughout an organisation. However, what this book has attempted to show is that there will always be opposing and, to an extent, contradictory tendencies within organisations and societies, towards both centralisation, and democratic action. To "centralise democracy" is an oxymoron. What we need, to better appreciate how the world is changing, is not to expect one sector of society to take up the challenge to the exclusion of others. Rather, we need to understand how these many forces interact, and all shape the resources and environments on which we will draw in the future.

There has always been a tension between the "liberal and critical dimension to education" (Robins and Webster, 1989: p. 110) and its productive benefits, supplying knowledge and personnel to industry and the state; from the earliest days of the Industrial Revolution. What I have tried to do in this book is not ignore the tension, designing a "liberal" curriculum which has little chance of being implemented in national education systems and even if it was, would be no more likely to arrive in the mainstream than has critical TV viewing, informatics, information literacy, emancipatory education or any other such approach. Rather,

---

[1] *http://ec.europa.eu/education/policies/2010/objectives_en.html* (last accessed 24 August 2008).

I have suggested a more holistic approach that involves seeing the connections and tensions between different stakeholders and educational settings. Parents, learners, local businesses, the government, community organisations, groups of friends; these will all have different perspectives on what "information", "technology", "literacy", "learning" and all these other seemingly common-sense – but in fact ambiguous and therefore divisive – terms mean to them, based on different needs and values. A positivist analysis would see these various tensions and relationships as things to be measured then managed; an interpretivist one, things to be understood. Only a critical approach, however, can truly help work out how they can be *changed*. And such change may be needed not just from an activist perspective, that of the social movement crying out its ideals, but for quite instrumental reasons, such as when an organisation must learn about changes in its market. There is a deep and direct contradiction between calls for active users of technology, flexible and creative learners, and committed citizens – and ways of organising education, and our use of information, which are oriented towards producing conformity to cognitive schema designed for us, not by us. It is in this contradiction that information obesity resides, and solutions to it have to be found in the lifeworld, not the system.

If it "seems quite frivolous and unrealistic to appeal even to liberal principles... [t]*hat* is the measure of the power of technocratic thought" (Robins and Webster, 1987: p. 270). But criticising the organisational basis of society, and showing how this affects the way we learn, make meaning, process information and think, has (1987: 273):

> ...nothing whatsoever to do with the defence of pure knowledge or the refusal to be involved in the "real world". Indeed it is very much about active engagement with the external world. But as such it is about acknowledging and insisting that this relationship to the world is complex and many-sided: it is cognitive, but it is also emotional, moral, imaginative and aesthetic. Because we have disavowed these dimensions of expertise, we have become competent only in certain areas of instrumental reason, whilst "at the same time we allow a scandalous incompetence in dealing with the fundamental recurring questions of human existence: How are we to live together? How can we live gracefully and with justice?" (Winner, 1986, p. 162).

As communities, we can learn to respond to shared threats, of which information obesity is one. Through communication, education, and the *selective, critical* application of science and technology, we can resist and turn back the colonisation of our lives by the steering media of money and power. Through such active work, we can rewrite technology in our own image, and as Feenberg (2002) demands, learn how to control past, present and future technological developments, rather than have them control us.

The system will not do any of this. It's up to us. It's up to you.

Annotated reading list

This section briefly summarises the major works that contribute to the argument of each chapter, and suggests some supplementary reading. Full references are given in the bibliography which follows. Note that I have been deliberately selective in creating this list: there will be many more relevant works and, like any other piece of scholarship, this should serve merely as a starting point for exploration. This list is repeated on the website, which also includes hyperlinks to online resources.

Introduction: Levine's chapter in Hess and Ostrom (2007) kick-started my writing this book, and its position as the first work cited is no coincidence. Putnam's work on social capital (2000) is well known, and important reading. Wenger's (1998) work on communities of practice is also important for appreciating how communities build knowledge in ways that are neglected by formalised organisational processes.

Chapter 1: Samson and Pitt (1999) is a superb resource for understanding the ideas of biosphere and noösphere, and contain many other references, including Vernadsky. For empirical illustrations – in a literal, and beautiful, sense – of how the spheres of the world interact and create environmental diversity over millions of years, see Redfern (2000).

Chapter 2: Thompson (2008) has been drawn on frequently in this book and is highly recommended reading. Kuhn's (1970) work on how science creates value is a classic, as is Lyotard (1984), although this is a more difficult work – it has the advantage of brevity, however. Bonnett's chapter in McFarlane (1997) is useful both here and for Chapter 4. Hess and Ostrom (2007) contains many essays that illuminate the nature of, and threats to, the idea of an information commons.

Chapter 3: The classic citation for the social shaping of technology is Mackenzie and Wajcman (1985); Williams and Edge (1996) is, in my opinion, even better. Star (1999) is a good companion piece as it discusses ways in which these insights can be applied. For forms of organisation and the role of metaphor in studying them, Morgan (1999) is invaluable. Robins and Webster (1987) has clearly been an influence on my work and presents clear, albeit depressing, evidence of how organisations restrict creativity and generally technologise social relations. For activity theory, see Engeström *et al.* (1999) and Nardi (1996): Bedny and Harris (2005) is difficult, but also valuable for showing the differences between CHAT and SSTA, which are often ignored by many other writers. Argyris (1999) is valuable throughout.

Chapter 4: Many relevant works exist and I here cite only those that I have particularly drawn on. Hafner and Lyon (1996), Randall (1997) and Berners-Lee (1999) are useful histories of the Internet. Bush (1945) should be essential reading for any student of technology, and Nyce and Kahn (1991) is an excellent commentary on it. Shenk (1997) is also very interesting. Stoll (1990), Roszak (1994) and Webster (2002) provide a more critical view. Bell (1976), Webster (2002) – again – and Bauman (2000) are useful reviews of the impact of the information society. Rheingold (1993 and 2003) is more upbeat, but very readable.

Chapter 5: Warschauer (1999) is a useful work and provides many other references to resources on literacy. I found Dorner (2002) to be an interesting review of how traditional ideas of writing and *literature* (as opposed to literacy, but the connections are clear) are being affected by ICT. McFarlane (1997) has some useful chapters in the middle regarding other forms of literacy, such as number and visual. Freire (1972) is the classic source for how literacy, oppression and power are interconnected. For the latter part of this chapter, revisit Thompson (2008) and, in a more specific way, Knight (2000). I find Sagan (1986) to be an eloquent source for the interconnections between science and other human values, as is Feynman (1998).

Chapter 6: For histories of ICT education see Robins and Webster (1987) and Beynon and Mackay (1992). Reffell and Whitworth (2002) is far from being a definitive statement but it will at least provide you with an idea of what other writers have influenced my personal perspective. For "how to" books I particularly recommend McFarlane (1997) and Laurillard (2002). Nevison's (1976) paper is definitely worth a read. Many resources exist in Jonassen *et al.* (2003), particularly pages 42–67. Many of these, if they still exist and even though they may seem old, are linked to from the website. They show that innovative, creative work can be done with the World-Wide Web (even in its "Web 1.0", less interactive incarnation). For information literacy see Andretta (2007), Bruce (1997), and various essays in Andretta's edited collection including Bruce and Edwards (2007) and Markless and Streatfield (2007).

Chapter 7: Fay (1975) is brilliant – and short. Burrell and Morgan (1979) is also useful for appreciating the differences between positivism, interpretivism and criticality, as is, with more specific reference to education, Carr and Kemmis (1986).

Chapter 8: No work on, or by, Habermas is easy and I modestly suggest that the book you hold is as good a layperson's introduction as is available. An exception is Forester (1985), a stunningly elegant summary of Habermas, and his collection as a whole is definitely worth a look. For collected extracts from Habermas's work, as well as useful commentary, see Outhwaite (1996). Goldblatt's (1996) chapter on Habermas is quite good, and helps connect his work to the environmental model. Blaug (1999b) is not straightforward but is very useful for any attempts to apply Habermas's theories in the "real world".

Chapter 9: Blaug is a very readable author and his works (1999a, 1999b, 2007) are all worth consulting. Morgan (1999) discusses forms of organisation generally: for alternative forms see Rothschild and Whitt (1986); Gastil (1993); and, if you can find it (and it is worth trying) Merrick (1996). Freeman (1984) is a classic critique.

Chapter 10: Egan (1990) has not yet appeared on this reading list but clearly that book has been a considerable influence on this one, particularly in this chapter. Cunningham's and Bonnett's chapters in McFarlane (1997) are also relevant here.

Chapter 11: For PBL see Jonassen *et al.* (2003). Mezirow (1990) is excellent for transformative learning and has many other references. March and Cohen (1976) is important for establishing the ambiguous nature of decision making, particularly in educational organisations. I remind you again of the value of Carr and Kemmis (1986) for action research, plus Schön (1991) and Reason and Bradbury (2001).

Chapter 12: Beck (1998) is good for describing, then critiquing, citizenship education, and Clarke (1996) for the value of active citizens: these complement other works mentioned already, like Putnam (2000).

References

ACRL (Association of College and Research Libraries) (2000) *Information Literacy Competency Standards for Higher Education*. Available at *http://www.ala.org/ala/acrl/acrlstandards/informationliteracycompetency.cfm* (last accessed 14 August 2008).

ALA (American Library Association) (1989) *ALA Presidential Committee on Information Literacy*. Available at *http://www.ala.org/ala/acrl/acrlpubs/whitepapers/presidential.cfm* (last accessed 14 August 2008).

Andretta, S. (2007) *Information Literacy: A Practitioner's Guide*. Oxford, UK: Chandos.

Apple, M. W. (1982) 'Curriculum and the Labour Process: The Logic of Technical Control', *Social Text*, 5: 108–25.

Arendt, H. (1958) *The Human Condition*. Chicago, IL: University of Chicago Press.

Argyris, C. (1999) *On Organizational Learning*. Oxford, UK: Blackwell.

Aufheben (1998) 'The politics of anti-road struggle and the struggles of anti-road politics: the case of the No M11 Link Road campaign', in McKay, G. (ed.), *DiY Culture: Party and Protest in Nineties Britain*. London, UK: Verso; pp. 100–28.

Augoustinos, M. and Walker, I. (1996) *Social Cognition*. London, UK: Sage.

Avis, J. (2007) 'Engeström's version of activity theory: A conservative praxis?', *Journal of Education and Work*, 20(3): 161–77.

Bakhtin, M. (1986) *Speech Genres and Other Essays*. Austin, TX: University of Texas Press.

Baker, D., Akiba, M., LeTendre, G. and Wiseman, A. (2001) 'Worldwide Shadow Education: Outside-School Learning, Institutional Quality of Schooling, and Cross-National Mathematics Acheivement', *Educational Evaluation and Policy Analysis*, 23(1): 1–17.

Bartlett, F. (1932) *A Study in Experimental and Social Psychology*. Cambridge, UK: Cambridge University Press.

Bassett, I., Pannowitz, D. and Barnetson, R. (1990) 'A comparative study of tea-tree oil versus benzoylperoxide in the treatment of acne', *Medical Journal of Australia*, 153(8): 455–8.

Bates, A. W. (2000) *Managing Technological Change: Strategies for College and University Leaders*. San Francisco, CA: Jossey-Bass.

Bauman, Z. (2000) *Liquid Modernity*. Cambridge, UK: Polity.

Beck, J. (1998) *Morality and Citizenship in Education*. London, UK: Cassell.

Bedny, G. and Harris, S. (2005) 'The Systemic-Structural Theory of Activity: Applications to the study of human work', *Mind, Culture and Activity*, 12(2): 128–47.

Bell, D. (1976) *The Coming of Post-Industrial Society*. Harmondsworth, UK: Penguin.

Benson, A. and Whitworth, A. (2007) 'Technology at the Planning Table: Activity theory, negotiation and course management systems', *Journal of Organisational Transformation and Social Change*, 4(1): 75–92.

Benson, A., Lawler, C. and Whitworth, A. (2008) 'Rules, roles and tools: Activity theory and the comparative study of e-learning', *British Journal of Educational Technology*, 39(3): 456–67.

Berners-Lee, T. (1999) *Weaving the Web*. London, UK: Sage.

Best, S. and Kellner, D. (1991) *Postmodern Theory: Critical Interrogations*. Basingstoke, UK: Macmillan.

Beynon, J. and Mackay, H. (eds) (1992) *Technological Literacy and the Curriculum*. Abingdon, UK: Falmer.

Bijker, W. (1989) *The Social Construction of Technological Systems*. Cambridge, MA: MIT Press.

Bjerknes, G., Ehn, P. and Kyng, M. (eds) (1979) *Computers and Democracy: A Scandinavian Challenge*. Aldershot, UK: Avebury.

Blaug, R. (1999a) 'The Tyranny of the Visible: Problems in the Evaluation of Anti-Institutional Radicalism', *Organization*, 6(1): 33–56.

Blaug, R. (1999b) *Democracy, Real and Ideal: Discourse Ethics and Radical Politics*. Albany, NY: SUNY Press.

Blaug, R. (2007) 'Cognition in a Hierarchy', *Contemporary Political Theory* 6(1): 24–44.

du Boulay, B., Coultas, J. and Luckin, R. (2007) 'How compelling is the evidence for the effectiveness of e-Learning in the post-16 sector?', working paper, IDEAS Lab, University of Sussex: available at *http://www.informatics.sussex.ac.uk/research/projects/reveel/files/Version4.1.pdf* (last accessed 24 August 2008).

Bruce, B. and Bishop, A. (2008) 'New literacies and community inquiry', in Coiro J., Knobel, M., Lankshear, C. and Leu, D. (eds), *The*

Handbook of Research in New Literacies. Hillsdale, NJ: Lawrence Erlbaum; pp. 703–46.

Bruce, C. (1997) *The Seven Faces of Information Literacy*. Adelaide, Australia: Auslib.

Bruce, C. and Edwards, S. (2007) 'Six frames for information literacy education: a conceptual framework for interpreting the relationships between theory and practice', in Andretta, S. (ed.), *Change and Challenge: Information Literacy for the 21st Century*. Adelaide, Australia: Auslib; pp. 37–58.

Burrell, G. and Morgan, G. (1979) *Sociological Paradigms and Organisational Analysis*. Aldershot, UK: Gower.

Bush, V. (1945) 'As We May Think', *Atlantic Monthly*, July: available at *http://www.theatlantic.com/doc/194507/bush* (last accessed 19 August 2008).

Calhoun, C. (ed.) (1992) *Habermas and the Public Sphere*. Cambridge, MA: MIT Press.

Callinicos, A. (1989) *Against Postmodernism*. Cambridge, UK: Polity.

Capel, R. (1992) 'Social histories of computer education: missed opportunities?' in Beynon, J. and Mackay, H. (eds), *Technological Literacy and the Curriculum*. Abingdon, UK: Falmer; pp. 38–64.

Carr, W. (2007) 'Educational research as a practical science', *International Journal of Research and Method in Education*, 30(3): 271–86.

Carr, W. and Kemmis, S. (1986) *Becoming Critical: Knowing Through Action Research*. Geelong, Australia: Deakin University Press.

de Castell, S. and Luke, A. (1986) 'Models of literacy in North American schools: Social and historical conditions and consequences' in de Castell, S., Luke, A. and Egan, K. (eds), *Literacy, Society and Schooling*. New York, NY: Cambridge University Press; pp. 87–109.

Catts, R. and Lau, J. (2008) *Towards Information Literacy Indicators*. Paris, France: UNESCO.

Clarke, P. B. (1996) *Deep Citizenship*. London, UK: Pluto Press.

Cleveland, H. (1982) 'Information as a resource', *The Futurist*, 16(6): 34–9.

Cohill, A. and Kavanaugh, A. (1997) *Community Networks: Lessons from Blacksburg, Virginia*. Boston, MA: Artech.

Conole, G., Carusi, A. and de Laat, M. (undated) 'Learning from the UKeU experience', e-Learning Research Centre working paper: available at *http://www.elrc.ac.uk/download/publications/ICEpaper.pdf* (last accessed 21 August 2008).

Cressy, D. (1980) *Literacy and the Social Order: Reading and Writing in Tudor and Stuart England*. Cambridge, UK: Cambridge University Press.

Dawkins, R. (1976) *The Selfish Gene*. Oxford, UK: Oxford University Press.

Dewdney, A. (1996) *200% of Nothing: An Eye-Opening Tour through the Twists and Turns of Math Abuse and Innumeracy*. London, UK: Wiley.

Dorner, J. (2002) *Creative Web Writing*. London, UK: A & C Black.

Douglas, M. (1986) *How Institutions Think*. London, UK: Routledge.

Eccles, R., Griffiths, D., Newton, C. and Tolley, N. (1988) 'The effects of menthol isomers on nasal sensation of airflow', *Clinical Otolaryngology*, 13(1): 25–9.

Egan, K. (1990) *Romantic Understanding: The Development of Rationality and Imagination, Ages 8 – 15*. London, UK: Routledge.

Engeström, Y., Miettinen, R. and Punamäki, R.-L. (eds) (1999) *Perspectives on Activity Theory*. Cambridge, UK: Cambridge University Press.

Evans, J. (1989) *Bias in Human Reasoning: Causes and Consequences*. London, UK: Erlbaum.

Fay, B. (1975) *Social Theory and Political Practice*. London, UK: Allen & Unwin.

Feenberg, A. (2002) *Transforming Technology: A Critical Theory Revisited*. Oxford, UK: Oxford University Press.

Feinstein, L. and Symons, J. (1999) 'Attainment in Secondary School', *Oxford Economic Papers*, 51: 300–21.

Feynman, R. (1998) *The Meaning of It All*. London, UK: Allen Lane.

Forester, J. (1985) 'Critical theory and planning practice' in Forester, J. (ed.), *Critical Theory and Public Life*. Cambridge, MA: MIT Press; pp. 202–30.

Foucault, M. (1980) *Power/Knowledge*. New York, NY: Random House.

Freeman, J. (1984) 'The Tyranny of Structurelessness', in *Untying the Knot: Feminism, Anarchism and Organisation*. London, UK: Dark Star.

Freire, P. (1972) *Pedagogy of the Oppressed*. Harmondsworth, UK: Penguin.

Furlan, A., Brosseau, L., Imamura, M. and Irvin, E. (2002) 'Massage for low-back pain: A systematic review within the framework of the Cochrane Collaboration Back Review Group', *Spine*, 27(17): 1896–910.

Garnett, F. (2008) 'Six ICT literacies', working paper: available at *http://lgc.pbwiki.com/papers/ICTLiteracies* (last accessed 29 August 2008).

Garson, G. D. (2000) 'The role of information technology in quality education', in Garson, G. D. (ed.), *Social Dimensions of Information Technology: Issues for the New Millenium*. London, UK: Idea Group; pp. 177–97.

Gastil, J. (1993) *Democracy in Samll Groups: Participation, Decision Making and Communication*. Philadelphia, PA: New Society.

Gee, J. P. (1996) *Social Linguistics and Literacies*. London, UK: Taylor and Francis.

Geras, N. (1999) 'Minimum Utopia: Ten Theses', *Socialist Register 2000*, 2000: 41–52.

Gleick, J. (1988) *Chaos: Making a New Science*. London, UK: Sphere.

Goldblatt, D. (1996) *Social Theory and the Environment*. Cambridge, UK: Polity Press.

Goldhaber, M. (1997) 'The Attention Economy and the Net', *First Monday*, 2(4).

Habermas, J. (1984) *The Theory of Communicative Action Volume 1: Reason and the Rationalisation of Society*. London, UK: Heinemann.

Habermas, J. (1987) *The Theory of Communicative Action Volume 2: Lifeworld and System – A Critique of Functionalist Reason*. Cambridge, UK: Polity.

Habermas, J. (1991) *New Conservatism: Cultural Criticism and the Historians' Debate*. Cambridge, MA: MIT Press.

Habermas, J. (1993) *Justification and Application: Remarks on Discourse Ethics*. Cambridge, UK: Polity.

Hafner, K. and Lyon, M. (1996) *Where Wizards Stay Up Late: The Origins of the Internet*. New York, NY: Touchstone.

Hardin, G. (1968) 'The tragedy of the commons', *Science*, 162: 1243–8.

Hasson, D., Arnetz, B., Jelveus, L and Edelstam, B. (2004) 'A randomized clinical trial of the treatment effects of massage compared to relaxation tape recordings on diffuse long-term pain', *Psychotherapy and Psychosomatics*, 73(1): 17–24.

Hess, C. and Ostrom, E. (eds) (2007) *Understanding Knowledge as a Commons: From Theory to Practice*. Cambridge, MA: MIT Press.

von Hippel, E. (2005) *Democratizing Innovation*. Cambridge, MA: MIT Press.

Horkheimer, M. and Adorno, T. (1972) *The Dialectic of Enlightenment*. New York, NY: Seabury.

Jacoby, B. (1996) *Service Learning in Higher Education*. San Francisco, CA: Jossey-Bass.

Johnson, G. (2000) *Strange Beauty: Murray Gell-Mann and the Revolution in Twentieth-Century Physics*. London, UK: Jonathan Cape.

Jonassen, D., Howland, J., Moore, J. and Marra, R. (2003) *Learning to Solve Problems with Technology: A Constructivist Perspective*. London, UK: Merrill.

Jones, S. (ed.) (1997) *Virtual Culture: Identity and Communication in Cybersociety*. London, UK: Sage.

Kahn, P. and Baume, D., ed. (2003) *A Guide to Staff and Educational Development*. London, UK: Kogan Page.

Keen, A. (2007) *The Cult of the Amateur: How Today's Internet is Killing our Culture and Assaulting our Economy*. London, UK: Nicholas Brearley.

Kemp, R. (1985) 'Planning, Public Hearings and the Politics of Discourse', in Forester, J. (ed.), *Critical Theory and Public Life*. Cambridge, MA: MIT Press.

Kennewell, S., Parkinson, J. and Tanner, H. (eds) (2003) *Learning to Teach ICT in the Secondary School: A Companion to School Experience*. London, UK: RoutledgeFalmer.

Kirschner, P., Sweller, J. and Clark, R. (2006) 'Why minimal guidance during instruction does not work: An analysis of the failure of constructivist, discovery, problem-based, experiential and inquiry-based teaching', *Educational Psychologist*, 14(2): 75–86.

Kitchener, K. and King, P. (1981) 'Reflective judgment: Concepts of justification and their relationship to age and education', *Journal of Applied Developmental Psychology*, 2(2): 89–116.

Knight, P. (2000) *Conspiracy Culture: From the Kennedy Assassination to the X-Files*. London, UK: Routledge.

Kohr, L. (1993) *The Academic Inn*. Aberystwyth, UK: Y Lolfa Cyf.

Kropotkin, P. (1955) *Mutual Aid: A Factor of Evolution*. Boston, MA: Extending Horizons.

Kuhn, T. (1970) *The Structure of Scientific Revolutions*, 2nd edn. Chicago, IL: University of Chicago Press.

Landow, G. (1992) *Hypertext: The Convergence of Contemporary Critical Theory and Technology*. Baltimore, MD: Johns Hopkins.

Laurillard, D. (2002) *Rethinking University Teaching*, 2nd edn. London, UK: Routledge Falmer.

Lawler, C. (2008) 'Action research as a congruent methodology for understanding Wikis: the case of Wikiversity', *Journal of Interactive*

Multimedia Education, May: available at *http://jime.open.ac.uk/ 2008/06/* (last accessed 19 August 2008).

Levinson, P. (1999) *Digital McLuhan: A Guide to the Information Millennium*. London, UK: Routledge.

Lin, H. (2000) 'Fluency with information technology', *Government Information Quarterly*, 17(1): 69–76.

Luckin, R. (2008) 'The learner centric ecology of resources: A framework for using technology to scaffold learning', *Computers and Education*, 50(2): 449–62.

Luckin, R., Underwood, J., du Boulay, B., Holmberg, J., Kerawalla, L., O'Connor, J., Smith, H. and Tunley, H. (2006) 'Designing Educational Systems Fit for Use: A case study in the application of human centred design for AIED', *International Journal of Artificial Intelligence in Education*, 16(4): 353–80.

Lukacs, G. (1971) *History and Class Consciousness*. London, UK: Merlin.

Lyotard, F. (1984) *The Postmodern Condition: A Report on Knowledge*, Minneapolis, MN: University of Minnesota Press.

Mackenzie, D. and Wajcman, J. (eds) (1985), *The Social Shaping of Technology*. Buckingham, UK: Open University Press.

MacKeogh, K. (2003) *Student Perceptions of the Use of ICTs in European Education: Report of a Survey*. Dublin, Ireland: Oscail.

March, J. and Olsen, J. (1976) *Ambiguity and Choice in Organizations*. Bergen, Norway: Universitetsforlaget.

Marcuse, H. (1964) *One-Dimensional Man: Studies in the Ideology of Advanced Industrial Society*. London, UK: Routledge & Kegan Paul.

Markless, S. and Streatfield, D. (2007) 'Three decades of information literacy: redefining the parameters', in Andretta, S. (ed.), *Change and Challenge: Information Literacy for the 21st Century*. Adelaide, Australia: Auslib; pp. 15–36.

Mason, R., Mason, F. and Culnan, J. (1995) *Ethics of Information Management*. London, UK: Sage.

Mavin, S. and Cavaleri, S. (2004) 'Viewing learning organizations through a social learning lens', *The Learning Organization*, 11(3): 285–9.

McCarthy, T. (1984) *The Critical Theory of Jürgen Habermas*. Cambridge, UK: Polity.

McFarlane, A. (ed.) (1997) *Information Technology and Authentic Learning*. London, UK: Routledge.

McLuhan, M. (1962) *The Gutenberg Galaxy: The Making of Typographic Man*. Toronto, Canada: University of Toronto Press.

McGarr, O. (200X) 'The influence of prevailing ICT culture on its historical development across the curriculum in Irish post-primary schools', *British Journal of Educational Technology*, in press.

McKay, G. (ed.) (1999) *DIY Culture: Party and Protest in Nineties Britain*. London, UK: Verso.

van Meer, E. (2003) 'PLATO: From Computer-Based Education to Corporate Social Responsibility', *Iterations*, 2: available at *http://www.cbi.umn.edu/iterations/vanmeer.html* (last accessed 19 August 2008)

Menninger, K. (1969) *Number Words and Number Symbols: A Cultural History of Numbers*. Cambridge, MA: MIT Press.

Merrick (1996) *Battle for the Trees*. Leeds, UK: Godhaven.

Mezirow, J. (ed.) (1990) *Fostering Critical Reflection in Adulthood: A Guide to Transformative and Emancipatory Learning*. San Francisco, CA: Jossey-Bass.

Michels, R. (1959) *Political Parties*. New York, NY: Dover Publications.

Miller, P. (2006) 'Library 2.0: The Challenge of Disruptive Innovation', Talis White Paper: available at *http://www.talis.com/resources/documents/447_Library_2_prf1.pdf* (last accessed 20 August 2008).

Mintzberg, H. (1989) *Mintzberg on Management*. London, UK: Collier Macmillan.

Morgan, G. (1999) *Images of Organization*, 2nd edn. London, UK: Sage.

Morson, G. S. and Emerson, C. (1990) *Mikhail Bakhtin: Creation of a Prosaics*. Stanford, CA: Stanford University Press.

Mumford, E. (1987) 'Sociotechnical systems design: evolving theory and practice', in Bjerknes, G., Ehn, P. and Kyng, M. (eds), *Computers and Democracy*. Aldershot, UK: Avebury; pp. 59–76.

Nardi, B. (1996) 'Studying Context', in Nardi, B. (ed.), *Context and Consciousness: Activity Theory and Human-Computer Interaction*. Cambridge, MA: MIT Press.

Nevison, J. (1976) 'Computing in the liberal arts college', *Science*, 194: 396–402.

Norman, D. (2002) *The Design of Everyday Things*. New York, NY: Basic.

North, S. and Hodson, P. (1997) *Build a Bonfire: How Football Fans United to Save Brighton & Hove Albion*. Edinburgh, UK: Mainstream.

Norton, F. (2008) 'Using library and museum materials in the pursuit of scientific literacy and public engagement', keynote speech, LILAC '08 conference, Liverpool, UK.

Nyce, J. and Kahn, P. (eds) (1991) *From Memex to Hypertext: Vannevar Bush and the Mind's Machine*. London, UK: Academic Press.

Outhwaite, W. (ed.) (1996) *The Habermas Reader*. Cambridge, UK: Polity.

Parsons, A. (2005) 'The Mundane Computer: Non-Technical Design Challenges Facing Ubiquitous Computing and Ambient Intelligence', *Tangentium*, 2(2): available at *http://personalpages.manchester.ac.uk/staff/andrew.whitworth/tangentium/may05/feature1.html* (last accessed 17 November 2008).

Partnership for 21st Century Skills. (2004). 'The Road to 21st Century Learning: Policymakers'Guide to 21st Century Skills', policy paper: available at *http://www.21stcenturyskills.org/images/stories/otherdocs/P21_Policy_Paper.pdf* (last accessed 19 August 2008).

Papert, S. (1980) *Mindstorms: Children, Computers and Powerful Ideas*. New York, NY: Basic.

Passey, D. and Samways, B. (eds) (1997) *Information Technology Supporting Change Through Teacher Education*. London, UK: Chapman and Hall.

Prensky, M. (2001) 'Digital natives, digital immigrants', *On the Horizon*, 9(5): 1–2.

Putnam, R. D. (2000) *Bowling Alone: The Collapse and Revival of American Community*. New York, NY: Simon & Schuster.

Randall, N. (1997) *The Soul of the Internet: Net Gods, Netizens and the Wiring of the World*. London, UK: International Thomson Computer Press.

Reason, P. and Bradbury, H. (eds) (2001) *Handbook of Action Research*. London, UK: Sage.

Redfern, R. (2000) *Origins: The Evolution of Continents, Oceans and Life*. London, UK: Cassell.

Reffell, P. and Whitworth, A. (2002) 'Information fluency: critically examining IT education', *New Library World*, 102(11–12): 427–35.

Rheingold. H. (1993) *The Virtual Community: Homesteading on the Electronic Frontier*. Reading, MA: Addison Wesley.

Rheingold. H. (2003) *Smart Mobs: The Next Social Revolution*. Cambridge, MA: Perseus.

Robins, K. and Webster, F. (1987) *The Technical Fix: Education, Computers and Industry*. Basingstoke, UK: Macmillan.

Rockman, I. (ed.) (2004) *Integrating Information Literacy into the Higher Education Curriculum*. San Francisco, CA: Jossey-Bass.

Roszak, T. (1994) *The Cult of Information*, 2nd edn. Berkeley, CA: University of California Press.

Rothschild, J. and Whitt, J. (1986) *The Cooperative Workplace: Potentials and Dilemmas of Organizational Democracy and Participation*. Cambridge, UK: Cambridge University Press.

Sagan, C. (1986) *Contact*. London, UK: Century Hutchinson.

Samson, P. and Pitt, D. (eds) (1999) *The Biosphere and Noösphere Reader: Global Environment, Society and Change*. London, UK: Routledge.

Schlosser, E. (2006) *Fast Food Nation: The Dark Side of the All-American Meal*. New York, NY: Harper Perennial.

Schön, D. (1991) *The Reflective Practitioner: How Professionals Think in Action*. Aldershot, UK: Ashgate.

Schuler, D. and Namioka, A. (eds) (1993) *Participatory Design: Principles and Practices*. Mahwah, NJ: Lawrence Erlbaum.

Scott, J. C. (1990) *Domination and the Arts of Resistance*. New Haven, CT: Yale University Press.

Selwyn, N. (1998) 'What's in the box? Exploring learners' rejection of educational computing', *Educational Research and Evaluation*, 4(3): 193–212.

Senn Breivik, P. and Gee, E. G. (2006) *Higher Education in the Internet Age: Libraries Creating a Strategic Edge*. Westport, CT: Praeger.

Shenk, D. (1997) *Data Smog: Surviving the Information Glut*. New York, NY: Harper Collins.

Shor, I. (1996) *When Students Have Power: Negotiating Authority in a Critical Pedagogy*. Chicago, IL: Chicago University Press.

Smith, M. and Kollock, P. (eds) (1999) *Communities in Cyberspace*. London, UK: Routledge.

Spurlock, M. (2005) *Don't Eat This Book*. London, UK: Penguin.

Stalder, F. (2008) 'Bourgeois anarchism and authoritarian democracies', *First Monday*, 13(7).

Star, S. L. (1999) 'The Ethnography of Infrastructure', *American Behavioral Scientist*, 43(3): 377–91.

Stoll, C. (1990) *The Cuckoo's Egg: tracking a spy through a maze of computer espionage*. London, UK: Bodley Head.

Taylor, F. W. (1911) *Principles of Scientific Management*. New York, UK: Harper & Row.

Thompson, D. (2008) *Counterknowledge*. London, UK: Atlantic.

Toffler, A. (1970) *Future Shock*. London, UK: Bodley Head.

Tuman, M. (1992) *Word Perfect: Literacy in the Computer Age*. Pittsburgh, PA: University of Pittsburgh Press.

Turkle, S. (1997) *Life on the Screen: Identity in the Age of the Internet*. London, UK: Phoenix.

Tyme, J. (1978) *Motorways Versus Democracy*. Basingstoke, UK: Macmillan.

Vernadsky, V. (1945) 'The Biosphere and the Noösphere', *American Scientist*, 33: 1–12.

Vidal, J. (1997) *McLibel: Burger Culture on Trial*. Basingstoke, UK: Macmillan.

Vygotsky, L. (1978) *Mind in Society: The Development of Higher Psychological Processes*. Cambridge, MA: Harvard University Press.

Walker, C. (2008) 'Information Literacy in the Home: A study of the use and understanding of information by parents of young children', paper, LILAC '08 conference, Liverpool, UK.

Warschauer, M. (1999) *Electronic Literacies: Langauge, Culture and Power in Online Education*. Mahwah, NJ: Lawrence Erlbaum.

Weber, M. (1947) *The Theory of Social and Economic Organization*. Oxford, UK: Oxford University Press.

Webster, F. (2002) *Theories of the Information Society*, 2nd edn. London, UK: Routledge.

Weick, K. (1976) 'Educational Organizations as Loosely Coupled Systems', *Administrative Science Quarterly*, 21(1): 1–19.

Weiser, M. (1993) 'Some Computer Science Issues in Ubiquitous Computing', available at *http://www.ubiq.com/hypertext/weiser/UbiCACM.html* (last accessed 19 August 2008).

Wellington, J. J. (1984) 'Computers across the Curriculum – The Needs in Teacher Training', *Journal of Further and Higher Education*, 8(3): 46–52.

Welton, M. (ed.) (1995) *In Defense of the Lifeworld: Critical Perspectives on Adult Learning*. Albany, NY: SUNY Press.

Wenger, E. (1998) *Communities of Practice: Learning, Meaning and Identity*. Cambridge, MA: Cambridge University Press.

Whitworth, A. (2003) 'Communicative Rationality and Decision Making in Environmental Organizations', *Research in Social Movements, Conflict and Change*, 24: 123–53.

Whitworth, A. (2004) 'Networking Democracy: IT and Radical Infrastructures', *Tangentium*, 1(4): available at *http://personalpages.manchester.ac.uk/staff/andrew.whitworth/tangentium/may04/feature2.html* (last accessed 19 August 2008).

Whitworth, A. (2005) ''Who wants to learn web design anyway?' Course design for student diversity in an ICT subdiscipline', *ITALICS*, 4(2): available at *http://www.ics.heacademy.ac.uk/italics/vol4iss2.htm* (last accessed 24 August 2008).

Whitworth, A. (2007a) 'Communicative competence in the information age: towards a critical theory of information literacy education', in Andretta, S. (ed.), *Change and Challenge: Information Literacy for the 21st Century*. Adelaide, Australia: Auslib; pp. 85–113.

Whitworth, A. (2007b) 'Researching the cognitive cultures of e-learning' in Andrews, R. and Haythornthwaite, C. (eds), *The Sage Handbook of E-learning Research*. London, UK: Sage; pp. 202–20.

Williams, R. and Edge, D. (1996) 'The Social Shaping of Technology', *Research Policy*, 25(6): 865–99.

Winner, L. (1986) 'Do Artefacts Have Politics?', in *The Whale and the Reactor: A Search for Limits in an Age of High Technology*. Chicago, IL: University of Chicago Press; pp. 19–39.

Wodak, R. (1996) *Disorders of Discourse*. Harlow, UK: Addison Wesley Longman.

Zeller, T. (2005) 'Measuring literacy in a world gone digital', *New York Times*, 17 Jan 2005.

Index

Lightning Source UK Ltd.
Milton Keynes UK
UKOW06f2132160715

255290UK00005BA/128/P

9 781843 344490